MW00777158

# Advance praise for *Timothy B. Dyk: The Education of a Federal Judge*

"Tim Dyk has done it all. Law clerk to a famous chief justice, a heavyweight advocate in First Amendment cases, and for more than two decades, perhaps the most literate judge on the U.S. Court of Appeals for the Federal Circuit. In this book, he tells all about his fascinating life in the law."

*—Nina Totenberg, Legal Affairs Correspondent,*
*National Public Radio, USA*

"What a joy to read a book by a practicing lawyer and now a judge that is candid, not egotistical, and eminently readable! Judge Timothy Dyk has enjoyed a charmed legal career in private practice and as a federal judge, but that does not prevent him from telling readers what is wrong with the legal profession and what makes judging difficult. His book includes discussions of the fascinating (and important) cases in which he was involved as well as his tortuous route to becoming a judge. Anyone who has intersected with the law (which means just about everyone) should read this insightful book."

*—David Dorsen, author of "Henry Friendly, Greatest Judge of*
*His Era" and "The Unexpected Scalia. The Liberal Opinions*
*of a Conservative Justice."*

"An engaging, thoughtful, and judicious reflection on the practice of law and the search for justice from Tim Dyk, one of the great Washington lawyers. Dyk's career spans more than a half century, beginning with a clerkship with the Warren Court, and his memoir offers a candid and compelling account of the legal profession, the judicial confirmation process, and the joys and challenges of judging."

*—David Cole, National Legal Director, ACLU, USA*

"Tim Dyk's memoir is a Coming of Age story about the legal community in Washington, D.C. that should interest anyone who wants to learn about law practice and the judiciary. It is a lucid, honest, and understated account of the 60-year journey of one very successful lawyer – from law school, to Supreme Court clerkship, work in the Executive Branch of the federal government, private practice in two leading firms, and service as a Federal Circuit judge – as the legal community in Washington evolved from a small gentlemen's club to one of the major centers of today's hugely lucrative global legal industry."

"Tim Dyk is interesting and smart, a man who has seen every angle of the law. From judicial clerk for Chief Justice Earl Warren to being an appellate federal judge himself, and in between a distinguished First Amendment practice and making money at the same time, plus some progressive politics along the way. You'll learn and read some yarns. You won't put it down."

"This gracefully written life story is filled with marvelous, engaging and candid insights, anecdotes and wisdom, drawing on Judge Dyk's six decades of impressive experience as a Supreme Court law clerk, government lawyer, Washington lawyer and highly regarded appellate advocate and federal appeals court judge. It is a wonderful read for anyone fascinated by the Washington legal world and the federal judiciary."

"Want to know how to become a Federal court of appeals judge? This book is worth reading for that chapter alone. Working from his daily notes, Judge Dyk tells a remarkable and somewhat frightening tale of our confirmation process—a process that has only gotten worse in the twenty years he has been on the bench."

Timothy B. Dyk

Timothy B. Dyk

# The Education of a Federal Judge

Timothy B. Dyk
with Bill Davies

ANTHEM PRESS

Anthem Press
An imprint of Wimbledon Publishing Company
*www.anthempress.com*

This edition first published in UK and USA 2022
by ANTHEM PRESS
75–76 Blackfriars Road, London SE1 8HA, UK
or PO Box 9779, London SW19 7ZG, UK
and
244 Madison Ave #116, New York, NY 10016, USA

*British Library Cataloguing-in-Publication Data*
A catalogue record for this book is available from the British Library.

*Library of Congress Cataloging-in-Publication Data*
Names: Dyk, Timothy B., author. | Davies, Bill, 1979– contributor.
Title: Timothy B. Dyk : the education of a federal judge /
Timothy B. Dyk ; with Bill Davies.
Description: London, UK ; New York, NY : Anthem Press, an imprint of Wimbledon
Publishing Company, 2022. | Includes bibliographical references and index. |
Identifiers: LCCN 2022004683 | ISBN 9781839982149 (hardback) |
ISBN 1839982144 (hardback) | ISBN 9781839982163 (epub) |
ISBN 9781839982156 (pdf)
Subjects: LCSH: Dyk, Timothy B. | Judges—United States—Biography.
Classification: LCC KF373.D95 A3 2022 | DDC 347.73/0234 [B]—dc23/eng/20220131
LC record available at https://lccn.loc.gov/2022004683

ISBN-13: 978-1-83998-214-9 (Hbk)
ISBN-10: 1-83998-214-4 (Hbk)

Cover Image: Painting by Brendan Kelly / reproduction photograph
by Andrew Smart of a.c.cooper(colour)ltd.

This title is also available as an e-book.

*To Sally Katzen Dyk, who made this and so many other things possible.*

# CONTENTS

# FOREWORD

Tim Dyk began writing this fascinating book with the simple idea of sharing with his children and grandchildren his experiences as both a top of the game lawyer and a respected federal judge. We should be grateful that he decided to share his memoir with the rest of us. His legacy is impressive, spanning American history from John F. Kennedy's New Frontier to the present day, but the *Education of a Federal Judge* is much more. In detailing Judge Dyk's own education, it educates the reader about the most interesting and significant aspects of the legal profession.

Judge Dyk's long legal career allows him to authoritatively describe the radical change in the legal profession over the past half century, particularly in what is fondly known as "Big Law." His experience in litigating critical cases involving the First Amendment and federal and state regulation demonstrates the challenges and rewards of private practice and how federal court litigation can rein in overreach by the executive and legislative branches. His well-documented excruciating path to confirmation as a federal judge provides a window into the broken judicial selection process. Judge Dyk's 20 years as a federal judge on one of our most significant court of appeals provides a detailed and inspiring description of the day-to-day operation of our federal appellate courts.

As a former law clerk to a federal judge and member of the bar, I found the description of the work of a federal judge and the changes in the legal profession in turn to be reassuring and revealing. As a former state attorney general, I found Judge Dyk's description of his career as a litigator to be a notable contribution to understanding how federal court litigation provides an essential check on the other branches of government. But, most significantly, as a former US senator, I found the description of the confirmation process to be both accurate and deeply concerning. Judge Dyk's remarkable career as a lawyer, litigating some of the most significant issues of our time, was ironically a source of problems for his confirmation, providing a warning of the increased political polarization of the selection process for federal judges.

Article III of the US Constitution establishes the federal courts as the third branch of government, in significant part to serve as a neutral arbiter between the executive and legislative branches and to create a nation of laws applicable to public officials and private citizens alike. Supreme Court Chief Justice John Roberts famously said in his confirmation hearing before the Senate, judges are like umpires who only apply the rules, not make them.

The fact is, however, that the judiciary plays an increasingly active role in articulating public policy on an escalating array of the important political, social and economic issues that come before it. As de Tocqueville observed in *Democracy in America*, "there is hardly any political question in the United States that sooner or later does not turn into a judicial question."[1] In addition, since Article III judges are not elected by the people and have, singularly among the world's democracies, life tenure ("during good behavior"), the selection process is critical.

Beginning after the landmark decision in *Brown v. Board of Education* and other seminal decisions of the Warren Court, politicians started paying more attention and have grown progressively more invested in attempting to mold the federal bench to suit themselves, fostering an increasing level of contention, acrimony and mistrust. As the partisan divide deepens and the consideration of nominations to the federal courts becomes more adversarial, the Senate's constitutional advice and consent role in the appointments to the federal courts risks losing any semblance of unbiased, thoughtful consideration of qualifications and suitability.

During my 12 years in the Senate from 2009 to 2020—the Obama and Trump presidencies—I watched as my colleagues blocked appointments, traded judicial votes for votes on unrelated issues, exploited the rules to unreasonably delay a nomination and otherwise exacerbated the partisan divide. The result has been too many long-term vacancies on an already overworked system, only sporadic improvements in much needed diversity, and the decision by qualified candidates to decline to stand for nomination or to eventually withdraw their names.

It is to Judge Dyk's enormous credit that he chose to step away from an obviously successful practice to engage (without losing his sense of humor) and ultimately triumph in a grueling process that lasted an astonishing 785 days from nomination to Senate confirmation. The diary he kept of this journey tells the judicial selection story as well as it can be told. It illustrates how close the system is to breaking and why it is deserving of our immediate concern.

This book will prove invaluable for lay readers and lawyers alike who will better understand how our legal system works, how our judges are selected and how they do their critical work and navigate the inevitable challenges.

Tom Udall
Santa Fe, New Mexico
October, 2021

## Note

1 Alexis de Tocqueville, *Democracy in America*. English edition. Edited by Eduardo Nolla. Translated from the French by James T. Schleifer (Indianapolis, IN: Liberty Fund, 2012), vol. 1. https://oll.libertyfund.org/title/democracy-in-america-english-edition-vol-1#Tocqueville_1593-01_2648.

# ACKNOWLEDGMENTS

Being a subscriber to the dictum attributed to Robert Graves that "there is no such thing as good writing, only good rewriting," this manuscript went through untold drafts. The rewriting benefitted greatly from the generous review and valuable suggestions by colleagues who read and commented on all or part of the manuscript. Those who read the whole "damn book," as one of them called it, include my fellow judge Richard Taranto, my law school classmate Sidney Rosdeitcher, Sarah Wilson (who as Associate White House Counsel guided me through the confirmation process) and my children Caitlin Palacios and Abraham Dyk. Those who read and made valuable comments on selected chapters include Ralph Goldberg (formerly with CBS), Peter Edelman (my law school classmate), Steve Hut (my former partner at Wilmer Cutler), my sister Penelope Carter, my daughter Deirdre VanDyk, my cousin Mary Greenacre and Ira Dosovitz. My thanks particularly to Richard Taranto, whose dedication to excellence and thoroughness has made this a better book.

There are, no doubt, errors in here, faults of memory that are attributable to me and not those who read the manuscript. Where sources are not cited for quoted material, the quotes are based on my best recollection.

Colin Shannon provided excellent help in cite checking the legal material. Those who ably assisted my co-author Bill Davies in his voluminous research include Hannah Brown, Sydney Lang, Austin Bartola, Chana Barron and Grant Thompson. Many thanks also to the Ehrenhaft family for permission to use the photograph of Chief Justice Warren and, particularly, to Brendan Kelly for allowing the use of his remarkable painting on the cover of this book. Archival assistance was generously provided by the Library of Congress, the National Archives and Records Administration, the Federal Communications Commission and the Historical Society of the US District Court for the Eastern District of Tennessee.

Finally, the person other than Bill or me who contributed the most to this memoir is my wife, Sally Katzen, whose care in reading and rereading the text, suggesting revisions and correcting my errors is appreciated beyond measure.

# Chapter 1

# INTRODUCTION

Every federal judge is the product of an earlier life in the law. On the bench you continue to learn from colleagues, litigants and many others, but your earlier experiences powerfully shape your view of judicial excellence and your own aspirations. No two judges followed the same path to the bench; no two judges have an identical jurisprudence. Yet there are commonalities. One of these is that we have great faith in the American legal system, imperfect as it is, and its ability to provide an impartial forum for the resolution of significant disputes and to thereby sustain our democracy. There is no other legal system in the world with the same authority, dedication to excellence, independence and honesty as our system of federal courts. For more than almost 60 years now, I have been a lawyer in practice and a federal judge, litigating and then adjudicating cases of some significance in the federal courts. This memoir describes the path that I followed to the bench from my earliest days, how I now pursue my craft, and my sense of privilege in having been able to serve this system from both sides of the bench.

There are relatively few memoirs or biographies of the legal careers of circuit judges during the period that I have been in active practice and on the bench—from the early 1960s to the present. The only non-Supreme Court comprehensive biographies of federal appellate judges in modern times that I am familiar with are those of Learned Hand, Henry Friendly, William Hastie, Jon Newman, Richard Posner and Damon Keith.[1] With the exception of Newman's, none of these is in the judge's own words, and the Hand, Friendly and Hastie biographies cover an earlier period. There is, therefore, a dearth of information about what it was like to be a lawyer and then a federal judge during my time in private practice and on the bench. I thought that it might be useful to record what I learned and what I experienced.

This memoir was not at the inception designed for the general public. Rather, it was originally designed for my children, my grandchildren and their descendants. It was motivated by my acute sense of loss that I do not have a detailed record of my parents' lives. My wife Sally, as a birthday present, connected me with Bill Davies, a legal historian and professor in the School of Public Affairs at American University, who was interested in working with me. Eventually, with Bill's excellent help, my planned family memoir morphed into a memoir suitable for publication. Our division of labor was that I would write, and Bill would research. He throughout insisted that we provide context, which was invaluable.

To be sure, describing my history to some extent involves a description of mundane events. But it is the everyday that is important to history, in what the Germans call *Alltagsgeschichte*, and these experiences are often lost because no one bothered to record them. For example, Justice John Paul Stevens, when he was writing *Five Chiefs*, a book about his experiences on the Supreme Court, was stumped by the absence of an historical record.[2] Try as he might he could not find any written record as to the order of speaking when the Justices held their conferences in the 1960s, whether junior to senior or vice versa.

In writing this memoir, I was reminded of how many things in my life are the results of accident rather than design. But for some small event, my professional life would have taken an entirely different direction. There are numerous examples of this: my inability before college to get into the Naval ROTC program and my inability after college to get a job in book publishing. My choice of law firm and city to practice law: if a large New York firm had not declined to raise my existing salary as a law clerk, I might have gone to New York, and my life would have been very different. If I had not chosen to go to Wilmer Cutler, I never would have worked on CBS matters, which became a central part of my professional life for two decades. If I had not been rejected for a district court nomination, I would never have been a circuit judge. All of these events had consequences I could not have foreseen.

Working on this memoir has brought back memories of the many people who helped to educate me and advance my professional career, and I am chagrined that it is too late now to thank them because they are no longer alive. These include my history teacher (Mr. Kosinski) and Principal Brunch at my high school in Brooklyn, the latter being responsible for my being admitted to Harvard College; Alfred Harbage, a professor of Elizabethan literature at Harvard, who kindled my interest in academic life; Paul Freund, a professor at the Harvard Law School, who was an inspiration and responsible for my getting the clerkship with retired Justices Reed and Burton; Chief Justice Earl Warren at the Supreme Court; Louis Oberdorfer at the Department of Justice Tax Division and Roger Wollenberg at Wilmer, Cutler and Pickering. Both Oberdorfer and Wollenberg taught me lawyering and generously advanced my career, with Wollenberg in particular teaching me how to be an appellate advocate. Fortunately, I am able to express my great appreciation to my wife, Sally Katzen, for her help and support in my professional career. Without her assistance, I would not have been as successful as I have been or have as fulfilling a life.

Yet with all the assistance and guidance that I received from many generous people and with the benefit of an excellent legal education, after law school I was, to a significant extent, self-taught in the law. For me, the learning process did not begin by sitting as second chair (assisting lead counsel). For example, I did my first deposition, my first examination at trial, my first argument in district court and my first appellate argument without training from a more experienced lawyer. That was not always a good thing, and led over the years to mistakes, some of which I still acutely recall. Self-sufficiency is a vice as well as a virtue. I later learned a good deal by being second chair, particularly for appellate arguments, learning the critical importance of listening with great care to the judges, witnesses, opposing counsel and other involved in the litigation process.

I very much enjoyed private practice though perhaps I devoted too much of my life to it. After my first wife, Inga, and I divorced, she wrote a somewhat autobiographical novel (titled *Memory and Desire*) with a husband character who works obsessively.[3] Fair enough, but the husband (I think unfairly) has no sense of humor. In practice, the challenges and non-monetary rewards of both trial and appellate litigation were substantial, as was the experience of working with able lawyers both senior and junior to me. In retrospect, I cannot fault myself for lack of energy or ambition or failure to pursue appropriately the best interests of my clients. I always wanted the responsibility of having the ball, and I cared less than most about what others thought of me. Nor have I lacked creativity in shaping legal or factual arguments. I did lack patience with younger lawyers during my years in practice and, as with many lawyers, somewhat lacked enthusiasm for business development with new clients.

It has been a great honor and joy to be a federal judge. It has been quite different from private practice, where there is no client interest that provides the lodestar. Instead, the lodestar has been precedent, the language of statutes and regulations and the public interest. As a judge, as I develop below, I have done my best to reach the right result defined largely by authority, pragmatism and fairness. I strive for simplicity and clarity in my opinions. It seems to me that one of the primary differences between an appellate judge and a trial judge is that a trial judge is much more of a referee between the contending parties, whereas an appellate judge has to look beyond the individual case and consider the impact of the decision on future cases. This leads appellate judges, I think, to be less willing to be cabined by any of counsel's inadequacies; to strive to achieve the right result so long as the issue was properly raised; and to take joy in fine briefs and good advocacy.

In reflecting on my long legal career and education, I find major changes and several drivers of those changes in the legal profession that are developed more fully below.

The first of these is that in private practice, money has become the central goal and measure of accomplishment for many lawyers. The profession has become a business. Decrying materialism and a focus on monetary rewards is as old as civilization itself. Yet in the legal profession, the increasing focus on monetary rewards has had profound effects. It has long been the case that most lawyers choose the legal profession to make a good living, and some have been obsessed by money. But when I started out, law firm associates and even young partners made far less than they do today, and the disparity between income in practice and in government service was far less stark. More significantly, lawyers in private practice generally did not measure their self-worth by their income. The primary reward for most lawyers was the nature and quality of work that they produced and the respect that they earned, still a prime motivator for many. Now for too many the quality of work is secondary to the compensation.

The second change is that there has been an enormous growth in the number of lawyers in our society (and particularly in Washington), and commensurate growth in the size and geographic reach of the major firms. The center of the legal world of litigation in the United States has to a large extent shifted from New York to Washington, DC. The primary cause of this I think is twofold: the vast expansion of litigation by the private sector against the federal government, and the pool of talented lawyers in Washington. At the same time, there have been positive changes in the demographics of the legal profession where women, minorities and those of differing sexual orientation are now more welcome. Problems still exist, but we are at least on a better path.

The third change is the liberal/conservative divide. In practice and thereafter, I prided myself in having close friendships with lawyers and judges with different outlooks from my own. But in many organizations, working relationships and friendships have been become strained or nonexistent between those holding different views. You join either the conservative Federalist Society or the progressive American Constitution Society, but not both. We are less inclined to learn from each other. That is a great loss.

The fourth significant change has been technological. Typewriters have given way to word processors and laptops, land lines to smart phones, books to computer databases, bringing about a sea change in the way lawyers do business, and making it possible to work remotely. The result has been greater efficiency, but at the cost of fewer opportunities for reflection and in-person interaction.

With all these changes, the legal profession's traditions and processes still bring great benefit to our country and great satisfaction to many lawyers in and out of government. I have been fortunate to have been a part of it, and almost always had interesting work to do and interesting people to work with. In some ways, I have been a kind of Forrest Gump of the legal profession: present in a minor role in some great events of our time. I hope that my description of my career will be both informative and entertaining.

## Notes

1   Biographies of Judges Jones and Aldisert were less concerned with judicial work than with the Judge's nonjudicial activities. See Nathaniel R. Jones, *Answering the Call: An Autobiography of the Modern Struggle to End Racial Discrimination in America* (New York: The New Press, 2010) and Ruggero J. Aldisert, *Road to the Robes. A Federal Judge Recollects Young Years & Early Times* (Bloomington, IN: AuthorHouse, 2005).
2   John Paul Stevens, *Five Chiefs: A Supreme Court Memoir* (New York: Little, Brown, 2011).
3   Inga Dean, *Memory and Desire* (New York: Viking, 1985).

# Chapter 2

# FAMILY HISTORY

I begin with a bit of family history on the theory that who you are is influenced by where you came from. My mother, Ruth Belcher, and father, Walter Dyk, came from different backgrounds. My father was an immigrant from Germany, arriving in this country at age 5. My mother came from New England. While I know a great deal about the ancestry of my mother, I know much less about her life. In the case of my father, I know almost nothing about his family history beyond his parents, but I know quite a bit about his life. My mother's family in this country can be traced back to Myles Standish and Priscilla Alden. Of course, they did not marry (Priscilla had famously asked "Why don't you speak for yourself, John?" when John Alden was courting her on behalf of Standish, and she married Alden), but their children married, and they were my ancestors. So I had always felt a strong connection to our country's history.

My mother was born in Portland, Maine, on March 25, 1901, into a family of Republicans. Her father was a lawyer. His name was Arthur Belcher, and he was born in Farmington, Maine, on April 24, 1861, about the time that the Civil War began.[1] He went to Andover and then Bowdoin College. He did not attend law school, but instead studied in various law offices, as was common in those days. Admitted to the bar in 1885, he practiced law in Farmington until 1896, when he moved to Portland and entered into a partnership with Frederick Hale. A lot of the work he did as a lawyer was for a telephone company. Unhappily, at a time when he reportedly was about to run for the US Senate, my grandfather contracted appendicitis and died of peritonitis on October 5, 1904, when my mother was just three years old. My grandfather's partner, Hale, was elected to the US Senate in 1916 and became famous for his opposition to Hugo Black's nomination to the Supreme Court because of Black's Klan affiliation, an opposition that was misplaced, given Justice Black's later record.[2]

If Henry Louis Gates were to provide me with my own Book of Life, as he has done for so many others, he would note that one of Arthur Belcher's relatives (his father's brother) was Clifford Belcher. Clifford stands out as a family embarrassment.[3] He left home to study at Harvard College at age 14 in 1833, a classmate of Henry David Thoreau. He then studied law at Cambridge and practiced for a while in New York City. In 1846, before the Civil War, he moved to Louisiana and bought a slave plantation in Thibodaux, near New Orleans. This was not unique among Bostonians, despite Boston's reputation for being the hotbed of abolition. He was a major in the Confederate army, losing everything in the war. After the war, he returned to Boston and made another fortune practicing law. He wore white linen suits, perhaps a holdover from his Southern experience. He eventually retired due to ill health and died on Christmas Eve 1879. He has the largest monument in our family graveyard in Maine. On the plus side, my mother's family was connected collaterally to General Howard who founded Howard University.

My mother's mother, Annie Manson Smith, was born in 1868 and graduated from Wellesley College in 1890. Interestingly, she was one of the first female students at the Tufts Medical School, but she never graduated, having been forced to leave school when she married. She was relatively old when she had children, being in her early thirties when my mother was born. After my grandfather died, she, my mother and my mother's sister (Margaret) moved first to Winchester, Massachusetts, and then to Newton Center outside of Boston. My mother also eventually went to Wellesley, pictured below in Image 1, where she graduated in the class of 1923 and earned a master's degree in Economics from Simmons College in 1924. She did further graduate work at the University of Wisconsin and at Berkeley. My mother was involved in the Women's Suffrage movement from a young age, marching with my grandmother in the Boston suffrage parade in 1915. They also voted together for the first time in the November 1920 election, when my mother was 19 years old.[4] My mother taught me to value, indeed, to expect education and professional accomplishment in women as well as men.

My father was born on September 30, 1899, in Halberstadt, Germany. The town resisted the American forces in World War II such that the town and all of its records were destroyed. An ancestor was reportedly a drummer boy in the Franco-Prussian war of 1870–71 and another was said to have made a violin out of matchsticks. My father's father, Wenzel, born in 1878, was a Catholic and an itinerant glove maker (a pattern cutter, the most important and skilled position). He originally came from Bohemia—what is now the Czech Republic. His wife, my father's mother, was Prussian and a Lutheran. She was named Emma Marcia Agnes Lange. They met in Germany when they were in their early twenties.

My grandfather visited the United States and was convinced to return to Germany and bring his family back with him. My grandfather was probably recruited by US glove makers to come to America. Another incentive was the

RUTH M. BELCHER
168 WARREN ST., NEWTON CENTRE,
MASS.
She studies hard. What's more, she
admits it.

**Image 1.** Ruth Dyk at Wellesley College, 1923

("Ruth Belcher Dyk," Suffrage at Simmons, The Wellesley College Legenda, last accessed June 9, 2021, https://beatleyweb.simmons.edu/suffrage/items/show/72.)

avoidance of military service in Europe. My paternal grandparents, my father and his brother Karl came to the United States in 1905 on the steamship SMS *Moltke*, which left Coxhaven, Germany, on June 1, 1905, and arrived in New York on June 11, 1905. There is some dispute about whether the family name was changed from Tyk to Dyk on Ellis Island. It appeared on the ship's manifest as Tyk, but that may have been a mistake. Interestingly, I visited the Czech Embassy in Washington some years ago and was told that the name Dyk was a common Czech name. Maybe there was no name change after all. The family secured citizenship on February 10, 1914, and they lived in Gloversville, New York, a center of the glove industry. Two other children (Hattie and Robert) were born in the United States.

During World War I, there was an enormous amount of anti-German sentiment in the United States, much more than there was during World War II. My father spoke only German when he came to the United States, learning English thereafter. When he was in high school, he worked at *The Leader-Republican*, which was an evening newspaper in Gloversville, and eventually ran a debt collection service for merchants, using a 1917 Harley Davidson motorcycle that he purchased. My father was a failure as a bill collector because he would pay the bills of hard-up customers out of his own pocket. He did not serve in the military during World War I, which is perhaps not surprising because of the hostility towards Germans at that time. Instead, he worked in the Camden, New Jersey, shipyards with the Ilion-Westchester Arms Company on the Riverton Iron Works, under the name of Walter O'Day, pretending to be of Irish ancestry, which was much more popular than German ancestry at the time. Presumably as a defense worker, he was draft exempt. He was a fast worker, and because it was piece work, he earned a lot until he realized that this was disadvantaging his coworkers, and he slowed down.

During the 1918 Spanish Flu pandemic, while working in Camden, my father contracted influenza and had a fever of 105–6°F. This may have caused him to develop Parkinson's disease later in his life, which I understand was not uncommon for people who suffered through the flu epidemic with very high fevers. After the war, my father joined the US Navy on August 4, 1919, in Philadelphia. He served on the USS *Camden* and the USS *Melville* and was discharged at age 21 in San Diego on August 3, 1921, having received the rank of Chief Petty Officer.

He then worked as a stevedore on the San Francisco docks and as a house painter. He eventually went to night school and earned a high school equivalency diploma. Influenced by the famous linguist and novelist Jaime de Angulo, he attended Berkeley, earning a BA in English in 1928. Berkeley was very cheap in those days.

At my father's suggestion, my grandparents moved to the Bay Area. My grandfather started his own glove business and, with my grandmother's help, was quite successful. My grandmother died in 1932 of stomach cancer. My grandfather died about six years later. He was found in a hotel room in San Francisco, after dining out at a tavern. Presumably, his death resulted from a blow to the head during a robbery. He was 60 years old and died on April 17, 1938. Here is the story from the *Oakland Tribune* on April 19, 1938:

"'B Girls" Sought in Tavern Probe

San Francisco police sought today to discover whether "B girls" have been employed at a tavern at 67 Taylor Street, where Wenzel Dyk, 60, Berkeley glove manufacturer, died Sunday evening. Officers questioned Rosalie James, divorcee with whom Dyk drank and dined before he died, and Steve Ireland, operator of the tavern. She denied that she was employed at the place and Ireland denied that he employed her. Mrs. James, held overnight for questioning, was released yesterday. She and others questioned said that Dyk fell in a washroom, injuring his head. Police were satisfied that Dyk's fall caused his death. He suffered a basal fracture of the skull, an autopsy showed.[5]

A "B Girl" was probably a prostitute. James was a known extortionist and shady character.[6] By this fatal event I was deprived of the opportunity to meet an exceptional and interesting man.

Well before my grandfather's death, my father had moved from the Bay Area. He received his master's degree in Anthropology from the University of Chicago, and a PhD in Anthropology from Yale in 1933.

My parents met in New Haven, Connecticut, in 1931 when my father was working on his doctorate. Their time in New Haven was notable. My father had been in an automobile accident in Utah, and his ear had been sheared off. The ear was reattached. He appeared at my mother's office in bandages. My mother was at the time working with juvenile delinquents. Her secretary said: "One of your delinquents is here to see you," referring to my father. They eventually married in the Yale chapel, and began life working on the Navaho Reservation, where my father was doing field work recording the life stories of Navaho people. He used a translator and recorded the stories in his own form of shorthand. In 1933, he stayed on the reservation while my mother worked in Berkeley, where my father's father, brothers and sister continued to live. The results of his research were published later as *Old Mexican: A Navaho Autobiography*.[7]

That project was followed by *Son of Old Man Hat*, based on the life of Left Handed, another Navaho. The first installment was published in 1938 and became a classic in the field.[8] It has been lauded as "the finest single account of the Navaho life and culture."[9] Many years later, when my wife Sally was working in the White House, she was at a meeting of many of the Native American chiefs. She was sitting next to the chief of the Navaho Tribe, and he saw her White House pass with her last name "Dyk." He looked surprised and asked if she was any relation to Walter Dyk. "Yes," she said, "he was my father-in-law." The chief nodded and smiled. I have been proud that my immigrant father in many ways lived the American Dream.

After my father's death, my mother (already the coauthor of two books on psychology as well as journal articles)[10] finished the second half of the Navaho ethnography, published in 1980 by Columbia University Press with the title *Left Handed: A Navaho Autobiography*.[11] We enjoyed my mother's intellectual company for almost 30 years after my father's death. Distant emotionally perhaps, but always interesting. Her New England reserve shaped my own personality.

I close the family history on a note of regret: that in a professional biography I lack the space to describe my immediate family, relatives and friends at greater length. My sister, Penelope, after serving in the Peace Corps, married Tony Carter, a professor of anthropology at the University of Rochester. She worked for years with disadvantaged children. They have two gifted children: Amanda and Eleanor. I was married first to Inga Shirer, and after Inga and I divorced, I married Sally Katzen. Inga later died tragically of glioblastoma. My three children lead meaningful and successful lives: Deirdre (an editor at Gannett magazines), Caitlin Palacios (senior attorney in the General Counsel's office of the Department of Health and Human Services) and Abe (formerly a political operative and now a lawyer in private practice). Their spouses are similarly engaged: Alex Palacios, a vice president at Balfour Beatty, and Christina, also in private practice, as are my grandchildren (Rebecca Palacios, a student at the Georgetown School of Foreign Service; Christopher Palacios at graduate school at Penn State, playing Division I soccer; and Matthew Palacios, a student at Oberlin). My father died in 1972, my mother in 2000.[12] In her last months she saw me join the bench (very meaningful to her) and was also featured at a Hillary Clinton for Senate rally in New York, facilitated by her grandson, Abe.[13]

## Notes

1    "Arthur F. Belcher," *Albums of the Attorneys of Maine* (Bethel, ME: News Publishing, 1902): 77.

2    "Hale, Frederick," Biographical Directory of the United States Congress, last accessed June 9, 2021, http://bioguide.congress.gov/scripts/biodisplay.pl?index=H000031.

3    Biographical information on Clifford Belcher is available both in Henry Williams, *Memorials of the Class of 1837 of Harvard University* (Boston, MA: Geo H. Ellis, 1887), 64–66; and Margaret Fuller, *The Letters of Margaret Fuller, 1817–1838* (Ithaca, NY: Cornell University Press, 1983), 169, n. 8.

4    "Ruth Belcher Dyk," Suffrage at Simmons, The Wellesley College Legenda, last accessed June 9, 2021, https://beatleyweb.simmons.edu/suffrage/items/show/72.

5    *Oakland Tribune* (Oakland, CA), April 19, 1938, 13.

6    "Woman Plans 4th Marriage Principal in 'Badger Game' Case Files Intention to Wed," *Oakland Tribune* (March 19, 1940), C-19.

7    Walter Dyk, *Old Mexican, a Navajo Autobiography*. Edited by Walter Dyk. Viking Fund Publications in Anthropology, no. 8 (New York: Viking Fund, 1947).

8    Walter Dyk, *Son of Old Man Hat: A Navajo Autobiography* (New York: Harcourt, Brace, 1938).

9    F. Eggan and M. Silverstein, "Obituary: Walter Dyk, 1899–1972," *American Anthropologist* 76, no. 1 (1974): 86–87, https://anthrosource.onlinelibrary.wiley.com/doi/pdf/10.1525/aa.1974.76.1.02a00220.

10   H. R. Klein, H. W. Potter and R. B. Dyk, *Anxiety in Pregnancy and Childbirth* (New York: Paul B. Hoeber, 1950) and H. A. Witkin, et al, *Psychological Differentiation: Studies of Development* (New York: John Wiley, 1962).

11   Walter and Ruth Dyk, *Left Handed: A Navaho Autobiography* (New York: Columbia University Press, 1980).

12   A summary of my mother's life appeared in the *New York Times*. See Douglas Martin, "Ruth Dyk, Champion of Women's Suffrage, Dies at 99," *The New York Times*,

November 26, 2000, https://www.nytimes.com/2000/11/26/nyregion/ruth-dyk-champion-of-women-s-suffrage-dies-at-99.html. A commemoration of my father's life, written by two of his fellow anthropologists, can be found in Eggan and Silverstein, "Obituary: Walter Dyk," 86–87.

13    Winnie Hu, "Invoking Suffragists, Mrs. Clinton Courts Women Upstate," *The New York Times*, August 23, 2000, https://www.nytimes.com/2000/08/23/nyregion/invoking-suffragists-mrs-clinton-courts-women-upstate.html.

# Chapter 3

# EARLY LIFE AND SCHOOLING, 1937–61

## Childhood

After the Navaho field work, my parents moved to Cambridge, Massachusetts, where my father had a research fellowship and later taught statistics at Simmons College. I was born in Boston at Massachusetts General Hospital on February 14, 1937. My parents were pleased. They wanted a boy first. I was independent; as my mother said, "not a cuddly child." My mother was 35 and my father 37. This was still the Depression, and although my parents were well off by the standards of the day (both parents being employed and my mother having a small inheritance), money was still a concern. Years later when I was filling out security clearance forms for the government, I learned from my parents that, in Cambridge, we moved repeatedly, taking advantage of the incentive provided by landlords of a month's free rent. Yet at the same time (not uncommon in those days for a middle-class family), my parents employed a nanny for me and for a time a butler as well. It was clear to me at an early age that my mother preferred working to housekeeping. We spent summers in Truro on Cape Cod at or near Longnook Beach, where my wife Sally and I now have a house, returning to my roots.

I do not have a lot of early memories. One was going out on a lobster boat in Maine with my father and eating lobster cooked on the engine of the boat. Another was trying to kill rats at a barn in Maine with a .22 rifle (no luck). Other early memories relate to health—splitting open my lip in a fall from a runaway tricycle, being hit above the eye with a baseball bat (stitches again) and being stung by many bees (requiring a hospital visit and an adrenaline shot). The scars from the first two are still with me. I also remember Thanksgivings at Uncle Melville's house on Beacon Hill in Boston. (He was the advertising manager for the *Saturday Evening Post*. He was my mother's cousin but had the honorific title of "uncle.") The house was grand and memorable.

My parents with me in tow moved to Brooklyn in 1942. I was 6 years old. The move was occasioned by my father's being hired to teach at Brooklyn College as an assistant professor, at a substantial raise over his Simmons College salary. My mother did not continue to work and was unenthusiastic about moving to Brooklyn because it was, for her, not a place with the caché of Boston or Cambridge. We lived in an apartment building on Remsen Street in Brooklyn Heights. My sister Penelope was born in Manhattan (at my mother's insistence). I recall that we had to use blackout curtains at night. For many years, I thought the purpose was to fool the supposed German bombers, but I later learned that the purpose was to prevent the city lights from silhouetting transport ships off the coast and making them stand out to German submarines. I recall riding alone in the apartment building elevator. It stopped. Despite a wave of panic, I kept pushing buttons until it started again, an early example of solving problems on my own.

## Early Schooling

Between second grade and graduation from high school I attended Adelphi Academy, a school not too far from where we lived. Each class was about 50 people, both boys and girls. I was on a scholarship. The school had existed for quite a while, and it was one of several small private schools in Brooklyn (Poly Prep being another one). Adelphi was close enough to our house that I was able to walk to school. I did well in school from the beginning save in one subject—handwriting. I first became aware of the issue in second grade when my teacher expressed considerable dissatisfaction with my cursive. There was no cure. I sometimes wonder whether in later schooling the inability of others to read my handwriting led to higher grades (because the teachers imagined that the answer was better than it was) or lower grades (because the teachers were unable to decipher the material). The handwriting continues to tax my law clerks, and I sometimes notice that mistranscriptions have even worked their way into the Federal Reporter. I am comforted by the fact that Justice Oliver Wendell Holmes, Jr. also had bad handwriting, but, unlike mine, Holmes's handwriting at least looked legible—sort of like his opinions: always beautifully written but sometimes opaque.[1]

An experience in second grade may have helped to steer me to the law later in life. Someone had set the boy's bathroom on fire by lighting the paper towel bin. I was naturally a suspect, having earlier brought matches to school, and having told other children that the existence of God was questionable at best. A trial was conducted by the school authorities, and I was acquitted. Justice prevailed. The system worked.

Despite my acquittal for arson, I was not in those early grade school years a model of probity. Three experiences shaped my future life in significant ways. The first of these concerns smoking. There was a neighborhood candy store near our house. As an accommodation to the children, most of whom had only pennies to spend, the store would break open packages of cigarettes, and sell individual cigarettes to the kids for a penny or two. For whatever reason, I did not like cigarettes, but the store also sold corncob pipes and small portions of pipe tobacco. I indulged. My smoking lounge was the basement of our house. After several smokes, the pipe became covered with tobacco residue, so I did what seemed natural. I washed the pipe with soap and water. But I failed to rinse away all of the soap. The next time I lit up, the fumes from the burning soap did me in. I stumbled upstairs literally green. My parents had the grace to regard this as terribly funny, but this pretty much cured me of smoking—to my great benefit. While in high school I did not frequent the smoking lounge set aside by the school authorities for the students.

Another important life lesson learned at that time also related to candy stores. It was customary among the neighborhood kids to steal candy and comic books from the stores. I was not entirely comfortable with this but felt that I had to prove myself to be one of the gang with which I had at best a tenuous connection. I swiped a candy bar, but was caught by the proprietor and sternly rebuked, scaring me out of my wits. Again, a great benefit. I never stole again and perhaps carry ethical concerns to extremes (my family fondly recalls disputes over my insistence on detailed customs declarations). But one more lesson was necessary to extend the honesty rule beyond an aversion to stealing. As a child, I was often sick with bronchitis. Because penicillin was unavailable to the general public until after 1945, I was treated with mustard plasters. No one thought to suggest that maybe some exercise would prevent the bronchitis (a lesson learned much later). So, I would stay home from school and fall behind in my schoolwork. Workbooks were brought home. I copied the answers from the back of the book. Caught on my return, I reformed so much that I got a reputation for being a disgustingly straight arrow.

We always took vacations, even later when my father's illness caused strained financial circumstances. I particularly remember during World War II and immediately thereafter going to Warm Pond in the Adirondacks. We rented one of two cabins on a lake, which had no electricity, plumbing or (at the beginning) running water. A taste of what life was like in an earlier time.

My schooling at Adelphi was interrupted at the end of the fifth grade by a trip to Arizona and New Mexico. After my father had been teaching at Brooklyn College for a few years, he earned a sabbatical, and he received a grant from the Wenner-Gren Foundation to continue field work with the Navaho. This was from June 1947 to September 1948. At about that time, I became aware that my father looked very much like Humphrey Bogart, as pictured in Image 2 below, and my mother said he was sometimes mistaken for him by autograph seekers. Since that time, I have been a big fan of Humphrey Bogart movies.

**Image 2.** Walter Dyk

(Fred Eggan and Michael Silverstein, "Obituary: Walter Dyk, 1899–1972," *American Anthropologist* 76 (1974): 86–87.)

With part of the grant from the Foundation, my father purchased a Willys Jeep station wagon, and we all drove across country stopping at the Grand Canyon, the Painted Desert and other tourist attractions. The first place we lived from August 1947 to May 1948, while my father worked on the reservation, was in the middle of a citrus orchard in Phoenix owned by the Olsens. We were allowed to eat whatever produce we wanted, and my sister and I were allowed to hawk grapefruit (being more plentiful than oranges and lemons) at a roadside stand. We kept chickens and ate the eggs, but not the chickens. The Olsens kept goats. When we left, we found a good home for the chickens, being told that they would not end up on the dinner table. I went to sixth grade in Arizona but was an outsider having not attended the school in earlier grades. My parents allowed me to buy a BB gun which I enjoyed, though the one time I managed to kill a dove I was stricken with guilt. My mother dutifully took me to Cub Scout meetings where I learned leather working (my grandfather would have been proud). I learned to ride horses, and learned a match trick from a real cowboy, who was disgusted that I talked too much and asked too many questions ('Why this?', 'Why that?'). (The lawyers who appear before me now might agree.) It was hot, and the living room of the house was cooled by a water evaporation system.

My father made frequent trips to the Navaho Reservation, now recording the material with a wire voice recorder (the precursor of tape recorders). While we were in Arizona, he went to the Mayo Clinic where he was diagnosed with Parkinson's disease—as I mentioned earlier, perhaps the result of encephalitis and a very high fever during the 1918 flu pandemic. He must have had symptoms before then that I had not noticed, and I later learned that he had actually been diagnosed earlier at Presbyterian Hospital in New York (a diagnosis that at the time he did not even share with my mother). My parents shielded me from knowledge of my father's illness until it was undeniable, an approach that did me no favors. It conveyed to me a sense that the illness was something to be ashamed of, and in later years I was embarrassed that my father was ill—an attitude that I now find wrenching to remember. The effect of the disease was gradual. He continued to teach until the early 1960s, even though he had difficulty speaking. The school kept him on so that he could earn a pension. Even with his disability, he mentored others, including Leonard Plotnicov, himself a distinguished anthropologist.

The disease affected both my father's physical state (difficulty walking and speaking) and his mental state, making him in later years prone to anger and paranoia. It was devastating for him and the rest of the family. It deprived me of his companionship and instruction. Most significantly, I was deprived of having the man who existed before his illness—warm, generous, funny and vital. One thing that we were able to do together both before and after his illness was to listen to the *Lone Ranger* on radio. My father must have thought that the Tonto character was a bit peculiar, but he never said anything. Perhaps the portrayal of Native Americans being like Tonto was better in his eyes than the traditional movie portrayal of Indians as bloodthirsty terrorists. I recall FDR's death in April 1945 because *The Lone Ranger* was cancelled that night.

After Arizona we spent a few months in New Mexico in an adobe house with ladders instead of stairs at 1210 Canyon Road, owned by my parents' friend, Jack Snow, a renowned photographer. My father worked on a sequel volume to *Son of Old Man Hat*, with Left Handed (the son of Old Man Hat) and his translator, Philip Davis (Left Handed and Philip were living in our basement). My father never learned to speak Navaho fluently as it was much too difficult (think of the World War II code talkers) though he knew enough to take note of an incomplete translation. I visited the reservation once with my father and remember it as a desolate and undeveloped place. Tuberculosis was common. Philip Davis later died from TB. After the summer in Santa Fe, we returned to Brooklyn. On the trip back my father, because of his illness, could not drive his beloved Jeep. Instead, my mother did the driving. My father was devastated when the Foundation insisted that the Jeep represented unused grant money and had to be surrendered. He hoped to return to the reservation. He never did. Nor did he have success in putting his newly gathered material into publishable form. This material was later used by my mother in producing the second volume of the Navaho biography.

On our return to Brooklyn, my father only taught part time at a reduced salary, and my mother had to go back to work. She became the family's primary breadwinner as my father's ability to work declined. It was very hard for a woman to get a job. Women professionals were uncommon in those days, and often suffered discrimination. I recall that my mother was fired from her first job (for reasons unknown to me) and her tears of anguish upset us all. The stress was considerable. My mother spent one year working at the City Youth Board, then four years at Sloan Kettering. My mother eventually became an assistant professor of psychology with the University of the State of New York (Downstate Medical School). My sister Penelope is quoted in my mother's *New York Times* obituary:

> Ms. Carter said her mother's strong will was evident when Mr. Dyk was suffering from Parkinson's disease and cancer and she was juggling two jobs and raising two children in the 1950's and 1960's. "What choice did I have? I did what I had to do," she said.[2]

Despite the financial circumstances, when my sister and I were younger we had a housekeeper, although they were so poorly paid that discharge for theft was not uncommon. After my parents could no longer afford any help, I was assigned the task of washing the dinner dishes, a job that I hated. Instead, I volunteered to do the cooking. One of my first meals was making chicken cacciatore for a dinner party that my parents were having. It turned out well—when I finally finished it at 10:00 p.m. This started a lifelong love of cooking that continues to this day. There are many memories of family economics, including the oft-told story of my parents' requiring me to return an unauthorized purchase of a 25-cent coffee cake from the local deli.

I did well in school; interestingly, my parents did not push me to succeed or even pay a great deal of attention to my school performance. No helicopter parents or tiger moms here. School success appeared to be assumed. My parents also gave me considerable freedom to travel with friends at age 10 to see movies in downtown Brooklyn, or later when I was 11 or 12 to take the subway myself to Manhattan to buy tropical fish. Tropical fish were my first hobby. When they died as a result of a thermostat malfunction (cooked), I turned to collecting classical music records and built myself a Hi-Fi set, as they were then known. This was made possible by my starting work at age 13, earning my own spending money. In high school, I took part in various extracurricular activities, including the yearbook, the school paper and the tennis team, though I think my tennis in those days was rather poor. It is now a consuming passion.

The movies in downtown Brooklyn were a regular activity. Classical music concerts were as well. I recall sitting on the stage at a Walter Geiseking concert. In 1954, the year I graduated from high school, I went with my sister to Toscanini's last concert with the NBC Symphony. My love of music (particularly opera) continues to this day.

My time in high school coincided with the rise of Joe McCarthy and the Red Scare. He grabbed the public's attention in 1950 and was not finally brought down until 1954. The atmosphere affected my political life and the lives of many others, even our own family. The name of Brownlee Shirek (my father's sister's husband and a communist and labor organizer in the Bay Area) appeared more than once in the House Committee on Un-American Activities records. During that time, I did not regularly read a newspaper or watch the television news (today, I read four papers every morning). I was not politically active, and joining any organization seemed a risk. I avoided the Thalia Theater movie house in Manhattan, which showed Russian films, because it was reported that the FBI photographed those entering and exiting.

## Harvard College, 1954–58

When I was in my last year of high school, I, like my classmates, confronted the question of college. There was no question that I would go to college; there was also no doubt at that time that I would be able to get into some of the top schools, having done well in high school and on my SATs. Entirely absent was any real anxiety about the outcome. I applied to Harvard, Yale, Columbia (my safety school) and MIT, and no other schools. I decided to withdraw my application from MIT because, even at that point, I was not convinced that I wanted to be a career scientist, though I planned to be a science major. I got into Harvard, Yale and Columbia. My getting into Harvard was a bit dicey. In those days and still, Harvard required that the applicants go through an interview process, and I was scheduled to have an interview with a man named Mahue, who was a lawyer in downtown Manhattan. I had the interview, and it did not go well for reasons unknown to me. He recommended that I not be admitted to Harvard, but my high school principal, Mr. Brunch, went to bat for me, and I was admitted. I have always been grateful to Mr. Brunch.

Once I was accepted to college, the question was how to pay for it. The financial aid packages at the three schools were quite different. I received no scholarship at all at Yale; I received a half tuition scholarship at Harvard; and I received a full scholarship to Columbia, I think, including room and board. Columbia was not attractive to me because it was in New York and too close to home. All along Harvard had been my first choice, and I accepted. The tuition at the time I entered Harvard in 1954 was a few hundred dollars, and while the scholarship was half of the tuition, there would be room and board on top of that.

I had worked for a number of years in junior high school and high school as a clerk at Pratt Institute (an art and engineering college) in Brooklyn, both summers and during the school year. I had not been careful about saving my salary. One possible solution to the cost of college was joining the Naval ROTC, which, in exchange for four years of active service, provided full scholarships including room and board. I took the written examination and passed it, and the next step was my physical exam at the Navy recruiting office. The problem was that, in those days, I was very thin and did not meet the minimum weight requirements for somebody as tall as I was. I was around six feet four. I was initially rejected because of the physical exam and told to come back in a month. In the meantime, I was to gain weight by eating bananas and ice cream, which I did. But I did not gain enough weight. So, when I went for the second weigh-in, my solution was to drink a great deal of water beforehand. Unfortunately, they kept me waiting for the physical, so I had to relieve myself, and there went that weight gain.

When I was weighed by the Chief Petty Officer, he was kind enough to lie about my weight and put it down as the minimum, so that I qualified. The only remaining hurdle was an interview with a Navy commissioned officer. If I passed, I would be in the program. I vividly recall the interview. There was a key question. He asked me: "Do you intend to spend the rest of your life in the Navy?" The correct answer to that would have been "Of course that is something I would consider seriously. My father had been a Chief Petty Officer in the Navy. I have always admired the Navy. I am not sure what I will do. It all depends on my experience, etc." That was not the answer that I gave. Instead, I said: "No, I do not intend to spend the rest of my life as a naval officer." Well, whether it was that or something else, I did not get accepted into the program, which would have been a life changing event. As I describe in later chapters, this was not the last time that I had problems with significant questions.

I decided to go to Harvard with the half scholarship that I had, making up the rest with loans, income from working and parental contributions. At that time, unlike today, the loan amounts were not so great as to cause anxiety about the repayments. My parents struggled to pay for college, and I am grateful to them. I think it was very special that I was able to go to Harvard. Of course, Harvard would not admit me today, as is true of most Harvard graduates of my generation (not having been concert violinists or solvers of previously unsolvable mathematical problems while in high school). This has led many of us to feel a bit alienated from the school.

In those days it was not common for people to visit a college before going there. I never visited Harvard, Yale or even Columbia, though it was local. So,

I accepted Harvard without ever having seen the school or attending sample classes or anything like that. It was in many ways a mystery to me what it was going to be like.

At the time I entered Harvard, the country was on the cusp of radical change which we could not remotely foresee. Nor could we fully appreciate the radical change that had already been experienced by our parents' generation—the changes brought about by the electric light, home appliances, cars and airplanes, and the upheavals of two world wars and the Great Depression.

I had done well in high school; I was the co-valedictorian of my class and won various prizes on graduation. But Adelphi was not in most respects an intellectually stimulating school; nor do I think that the education was particularly rigorous. I suffered from that when I went to Harvard, where, unlike people who went to Andover or St. Paul's or other prep schools, I was not particularly well prepared, and my performance in the beginning was average at best. When I started my classes, there was a real sense of having to play catch-up because of my high school education. I was used to being the smartest student in the room and was a bit surprised that there were others at Harvard far smarter than I was.

I also took the wrong courses, concentrating on philosophy which interested me hardly at all. This was in the days before grade inflation, and I had a mixture of Bs and Cs. I do recall receiving one very bad grade in my first year—an E on a paper in the first-year writing course. We were assigned by the instructor to write an essay on "prejudice." I wrote a paper of about 10–15 pages, and it was quite good. I can vouch for that because I ran across it a few years ago and re-read it. The theme was that prejudice could be manifested when individuals treated people better, rather than worse, based on skin color, religion or ethnicity. It came back with a failing grade. I thought this was unfair and went to speak to the instructor. He informed me that the grade was the result of the repellant content. My explanation did not change his mind, and he had apparently never considered that my point exactly described white privilege, a foreign concept at the time.

My interests in high school and at Harvard were affected in significant part by my friendship with a man named Emile de Antonio, who later became a filmmaker of some renown and a significant figure in the counterculture of the 1960s.[3] He was nominated for an Academy Award in 1969 for his Vietnam War documentary, *The Day of the Pig*, and produced *Millhouse: A White Comedy* (about Nixon) and *Point of Order* (about McCarthy). I knew him simply as "d." That friendship was important in shaping my own intellectual development. I had met d because he moved in with and later married a woman named Lois Long, who lived in one of the Pratt faculty houses that lined our street in Brooklyn.

d had attended Harvard in the same class as the future President Kennedy and had been expelled for some kind of misconduct. Misconduct was a theme in his life. d had been in the army during World War II, originally in training as a pilot, but he had been kicked out of the pilot program for leading the cadets in a rendition of *"Deutschland, Deutschland über Alles."* He was demoted to sergeant and ended up being a B29 bombardier, flying bombing runs over Japan. He had joined the Communist Party at some point, and when I first met him, he had just lost his job as a rat inspector for some federal agency because of his communist affiliation. He was placed under surveillance by Hoover's FBI, which reportedly produced a 10,000-page dossier on his activities. His last film, *Mr. Hoover and I*, poked fun at this egregious waste of public resources.

d knew a remarkable number of interesting people. I got to know many of them through him—Robert Rauschenberg, Jasper Johns (painters), Merce Cunningham (dancer), John Cage (composer). I visited the Rauschenberg/ Johns studio in a Manhattan loft building several times. They had not yet been discovered by Leo Castelli, and I was offered the chance to buy a painting for $100. I declined, buying instead a pen and ink sketch by another artist for $25. I refer to the latter as my $250,000 work of art (that is at least what the Rauschenberg or Johns would be worth today if I had had the wit to buy it). d was responsible for my interest in classical music, and he and my family would attend the Frick collection concerts on Sundays and sometimes the New York City Opera. I learned many important life lessons from d, and some less useful, including how to consume too much alcohol (a skill lost years ago).

At Harvard at that time, if you were on scholarship, you were expected to work at school. At least in my first and second year, I worked at the dining hall at Dunster House on the breakfast shift. I loathed having to get up really early, but there were compensations beyond the money. Originally, I started with the job of dishwasher of the compartmentalized plastic trays on which dinner was served. This involved scrubbing off the loose food with a brush, loading the trays into racks and running them through the dishwasher. The era of eating on china at Harvard had disappeared at the end of World War II (though it has since been revived for students demanding better amenities). I recall the first day I was working in the dining hall, one of my coworkers (a "townie," as they were then known) walked up to me, buttonholed me and said, "What do you think of Plato?" I thought he was mocking me for being a Harvard student. But he was not. He actually was interested in Plato and had done well in his high school and was more taken with the study of traditional philosophy than I was. Eventually he was admitted to Harvard. Unbeknownst to me at the time, Harvard was making a real effort to admit students who did not fit the traditional mold. For example, Harvard had a program that admitted some students every year who were graduates of reform school or products of the juvenile justice system (not my friend). I know this because years later I met somebody who was in the class behind me, the class of 1959, who was one of those students who had been accepted at Harvard from reform school. He did very well in his later life, becoming one of the administrators of the Massachusetts juvenile justice system.

Several years after our work together, I ran into my coworker from Dunster House in the Harvard Yard, and he was wearing a tweed jacket and looked the part of a Harvard student. Sadly, he flunked out, which was hard to do. Harvard failed him as it failed many during that time. When I was there, Harvard was a cold place. As far as the administration was concerned, you had to sink or swim on your own without the school's help in navigating the choppy waters. In the end, my coworker friend sank. I swam.

In the dining hall, I was eventually promoted to food preparation, which I enjoyed much more than dishwashing. This mirrored my switch in household chores years earlier. I recall that one of the other food workers claimed to have been a Cossack and to have emigrated to the United States from Russia as a result of the Russian Revolution, which at that point was about 40 years earlier. I do not know whether that was true or not, but it was plausible as he did have a Russian accent and was of the right age. So, I met an interesting group of people at the Dunster House dining hall—compensation for the early hours.

If you were a scholarship student at Harvard, you really felt that you were in a different world than the students who came from rich families. You were not allowed to own a car. Being a scholarship student, you could not afford to go on ski weekends or go down to New York for parties or whatever. It was separating. You felt like a kid with his nose pressed against the glass of a candy store unable to afford the merchandise. My problems in this regard were compounded by the fact that I had been asked to join one of the final clubs but had declined because I thought I could not impose the cost on my parents. The club mentality was not limited to actual clubs. In those days, there was no random assignment of undergraduates to the house residences. You applied to be admitted as if to a club. My roommate (Tom Purvis) and I were consigned to Leverett House with other cast offs, like the future Aga Khan (my roommate's friend).

At the time I attended Harvard, there was not a huge divide between the Republicans and the Democrats. As noted earlier, I was not politically active when I was in high school and was not politically active when I went to college. I did not participate in any political campaigns or political organizations. What I did do, starting in my first year, was to join WHRB, the Harvard radio station. Ultimately it was awarded an FM license. But in those days, it broadcast through the power lines that went into the Harvard buildings and dormitories, so you could tune into it with an ordinary radio, though it was only available within Harvard buildings. WHRB was a classical music station, and I read the news on air regularly. Often there was no time to read the copy in advance. I learned to read ahead of pronouncing the words and how to use the cough button. I also announced the playlist for various music programs. Sometimes I played more than one role. I would assign myself a different handle for different roles: Jeffrey Kline Belcher Smith was one of those. I remember the experience with WHRB as being one of the best experiences that I had at Harvard College.

At the time, the Cold War had led to a missile race between the United States and the USSR. The Soviets launched Sputnik 1 in 1957, while the US program, Project Vanguard, frequently misfired. Only 3 of the 11 attempted launches were successful. We made constant broadcasts about Project Vanguard and its failures at Cape Canaveral, which we took to calling "Cape Carnival."[4] That was the virtue of not being regulated by the Federal Communications Commission (FCC) as an over-the-air broadcaster. I also remember election night in 1956 when Stevenson lost to Eisenhower for a second time after their previous match-up in 1952. Eisenhower's victory in 1956 was slightly stronger than in 1952. He won 41 of the then 48 States (Hawaii and Alaska would only become states in 1959).[5] I was broadcasting from Eisenhower headquarters. The station had set up a feed, and those of us who were Stevenson supporters managed to put in some skeptical commentary about the continuing Eisenhower presidency. The content of those broadcasts was to some extent fueled by the alcohol which was available at the headquarters party. Years later, I met Stevenson at a wedding in South Carolina, and came to appreciate that he did not embrace leadership. He was even reluctant when asked to lead guests into dinner.

The highlight of my WHRB experience was producing a John Cage concert at Sanders Theatre in Memorial Hall at Harvard on April 20, 1956.[6] The concert consisted of prepared piano pieces where various articles were stuffed into the piano to dramatically alter its sound; there were also long periods of silence.[7] To promote the concert, we ran spots on WHRB for John Cage's "Water Music" featuring the sounds of a flushing toilet. The concert was fairly well attended, but to Cage's delight, the music critics walked out in disgust early in the concert.

At some point toward the end of my time at WHRB, I called WQXR, which was a classical music station in New York City, and asked for an interview for a summer position as an announcer. I guess my voice sounded older than I was, and I was offered an interview. I recall going to WQXR and being given this long questionnaire about classical music—who was who and what was what. While I knew a fair amount of classical music, I was stumped by many of the questions. They were kind enough to allow me to go through the audition. Obviously, I was not offered a job. At the time, it was a somewhat humiliating experience. I recuperated by seeing a movie about giant ants.

I started at Harvard as a chemistry major. I had been successful in the sciences and math at high school, so it seemed logical to major in chemistry, even though I was not sure I wanted to become a professional scientist. Harvard in its wisdom assigned George Kistiakowsky, a member of the Manhattan Project and Eisenhower's science advisor, to be my freshman advisor. My first meeting with him was my last. He probably saw insufficient talent in me as a scientist, and he was right. I did not find chemistry to be very engaging. I enjoyed the laboratory work (it was a bit like cooking), but the lectures were not very interesting to me. Math class became uninteresting too. Perhaps because of my involvement with a Wellesley girl in the second half of my sophomore year, while taking a course in advanced calculus, I decided not to go to class or to open the book and tried to take the exam based on my knowledge of the first semester, which did not work. I got a failing grade of E. I lost my scholarship for a semester, which was not a good thing, but I decided at that point to become an English major, which was a very good decision because, if I had gone into chemistry, I would have been, at best, only an ordinary chemist. Being an English major led to a legal career, for which I was better suited.

Sadly, there was a great deal available at Harvard College that I did not take advantage of. Though on my housing form I requested (and was refused) a Black roommate in my freshman year, I did little to get to know classmates with different backgrounds. Nor was I more than distantly aware of the Supreme Court's decision in *Brown v. Board of Education of Topeka*, 347 U.S. 483 (1954), and the profound change that it would bring about. There were many lectures by famous people. I attended some of them—I remember going to hear T. S. Eliot and Learned Hand. I wish I had gone to more. There were really outstanding professors, whose courses I did not take. There were also outstanding professors, whose courses I did take. I recall taking courses from Alfred Harbage, the well-known Shakespeare scholar, and taking courses from Bartlett Whiting, who taught Chaucer. I also took courses from John V. Kelleher, the noted Irish scholar, including auditing his seminar on Joyce's *Finnegan's Wake*. Like many others, I found the novel incomprehensible, but always recall a line from the final page: "My leaves have drifted from me. All. But one clings still. I will bear it on me. To remind me of."

In my time at Harvard, while the students drank to excess, there was nothing as far as I was aware in the way of drinking games that are now prevalent. People just drank and got drunk without trying, and there was almost no use of recreational drugs. Marijuana, of course, was known, and yet I do not recall at any time in my four years at Harvard College going to a party where people were smoking or even hearing about people who smoked marijuana. I knew many people who smoked pot regularly in the 1960s, but not at Harvard College at that time. We knew about Timothy Leary and his promotion of peyote. I remember one of my friends experimenting with that. In my senior year at Harvard, a young woman had been with some of the college football players and had taken LSD. She had to be carried out of the room wrapped in a rug when she became psychotic. But by and large there was no drug culture at that time. It is interesting to wonder why that was true and what the reasons were for the later creation of a drug culture as part of the resistance to the Vietnam War.

One of the singular things that happened to me at Harvard College in my junior year was meeting a woman who later became my first wife. Her name was Eileen Inga Shirer. I met her because it was the tradition in those days to buy a copy of the Radcliffe Freshman Register, look at the pictures, and call the better-looking girls for dates. Inga had a good picture. So, I called her up, and we started dating.

Her father was William L. Shirer, who had been well known as one of the 'Murrow Boys,' the group of CBS broadcasters closely linked to Edward R. Murrow during World War II. He had authored a successful book called *Berlin Diary*, his record of what it was like to be a correspondent in Germany before World War II.[8] He eventually went to work at CBS radio in the States. After a while, he was forced out (effectively fired). At the time that I met him, he was largely unemployed and struggling and working on his book that became *The Rise and Fall of the Third Reich*.[9] That book made him well known again and financially successful.

Bill always claimed that he was fired from CBS News by William Paley, the CBS CEO, because he was too liberal. After he left CBS, he appeared on a list during the McCarthy era called Red Channels.[10] The list purported to identify media personalities who were supposedly Communist or fellow travelers.[11] That listing made it impossible for him to work in broadcasting. I accepted that version of his firing as gospel, though as we shall see later, it might not have been the whole story.

Through my time at law school, with Bill and his wife Tess (a particular favorite of mine) living in relative obscurity, Inga was roughly in the same financial circumstance that I was. Although she did not have much money, her family lived at 27 Beekman Place in New York, which was a three-story townhouse with a view of the East River. For this house they paid the grand total of $125 a month, courtesy, I think, of the generosity of the Shiff Family that owned the property. I guess the Shiffs liked to help a struggling journalist.

Now, 60 years later, when I look back at it, I am grateful that I had the opportunity to go to Harvard College. It was a wonderful time, but it was not the high point in my life. Three of my now colleagues on the Federal Circuit also went to Harvard College (Lourie, Bryson and Hughes). We share that strange experience.

## Harvard Law School, 1958–61

I graduated from Harvard College in June 1958. The graduation was on a beautiful spring day, and my parents and sister attended. During my time at Harvard, like many of my classmates (except, for example, pre-meds and future academics), I had given very little thought as to what I would do after graduation. The anxiety about future employment that pervades college today was absent. We thought there would always be a job. I am not sure whether I began looking for a job before or after I graduated. I had been an English major for the last two years. Although I had done well at Harvard College—I was in the top quarter of my class and graduated cum laude—I was not one of the stars of the class. As a result, I was not marked for a PhD or a career in the academy, which in those days was what the top of the class often pursued. For some, it was a mistake to go on to get PhDs in English or History or other humanities because, as it turned out, there were not enough jobs for them in later years. I was spared that difficulty by not having good enough grades to be a PhD candidate.

Instead, I decided to go into book publishing. That was influenced by the fact that Bill Shirer knew people in publishing, and I thought that he would be helpful in getting me a job in publishing because I was his daughter's boy-friend. He was not particularly helpful, having still not emerged from his own wilderness. I do recall that I had an interview at one publishing house where I was given a manuscript on which to comment. I do not think I did a good job. What I should have said was that it was boring, nobody would read it, and they should not publish it, but I did not. I was not as forthright about it as I should have been. In any event, the problem was that bright English majors from Ivy League schools were a dime a dozen.

Being unable to get a job at a publishing house, I was told that I should apprentice by working in a bookstore. I went to work at Doubleday bookstores, first at Fifth Avenue and then later in Penn Station, earning $44 a week in the summer of 1958, even then not a good salary. It was also not interesting or educational. Other clerks at the store supplemented their income by stealing from the cash register. Publishing looked less like a good career for me.

Though my first interest was in publishing, I had applied to Harvard Law School in my senior year at Harvard College. So, when working at Doubleday, it occurred to me that law school might be a better alternative. I had initially thought about going to law school because Learned Hand had given the Holmes Lectures at the Harvard Law School during the spring of my senior year in college, and I went to hear one or two of those lectures.[12] While I did not understand very much (and indeed the lectures were deemed a bit of a failure), I could see that Hand was a charismatic figure. Also seeing Henry Fonda in the movie *12 Angry Men* kindled my interest in law school. Applying to law school required taking the LSAT. The first time that I took the exam I had a 103-degree Fahrenheit fever. The proctor noticed this and suggested that I reschedule for a later date, which I did. That likely proved to be a life-changing piece of advice. I ultimately did well on the exam and was admitted. I did not apply to any other law schools.

None of my immediate family members had been a lawyer, except for my grandfather, Arthur F. Belcher, who, as mentioned earlier, had been a prominent lawyer in Maine at the turn of the last century. But he had died long before I was born, so I did not have that example to follow. The only lawyer that I knew at the time was Orrin Judd, the father of one of my high school classmates. He was known by the students as the "abortion lawyer," the lawyer who would help high school students get an abortion if needed. That, of course, was not what he was. Rather, Judd was a distinguished lawyer who was later appointed to the federal district court, sadly dying soon thereafter.[13] But when I was in college, I did not know him well enough to seek his advice, nor did I speak with anyone else about what law school was like. This reluctance to seek advice from others was a pervasive feature of my early life. I am better at it now.

Since publishing was not working out, I decided to step into the unknown. I used my Doubleday book discount to buy the necessary law books, left Doubleday, and went to law school. At least when I started Harvard College, mysterious as it was, I had some general idea of the curriculum. When I arrived at Harvard Law School in August 1958, I did not know what to expect. I just showed up and started. From the first moment, I loved it, and it was really, really easy for me. Understanding larger principles through the study of individual cases was far more congenial to me than the study of principles in the abstract.

During that first year I lived in the Gropius Center, supposedly a gem of modern architecture that has achieved landmark status. It was awful—small rooms with cinderblock walls that provided little in the way of a noise buffer. Unlike the Hollywood fantasy depicted in the movie about Justice Ginsburg, *On the Basis of Sex*, the male students did not wear suits, ties and white shirts to class; khaki pants and sports jackets with no ties predominated. At the beginning I participated in a study group but abandoned that after a while. I had no scholarship during the first year, but the tuition was only $800. In the second and third years, the tuition was $1,000 and I had a partial scholarship. Living expenses were an additional cost. In college and law school I took out some loans, but the aggregate was only a few thousand dollars, easily repaid later.

The dean of the law school was Erwin Griswold, a very formidable figure, who still taught tax, though it was said that he taught the 1939 Tax Code rather than the 1954 Code that was then in effect. Griswold would later become solicitor general in both the Johnson and Nixon administrations, and eventually a colleague of mine at the law firm of Jones Day many years later. In those days (and probably still today), the Harvard Law School faculty was a mixture of really great teachers and not so great teachers. The uneven quality was perhaps the result of the hiring process. Recruiting for the faculty at Harvard Law School mostly involved hiring people who had been Supreme Court law clerks and maybe had been in practice for a couple of years. They had rarely proven themselves at another law school, though there were exceptions like Jack Dawson, a wonderful professor of contract law, who came to Harvard from Michigan. In addition to Dawson, I had Paul Freund (who declined the solicitor general position under Kennedy thereby killing his chance of a Supreme Court appointment), Henry Hart (the father of the study of federal courts), Albert M. Sacks (later dean of the law school) and Don Turner (antitrust, and later a member of a tennis group Sally and I played with), who were all remarkable.

Others were not so good despite their major accomplishments outside the classroom. The reaction of the students to poor quality teaching was interesting. In those days, you were assigned to sections in the first year. All sections took the same courses, and you had no choice of professors. Even in the second and third years, core courses were taught by different professors, and you took the luck of the draw. If you were assigned to a professor who was not well regarded, the tradition was simply not to go to that professor's class. You would go to a better professor's class instead. In my first year, I had John McNaughton (later assistant secretary of defense in the Kennedy Administration and one of the architects of the Vietnam War strategy[14]) for civil procedure, and because McNaughton was not a good teacher, I went to Ben Kaplan's class (Kaplan helped develop the prosecution strategy in the Nuremberg trials). When I took constitutional law in the second year (another required course with no choice of professor), Arthur Sutherland (a former clerk of Justice Oliver Wendell Holmes Jr.) was my assigned teacher. Again, his lack of teaching proficiency meant that few students would go to Sutherland's class. There would be roughly 25 students in the classroom, when he was supposed to have 125 students. The rest of his students would sit on the classroom steps to hear Paul Freund, who would have a couple hundred students instead of 125. We returned to Sutherland only in the last couple of classes and volunteered to answer questions, hoping that our absence would be forgotten. I think that is not something that happens today, but it really shows the attitude of the students: We were there to learn, and we wanted to be taught well.

In my first-year section, as mentioned, contracts was taught by Dawson and civil procedure by McNaughton. Torts was taught by Milton Katz (earlier in the Office of Strategic Services, the precursor of the CIA). Property was taught by A. J. Casner, whose intimidating teaching style was caricatured in various books about what it was like to be a student at Harvard Law School (He was said to be the inspiration for Professor Kingsfield in *The Paper Chase*, for example[15]). Agency was taught by Archibald Cox, later solicitor general in the Kennedy Administration and the counsel in the Nixon impeachment investigation. Nixon's decision to fire him led to the Saturday night massacre in October 1973 and then to Nixon's resignation 10 months later.[16] Criminal Law was taught by a visiting Australian, indicative of the importance assigned to the course.

Early in the first year of law school, Inga and I had broken up. I was a bit distracted by that and did not study as much as I should have in the second semester. Nonetheless, I ended up being 25th in my class of some 500 students. The Law Review in those days was chosen entirely by grades, with the top 25 people in the class being invited to join. I still recall vividly when I learned that I made the Law Review. The mail arrived one morning in June, including a letter from the president of the Review inviting me to join. I was stunned. This possibility was not something I had contemplated.

Interestingly, that year the Law Review secretary (who became a close friend in later years) miscounted and mistakenly sent out 26 invitations to join the Law Review. This was soon discovered. Now you would think that perhaps the Law Review would overlook the mistake and admit 26. But no. The 26th person was told that "whoops, you are not invited to join." He later became a partner in a prominent Washington firm.

In those days, participation in all the primary extracurricular activities was determined by grades, so the top 25 went to the Law Review, the next few went to the Board of Student Advisors and the next group through to number 50 went to the Legal Aid Society. Everybody in the class had a class rank from number one to 500 and whatever, and you were told your class rank. It is something that is not now done in any law school I am aware of. People would compare their class ranks. So, it was very much at the top of your mind. But it was not a source of great stress because even people who were in the bottom of the class at Harvard were able to get good jobs at law firms and became partners at law firms. One of those near the bottom of our class was

Phil Bostwick, who later became a friend and a very successful partner in a Washington law firm and a preeminent go-to lawyer in his field.

I spent the summer after my first year working at a small New York firm, Jacobs & Persinger. They were good people, but I probably was not much help to them since I was just learning to be a lawyer. When I left, they gave me a copy of Whitney Darrow's cartoon of *Pierson v. Post* (a case about wild animal ownership), which I still have.

I returned early in August for the second year because if you were on the Law Review, you began a couple of weeks earlier than the others. At that time, I reconnected with Inga. In those days, the *Harvard Law Review* occupied a position much different than it does now. There were many fewer law review publications, and the *Harvard Law Review* was read by the bench and bar. A lot of lawyers subscribed to it. The Review existed to serve the profession, and it was very influential. Today law review articles often tend to be very theoretical and written for other law professors. Judge Harry Edwards made this point in his 1992 article in the *Michigan Law Review*, "The Growing Disjunction between Legal Education and the Legal Profession."[17] This phenomenon has become the focus of much debate over the years.

The task of second-year students on the Law Review was to write case notes that were summaries of recent cases, to prepare memoranda for longer notes and to write those notes, and to cite check articles and other pieces that were going to be published in the *Harvard Law Review*. The goal of most 2L students on the Review was to become an officer in the third year. I did not become an officer on the Review. I think the reason was that I put no effort into trying to become an officer, as evidenced by my attitude toward one assignment that I received. I was asked to write a memo on the significance of signs that you see in restaurants that the establishment is not responsible for hats and coats. I thought it was absurd that anyone would write a note about the significance of those signs, and I said that I was not going to prepare a memorandum on that subject. That was not well received, and I definitely was not viewed as very cooperative. That incident probably ruined my chances. Perhaps it was genetic since my father and cousins all had trouble as a result of talking back to supervisors. Eventually, I wrote a memo on unconstitutional conditions, a good memo that ultimately was the basis for a very good note written by Sidney Rosdeitcher.[18] Looking back, I feel intensely frustrated with myself for not being more directed in achieving the goals to which I aspired. Nonetheless, I learned a great deal from my experience on the Review—the importance of thinking and rethinking difficult problems, paying close attention to detail, and comprehensive research.

At the end of my second year in June 1960, Inga and I were married. The ceremony was performed at St. Marks's in the Bowery in New York. We honeymooned in Canada driving an old Pontiac that was a wedding gift from her father. He had been swindled. The Pontiac had a defective water pump, faltering on the honeymoon and dying soon after, destroying the engine. We returned to the States, and I began work as a summer associate at Winthrop Stimson. Henry Stimson, the distinguished former Secretary of War under Roosevelt and a pillar of the New York bar, was still alive, though I do not recall ever meeting him. The firm touted that there was a Jewish associate, who was about to become the firm's first Jewish partner. This was a matter of some significance given the Wall Street firms' historic anti-Semitism (though not a feature of Stimpson's own make-up). The highlight of the summer came when I was assigned to find a case where a US court refused to enforce a foreign judgment on grounds of fraud. After an exhaustive search I finally found a case on point and proudly showed it to the partner. He gently told me that he was looking for something more authoritative that a New York County Court (trial court) opinion, a lesson in the hierarchy of court authority.

Back at school, I took little advantage of opportunities to meet the law school faculty outside of class. While I did not get to know any of the Harvard professors outside of class, I did meet a Yale Law School professor. We had dinner one evening with Charles Reich, then a professor at Yale and dating one of Inga's friends. He was soon to be the author of *The Greening of America*, the best-selling book that was seen as the culminating expression of late-1960s counterculture.[19] At dinner, Reich pretended to be a Yale law student.

After placing 25th in my class after the first year, I was 13th in my class for the second year, and I must have been in the top 10 in the final year (though there was no separate ranking in the third year). By the end of the third year, my overall class rank was 16.

I had done well enough in law school to make a judicial clerkship a possibility. In those days, the applications for clerkships were not made at the end of the first or second years of law school but rather during the third year. I applied unsuccessfully for a clerkship with Justice Douglas (a friend of Bill Shirer). He wrote back promptly rejecting my application and explaining, "it has been my practice since coming to the Court to select my law clerk from amongst the graduates of schools in the Ninth Circuit." Many of the Douglas clerks did not enjoy their time with the Justice; I was saved. Clerkships with other Supreme Court Justices seemed to be out of the question, as did the very best clerkships at the court of appeals level. Why I did not consider other court of appeals or district court clerkships is a mystery. Instead, I assumed that I would join a firm. Even though I had an offer from Winthrop Stimson after my summer, I had not thought of returning there permanently. Instead, I interviewed with another large New York firm known for its active litigation practice. I was offered a job and accepted.

At some point later during the third year, I was approached by Professor Freund, and he asked whether I would be interested in clerking for retired Justices Stanley Forman Reed and Harold Hitz Burton. I was then a student in Prof. Freund's Supreme Court seminar, had done very well and he apparently thought well of me. I traveled to Washington and interviewed with Justice Reed. He offered me the position. I accepted, telling the New York firm that I would postpone joining the firm. I had only been to Washington once before, to deliver a package to the Securities and Exchange Commission (SEC) when I was a summer associate at Jacobs & Persinger. It was exciting to be coming to Washington during the early years of the Kennedy administration.

I took with me training in legal analysis (taught through the Socratic method) and vivid memories of Professor Freund's seminar (dealing with many of the Roosevelt New Deal cases) and two of his favorite sayings: (1) we can argue about it or look it up; and (2) *ignotum per ignotius* (reasoning about the unknown from the more unknown). As noted earlier, Freund himself was not to make the trip to Washington, having rejected Kennedy's importuning to be solicitor general. Freund became the overall editor of the Holmes Devise, a history of the Supreme Court funded by a bequest from Justice Holmes. Freund, suffering from depression, did not finish his own volume on the New Deal Court. Professor Hart, another great professor at Harvard Law School also suffered embarrassment, stepping aside in the middle of his Holmes lecture in 1963, remarking, "This isn't right."[20] Though these events happened years after I graduated, the memory of them brings great sadness.

Three other people in my class ended up clerking on the Supreme Court. Robin Homet clerked for Justice Frankfurter in my first year at the Court. He had a nervous breakdown during the clerkship, and he was never the same after that (though he had later significant successes in the area of foreign policy). There was an important lesson here. Law school and clerkship success does not necessarily translate into success in the legal profession. Inner demons (Robin), simple bad luck or (surprisingly) an unwillingness to put in the long hours can lead to dead-ends even for the most accomplished. In my second year clerking, others from my Harvard class with more success in later life included Bob O'Neil, later president of the University of Virginia, who clerked for Justice Brennan and Peter Edelman, a distinguished Georgetown law professor, who was going to clerk for Justice Frankfurter. When Frankfurter retired, Peter clerked for Frankfurter's replacement, Justice Goldberg. Many talented people in my Harvard class did not clerk. Obviously, there was a lot of luck involved.

Six members of my class eventually became federal appellate judges. Of all those people who became appellate judges, only Judge Stephen Williams (D.C. Circuit) and I had been on the Law Review. Williams, like me, had not been an officer, so being an officer of the Law Review or even being on the Review was not a requirement for being a federal judge, nor should it have been. Law school grades are not a good predicator of excellence in judging. The other four classmates who became appellate judges were Justice Kennedy and Circuit Judges Silberman (D.C. Circuit), Anderson (Eleventh Circuit) and Tashima (Ninth Circuit). Peter Edelman almost became a seventh (D.C. Circuit), but the Senate turned Republican in 1994, and he was perceived as too liberal to be confirmed and was therefore never nominated.

There were other Justices and judges in the classes ahead and behind me. Two classes ahead of me was Justice Ginsburg. In the class ahead of me were Justice Antonin Scalia and Judge Richard Arnold (Eighth Circuit), who almost became a Supreme Court Justice, and would have if he had not had serious cancer. Richard Posner was in the class behind. He became a Seventh Circuit judge and potential candidate for the Supreme Court. There were many other interesting people at Harvard Law School: One of my classmates, Bernard Nussbaum, became the White House Council for President Clinton. Several others became trial judges, public officials and distinguished law professors. Many became successful law firm partners. So, it was a very illustrious group of people who attended Harvard Law School. Harvard was viewed as pre-eminent at the time. The best alternative in those days was the Yale Law School, which was then viewed as being more concerned with public policy than with law. The notion then was that if you went to Yale, you did not get as good a legal education as you would get if you went to Harvard.

Most of those who went to Harvard Law School in the early 1960s feel very connected to the law school, and many of my friends today were classmates at that time, including Justice Kennedy, Judge Silberman, Jim Springer, Sidney Rosdeitcher, Peter Edelman and many others. David Grossman, Bob Pelletreau (distinguished at the State Department), Tony Essaye and until his death Phil Bostwick and our spouses have a reunion each summer on Cape Cod. In one instance, a former spouse of a classmate, Jill Cooper (now Udall) and her second husband, Tom Udall, are the closest of friends. Connected to the school or not, in those days it was common not to attend law school graduation, and I did not do so. Instead, I took the bar and then traveled to Washington.

## Notes

1   Todd C. Peppers, Ira. B. Matetsky, Elizabeth R. Williams and Jessica Winn, "Clerking for 'God's Grandfather': Chauncey Belknap's Year with Justice Oliver Wendell Holmes, Jr.," *Journal of Supreme Court History* 43, no. 3 (2018): 264.
2   Martin, "Ruth Dyk, Champion of Women's Suffrage, Dies at 99."

3   C. Gerald Fraser, "Emile de Antonio Is Dead at 70; Maker of Political Documentaries," *The New York Times*, December 20, 1989, https://www.nytimes.com/1989/12/20/obi tuaries/emile-de-antonio-is-dead-at-70-maker-of-political-documentaries.html.

4   On Project Vanguard, see Constance McLaughlin Green and Milton Lomask, *Vanguard. A History* (Washington, DC: NASA Historical Series, 1970).

5   1956 Presidential Election, https://www.270towin.com/1956_Election/index.html.

6   "Experimental Music in Sanders Tonight," *The Harvard Crimson* (April 20, 1956).

7   David Tudor, "Music for 2 Pianos; Water Music," *Music for Piano 4–19 and Music for Piano 21-36/37-52* (Cambridge, MA: Harvard University, Sanders Theatre, 1956), https://cagecomp.home.xs4all.nl/chronology_1912-1971.html.

8   William L. Shirer, *Berlin Diary. The Journal of a Foreign Correspondent 1934–1941* (New York: Alfred A. Knopf, 1941).

9   William L. Shirer, *The Rise and Fall of the Third Reich* (New York: Simon and Schuster, 1960).

10  John McDonough, "Eyewitness Historian," *Chicago Tribune*, February 2, 1990, https://www.chicagotribune.com/news/ct-xpm-1990-02-02-9001100059-story.html.

11  Counterattack (Organization), American Business Consultants, *Red Channels: The Report of Communist Influence in Radio and Television* (New York: American Business Consultants, 1950), 135–36.

12  Learned Hand, *The Bill of Rights* (Cambridge, MA: Harvard University Press, 1958).

13  Edward Hudson, "Judge Orrin G. Judd Dies; Cited Willowbrook Abuses," *The New York Times*, July 8, 1976, https://www.nytimes.com/1976/07/08/archives/judge-orrin-g-judd-dies-cited-willowbrook-abuses.html.

14  Art Drake, "The Man behind the Name," *Pekin Daily Times*, January 29, 2011, https://www.pekintimes.com/article/20110129/NEWS/301299988.

15  John Jay Osborne, *The Paper Chase* (Boston: Houghton Mifflin, 1971).

16  Ron Elving, "A Brief History of Nixon's 'Saturday Night Massacre,'" *NPR*, October 21, 2018, https://www.npr.org/2018/10/21/659279158/a-brief-history-of-nixons-saturday-night-massacre.

17  Harry T. Edwards, "The Growing Disjunction between Legal Education and the Legal Profession," *Michigan Law Review* 91, no. 8 (1993): 2191–219.

18  Note, "Unconstitutional Conditions," *Harvard Law Review* 73, no. 8 (1960): 1595–609.

19  Charles A. Reich, *The Greening of America* (New York: Random House, 1970).

20  This episode is confirmed by William N. Eskridge, Jr. and Philip P. Frickey, "The Making of 'The Legal Process,'" *Harvard Law Review* 107 (1994): 2046, note 92.

# Chapter 4

# CLERKING AT THE SUPREME COURT, 1961–63

## Arriving at the Court

The central figure at the Supreme Court in those days was, of course, Chief Justice Earl Warren. Warren was a Californian, trained in law at Berkeley.[1] He served in a number of leading positions in state government before being elected attorney general in 1939. When World War II broke out, Warren opposed the isolationists and supported Roosevelt's campaign to enter the fight. After Pearl Harbor, Warren was a leading proponent of the internment of Japanese Americans. By 1943, he had become governor, a position he held for 10 years. During this time, Warren had a national political profile, running as Thomas Dewey's vice presidential candidate in 1948 and losing to Eisenhower for the 1952 Republican presidential nomination, a defeat for which he held Richard Nixon responsible.[2]

Because of Warren's ultimate support of Eisenhower's candidacy, Warren was promised the next vacant spot on the Supreme Court. In 1953, when Chief Justice Fred Vinson died from a heart attack, Eisenhower was reluctant to appoint Warren, but Warren insisted. He was given a recess appointment (unheard of today) and was confirmed for the position in March 1954. Warren had not been a Supreme Court advocate, arguing only one case before the Court in his time at the bar—*Central Pacific Railyard Company v. Alameda County*, 284 U.S. 463 (1932)—a quiet title action involving the right to real estate in California's Alameda County, where Warren was then the district attorney.

If the central figure at the Court in 1961 was Warren, the central issue was racial discrimination in the aftermath of *Brown v. Board of Education of Topeka*, 347 U.S. 483 (1954), decided seven years earlier. At the end of the previous century, the Supreme Court had decided the notorious *Plessy v. Ferguson*, 163 U.S. 537 (1896), which held that state-enforced racial segregation was consistent with the Constitution's equal protection clause. With the blessing of *Plessy*, the Southern states enforced "separate but equal" racial segregation in the school systems. Subsequent Supreme Court decisions had chipped away at *Plessy* in higher education cases, holding that graduate and professional programs could not exclude students or segregate them on the basis of race in *McLaurin v. Oklahoma State Regents*, 339 U.S. 637 (1950) and *Sweatt v. Painter*, 339 U.S. 629 (1950), because equal facilities were not available to Black students. Those cases nonetheless left *Plessy* in place. In the aftermath of many African-Americans' having served with great distinction in World War II, and the desegregation of the military in 1948, change was in the air.

*Brown* presented the question whether public elementary and high schools could continue to be segregated. The cases had been argued the previous 1952 term when Fred M. Vinson was the chief justice.[3] The conference results were not encouraging. While a majority of the justices favored holding state segregation of public schools unconstitutional, the Court was not unanimous, and Vinson seemed unable or unwilling to achieve unanimity. The justices recognized that a split court would encourage resistance from the Southern states and that only unified support for desegregation could overcome that resistance. Just before *Brown* was to be reargued in September 1953, Chief Justice Vinson died from a heart attack. Warren was given a recess appointment a month later. Frankfurter is reported to have said that Vinson's death was "the first solid piece of evidence [...] that there really is a God."[4] Others saw Warren's ascent as God's punishment, leading Eisenhower to remark years later, again somewhat apocryphally, that appointing "that dumb son of a bitch Earl Warren" was the greatest mistake he made as president.[5]

The *Brown* cases were reargued on December 8, 1953, just weeks after Warren had been given his recess appointment. Where Vinson had failed, Warren succeeded. He wrote a unanimous decision holding that racial school segregation was unconstitutional in *Brown v. Board of Education of Topeka*, 347 U.S. 483 (1954). Some criticized the opinion as not being a work of legal scholarship; it was only 11 pages long and rested on the increased importance of public education since the adoption of the 14th Amendment, and the fact that segregated education was inherently unequal. But it was one of the most consequential decisions in the Court's history and represented the astonishing effectiveness of Warren as a chief justice. Yet the work of *Brown* was not over, given the resistance of many in the South to its implementation.

In the early 1960s, Washington was a bit of a backwater compared to Boston or New York. I remember the Center City Market, which was a farmer's market downtown on K Street. There were trolley cars still running around the city and out to Glen Echo Park in nearby Maryland. Although World War II had been over for 16 years, and the Cold War was in full swing, the Mall was still home to temporary World War II buildings that Roosevelt had been assured would only last for 10 years. Washington just did not have the bustle that came later on. I also learned that, even with *Brown*, there was still a lot of de facto segregation in Washington. There was segregation in housing and, as a result, in education, and also in private clubs, but not in public accommodations, at least not visibly so.

## First Year Clerking, 1961–62

I began work at the Court in August 1961. I do not know at what point I became aware that the Reed/Burton clerk also worked for Chief Justice Warren, but that was the case. I did become aware very quickly that I was not well prepared for my role as a clerk for at least two reasons. First, I had not learned to write or research well, at least to my current standards. Second, the criminal law course at Harvard Law School, taught by a visiting Australian professor, was limited to substantive criminal law and did not cover constitutional procedure. The Supreme Court criminal docket was then populated with many constitutional procedure cases.

Justice Stanley Reed was born in Kentucky.[6] He had been a leading figure in Roosevelt's New Deal, and the solicitor general responsible for arguing many of the most important challenges to New Deal Programs. Appointed to the Court in January 1938 by Roosevelt, he had taken senior status in February 1957 allowing him to sit in the lower Article III federal courts (but not the Supreme Court) and to have law clerk assistance. Justice Harold Burton had been a leading figure in Ohio politics, first as mayor of Cleveland and then as senator starting in January 1941.[7] He was appointed to the Court by Truman in September 1945. He had taken senior status in October 1958. My duties for Justices Reed and Burton were not time-consuming. My recollection is that Justice Reed sat a couple times on the Court of Claims and wrote a few opinions that I drafted for him. He ate rice for lunch every day as a treatment for high blood pressure. Justice Burton sat once on the D.C. Circuit, and I drafted an opinion on common-law marriage for him (*Matthews v. Britton*, 303 F.2d 408 (1962)). I assume that I prepared bench memos for them on the argued cases. My only other recollection of doing work for Justice Reed was helping him research rights to his tobacco allotment on his Kentucky property. I was not much help. Justice Reed ultimately resolved the problem by speaking directly to the secretary of agriculture.

In the chief's chambers were Mrs. McHugh and Maggie, who were secretaries (their relative status shown by the names by which they were known). Warren also had a messenger named Jean Clemencia, who doubled as a driver of his limousine that had the District of Columbia plate number 10. None of the other justices had cars provided by the Court, though they often used their messengers as chauffeurs in their own cars. Mrs. McHugh saw her role as supervising the Warren clerks in nonlegal matters. My co-clerks in the Warren chambers were Peter Ehrenhaft, Gordon Gooch and Hank Steinman.[8] Peter was short, Jewish and from New York City. Earlier, Peter and his family had escaped from Vienna when Hitler had annexed Austria in 1938 (the *Anschluss*). Gordon and Hank were extremely tall and heavyset and from Texas and California, respectively. Peter had clerked previously for then Judge Warren Burger on the D.C. Circuit, and he was the chief clerk for Warren. Neither Gooch nor Steinman had clerked before. Steinman had been a navy carrier pilot and that defined his attitude toward life generally—that is, he had a devil-may-care attitude. The three of them were completely different in experience and outlook.

The clerks' office was not adjacent to the chief justice's chambers but rather located on the second floor of the Court, which meant that the clerks were largely unsupervised. In my first year with Justices Reed and Burton, my office was located next to Justice Reed's chambers on the same floor as Warren's own chambers. The Warren clerks had a secretary, who typed various memos and drafts for the chief and the Court to review. This was a good thing because my typing skills were, and are, quite poor, like my handwriting.

I did not know then, and I do not know now, how Warren selected his clerks. My guess is that he and Mrs. McHugh made the choices; what I do know is that Warren's current clerks at the time played no role in the selection process. The result of this was that no consideration was given to selecting clerks with the ability to work with one another, as far as I could tell. The lack of clerk collegiality in chambers during my two years at the Court was a significant loss.

In my first year, Warren's clerks could not stand each other—that is, Gooch and Steinman could not abide Ehrenhaft because they viewed him as a bit pompous and resented Peter's efforts to supervise their work. Peter must have viewed the other two as impaired adolescents. Steinman and Gooch made Peter's life unpleasant. I recall one time their balancing a bucket of water on the door so that it would fall on Peter's head when he opened the door to come in. Ehrenhaft has reported that he and Steinman had a fist fight over some disagreement.[9] Though Peter later became a good friend, I was at the time a bystander to this and did not try to intervene on either side. Unbeknownst to me at the time, Gooch and Steinman's pranks were not limited to Peter, and at some point they even irritated Warren. He found out that they had a secret hobby pretending to be the chief's bodyguards.[10]

At that time, the Court heard argument in well over 100 cases. In the two terms that I was at the Court, the Court heard 137 cases in the first term[11] and 151 in the second[12] (a level of cases that was to continue for another 20 years thereafter). The number has since precipitously declined. Only 53 cases were signed in the 2019–20 Term.[13] Each justice had two clerks (with the exception of Warren, who had three and part of the Reed/Burton clerk, and Douglas who chose to have only one). Today each justice has four clerks. So, while today's cases may sometimes be more complex and the number of certiorari (cert) petitions is greater, it still could be said that in the early 1960s compared to today, the justices did twice the work with half the clerks. One result was that the clerk memos and draft opinions were a good deal shorter and less searching than they are today.

The tasks of the chief's clerks were several. We prepared cert memos for Warren for the regular docket, describing the cert petitions and responses. We included recommendations to grant or deny. We prepared cert memos for the entire Court in *in forma pauperis* (IFP) cases (submitted by individuals who could not afford counsel). This task was a precursor to today's cert pool where the clerks for most of the justices are pooled to prepare a single memorandum discussing the petitions for certiorari. The IFP cases typically came to the Court in a single copy. The Court had no Xerox machine at that time (the chief's being a traditionalist), so copies of our memos for the justices were prepared using onion skin paper and carbon paper and were appropriately known as "flimsies." Needless to say, the eighth carbon copy—going to the junior justice—was difficult to read. We made recommendations as to the disposition of those IFP cases, advising whether they should be granted or denied certiorari or put on what was called a "special list." Being on the special list was not a good thing because this meant that the case was not even discussed at the conference. The special list, otherwise known as the "dead list," had been an invention of Chief Justice Hughes in the 1930s.[14] I recall that one case was placed on the special list at my suggestion, but the case was removed from the list and cert was granted. I was happy to see that it was later dismissed as having been improvidently granted, seeming to vindicate my view that the case should not have been considered in the first place.

We also prepared bench memos for the chief on all argued cases, and the clerks prepared draft opinions for the cases that the chief justice undertook to write, with guidance from the chief only as to how the case was being decided and the basic approach of the decision. In my experience, a single clerk worked alone on the draft, with comments from co-clerks depending on the writing clerk's preference. There was no rigorous cite-check by another clerk within chambers. There was limited feedback to speak of from the chief justice once a draft was submitted, though he read the drafts carefully, objecting to my failure to date and number the drafts so that he could keep track of them. Warren was interested in results, not in finely crafted opinions that were so admired at the Harvard Law School and by acolytes of Frankfurter. With rare exceptions, the draft the clerk prepared (with Warren's edits) was the draft that was circulated to the Court. In my first year with the chief, I prepared a single draft opinion in *Enochs v. Williams Packing & Navigation Co.*, 370 U.S. 1 (1962), which concerned the Tax Injunction Act.

I did not have a great deal of contact with clerks from other chambers, and the chief made it clear that we were not to discuss what the Warren chambers was doing with other chambers—particularly Frankfurter's. Warren, because of experiences in earlier years on the Court, was much concerned that his clerks not fall under Justice Frankfurter's spell, and we were also forbidden to speak with Justice Frankfurter privately. This concern about clerks falling under the Frankfurter spell was not confined to Warren. My later partner at Wilmer Cutler, Roger Wollenberg, who clerked for Douglas after the war, received similar instructions.[15]

Several memories particularly stand out about my first year. This was the time of the civil rights revolution in the aftermath of *Brown*. One of the clerks came from the South and had not yet accustomed himself to the new reality of desegregation. At that time, there was a barber shop in the Supreme Court. The barber cut the justices' and clerks' hair by appointment, and the barber was open to the staff as well. But this particular law clerk refused to have his hair cut by the Supreme Court barber because the barber was Black. The result was that he was shunned by the other clerks.

Warren was very generous in taking his law clerks to lunch on a regular basis on Saturdays, when we would work a half day. Although Justices Reed and Burton sometimes invited me to lunch, I mostly joined the Warren clerks. Warren loved sports and loved to talk about sports. One of my deficiencies as a clerk at that time was my continuing lack of interest in, and knowledge of, sports. Often after lunch in the fall, Warren would invite us to his apartment to watch college football games. Occasionally he would take us to the Washington Senator's stadium to watch baseball games, as shown in Image 3. There is a photograph of me at one of the Senators' games with the chief justice in our suits and ties. Warren did not invite us to go to the then-Redskins' games, at which the chief was a regular attendee courtesy of the famous trial attorney Edward Bennett Williams, presumably because the tickets were expensive and difficult to get and the clerks did not fit in with the famous good old boys club.

Oddly for someone who had been so successful in public life, Warren, at least in later life, was not good at remembering names, unless prompted by Mrs. McHugh. When we were with him, he was frequently approached on the street by some friend or acquaintance from his past life, and it was clear to us that he had forgotten the name. But because Warren embraced the person with a warm bear hug, the person hugged was unaware of the memory lapse. Sometimes in chambers, Warren would call me Peter (after Ehrenhaft). As I now know, difficulty with names is the result of the aging process, not dementia.

**Image 3.** The chief justice and the clerks at the baseball park

(With permission from the Ehrenhaft Family.)


Warren was always very discreet about commenting on his colleagues. But it was clear that he was not a great fan of Douglas or of Douglas's unconventional lifestyle. I recall one time in particular, when Douglas and a group of Kennedy Administration officials (including Stewart Udall, Secretary of the Interior) had gone to the Old Anglers Inn at lunchtime in muddy boots after walking the C&O Canal towpath and had sat at tables without ordering food. He and the others were asked to leave. I recall the chief's taking us to the Old Anglers Inn the next week and being much amused by the fact that Douglas had been evicted from the premises. Warren reportedly kept a standing reservation at the Inn and gave the proprietor his office phone number in case she ever needed help.[16]

Warren was quite candid with us on a whole range of subjects concerning his work on the Court and politics in general and his loathing of Nixon. He trusted his clerks to maintain his confidences, a trust between justices and clerks that has been largely lost as a result of a number of tell-all books about the inner workings of the Court. Our lunches and other meetings provided a window into Warren's character. He held prudish views but would not let those influence his decision-making. He felt that fair criminal process was not inconsistent with effective law enforcement. After all, he had successfully prosecuted crime in California while protecting defendants' rights. The protection of minorities from government oppression was the highest responsibility of the judiciary. The one subject that was not discussed was the Japanese internment cases that resulted in the *Korematsu* decision (*Korematsu v. United States*, 323 U.S. 214 (1944)). Warren had been in significant part responsible for placing the Japanese in the camps. The Court upheld the conviction of Fred Korematsu for attempting to evade the exclusion order that interned Japanese Americans after the start of World War II. That decision was explicitly repudiated by the Court in its recent *Trump v. Hawaii* ruling (*Trump v. Hawaii*, 585 U.S. ___, 138 S. Ct. 2392 (2018)). While Warren in his later published memoirs said that he regretted his role in *Korematsu*,[17] we were too embarrassed to raise it with him since it seemed like a blot on his otherwise commendable record as a public servant.

Another noteworthy event from my first year was taking a trip to New York to watch the chief justice give the third James Madison Lecture at the NYU School of Law when Russell Niles was the dean. The chief flew up to New York, but he had Jean take his limousine with his number 10 license plate to New York so it would be available to him in the city. The chief generously allowed his clerks to ride to New York in the limousine. The lecture concerned the Bill of Rights and the military and what role the Supreme Court had in ensuring that the exercise of military power did not erode the freedoms guaranteed by the Bill of Rights.[18] At the reception after the speech, I met Telford Taylor, a Columbia law professor, who had participated in the war crimes trials in Germany after World War II and was an acquaintance of my father-in-law, Bill Shirer. Taylor invited me to come to Columbia the next morning to talk about possibly teaching. After the speech was over, Gooch, Steinman and I went barhopping in New York and did not go to sleep that night. I was not in any shape the next morning to be interviewed by anyone for anything, but I showed up anyway. I never heard further about teaching at Columbia Law School, which was probably just as well.

Another memory from my time as a clerk was watching oral arguments at the Supreme Court. There were some very distinguished advocates, such as Solicitor General Archibald Cox and Dean Acheson, Truman's secretary of state and then at the Covington law firm. Archibald Cox was not viewed by the Court as outstanding, in large part because of the perception that he was talking down to the Court,[19] something which Warren in particular found irritating. I do not think that Cox intended to come across this way. It was his awkward manner that made him appear condescending. Bobby Kennedy, the new attorney general, gave his one and only argument (*Gray v. Sanders*, 372 U.S. 368 (1963)). Some years after clerking, I remember watching Richard Nixon's one Supreme Court appearance in *Time, Inc. v. Hill*, 385 U.S. 374 (1967). He was a fabulous advocate. Memorable cases that first year included *Baker v. Carr*, 369 U.S. 186 (1962) (whether the Court would consider political malapportionment of state legislatures) and *Engel v. Vitale*, 370 U.S. 421 (1962) (on prayer in public schools).

Another significant case that year involved states' exclusion of women from jury service unless they volunteered (*Hoyt v. Florida*, 368 U.S. 57 (1961))—a bête noir of the young Justice Ginsburg in her efforts to advance women's rights. A bench memo that I wrote for that case, being part of the Warren archives, came back to life in the early 1990s, when a leading historian, Linda Kerber, asked to interview me about the memo and the case. I agreed to be interviewed, and she showed me my bench memo. In the memo I had said the only thing that could justify this automatic exclusion of women from juries was to ensure that they had adequate time to perform their domestic duties. When she showed me this, I remember being appalled that I had said that, and she said, "I think you were joking." She was right—I recalled that I had meant it as a sarcastic remark, and she wrote this up in her book.[20] My bench memo recommended reversal—that is, I recommended holding the exclusion unconstitutional. Ironically, the Court, in sustaining the exclusion, relied on the fact that a woman is still regarded as the center of home and family life (*Hoyt*, 368 U.S. at 63). Another memorable aspect of *Hoyt* is Warren's concurrence which "concur[s] in the result for the reasons set forth in Part II of the Court's opinion" (*Hoyt*, 368 U.S. at 69). Part II of the opinion held that the statute as applied to the facts of the case was not unconstitutional. I pointed out to Warren that he could not concur in the result without taking a position on the first argument rejected in Part I, concerning the validity of the statute on its face. This logic fell on deaf ears. Warren was saving his powder for a later case involving the same issue—that is, he joined so that he could later say, "I joined only because of the facts of the particular case." But it was not to be. *Hoyt* was not overruled until *Taylor v. Louisiana*, 419 U.S. 522 (1975)—a year after Warren died.

## Second Year Clerking, 1962–63

In the middle of the first year, I asked Warren if I could stay on as clerk for a second year. In those days, the selection of the following year's clerks did not happen until the spring of the preceding year. Though I had graduated from Harvard (and was at risk of being a Frankfurter disciple), Warren said that he would be happy for me to stay for a second year, and so I became his chief law clerk, and again postponed going to the New York firm. The chief's other clerks for the new term were John Niles, the son of the NYU dean, and Peter Taft, the grandson of Chief Justice Taft.[21] John was married and had two children; but John was gay. Later on, when he was a partner at Debevoise & Plimpton, he came out. In the early 1980s, he contracted AIDS and died in 1990. I recall going back to NYU with Gooch and Steinman for the memorial service, which dealt candidly with John's journey. I was struck by the firm's decency. The Reed/Burton clerk was Stuart R. Pollak, who later became a distinguished trial and appellate judge in California.[22] Jim Adler, who was a college roommate and friend of later Justice Stephen Breyer, was originally hired to clerk with Justice Whittaker, but also helped out in the Warren chambers. As with the 1961 Term, there was an absence of collegiality among the three Warren clerks (John, Peter and me), though without the overt hostility. No water buckets and fist fights. The lack of collegiality was a loss to all of us, and I wish it had been otherwise. Ironically, I had been closer to the clerks from the previous year.

During the summer between my first and second years, Inga and I moved to an apartment on 35th Street in Georgetown, on the second floor of a house owned by an elderly couple. They seemed unexceptional, though it turned out that the wife kept a card catalog of the many communists in the neighborhood. When we were there, our daughter Deirdre was born (August 15, 1963). This presented the usual challenges of fatherhood. In those days, cloth diapers were standard. After use, they were sent back to be washed by the diaper service. But the parents were expected first to rinse the excrement off the diapers in the toilet. One day I lost my grip on the diaper, and it went down the drain. How much damage could this cause? A lot. The property owners' apartment was soon covered in six inches of sewage. We must have made the card file.

When I began as a law clerk, the justices, in addition to Warren, were Black, Frankfurter, Douglas, Clark, Harlan, Brennan, Whittaker and Stewart. Warren was one short of a liberal majority. When I started my second year as clerk in July 1962, there had been two significant changes in the composition of the Court. First, Justice Whittaker had had a nervous breakdown and had retired from the Court. Whittaker had been very much the swing vote on the Court, which I think is what led to his breakdown. Whittaker was replaced by Justice White on April 16, 1962, at the very end of my first year of clerking. Then Justice Frankfurter had a stroke and was incapacitated and resigned from the Court. Justice Goldberg replaced him on October 1, 1962. With White and Goldberg, it seemed as though Chief Justice Warren for the first time had a liberal majority of six. But Justice White did not turn out to be as liberal as Warren had hoped. In later years, I am told, Warren was quite dissatisfied with White's voting record and exercised his prerogative as chief justice to assign dog opinions to White. But in the fall of 1962, there were Black, Douglas, Brennan, Goldberg and Warren himself. Even without White, Warren had his liberal majority. This changed enormously what Warren was able to do with the Court.

Warren as chief justice saw himself to some extent as setting an agenda and not just reacting to events. This was natural for Warren with his political background as the governor of California. Sometimes the Court moved quickly, and at other times more slowly to allow public opinion to catch up. The delay in implementing *Brown* is an example of the latter, as was the delay in outlawing bans on interracial marriage—an issue not resolved until *Loving v. Virginia*, 388 U.S. 1 (1967). The Court is always reactive in the sense that it has to wait for a case to come before it, but in the selection of cases that it chose to hear and the way the decisions were written, it was very assertive, particularly so when Warren finally had his majority.

At the beginning of the second term, other graduates of Harvard Law School came to clerk on the Court, including Richard Posner, later a professor at Chicago and judge on the Seventh Circuit; Peter Edelman; and Bob O'Neill. Edelman clerked for Goldberg, Posner and O'Neill clerked for Brennan and Stuart Pollak, who as I noted was the Reed/Burton clerk, was in the class at Harvard behind me. Justice Goldberg was interested in getting to know the clerks of other justices. Occasionally we would be invited to his chambers to celebrate a birthday or something like that. He was very gregarious. He was also both ambitious and naïve. Johnson eventually suckered him into leaving the Court to head the UN delegation with hints of a "President Goldberg." Goldberg's leaving made room for Johnson's friend, Abe Fortas, who joined the Court reluctantly in October 1965, after my time.

My second year as a clerk included a number of significant cases, including *NAACP v. Button*, 371 U.S. 415 (1963) (overturning a Virginia state law barring lawyers from promoting antidiscrimination litigation), *Gideon v. Wainwright*, 372 U.S. 335 (1963) (establishing the right to counsel for indigent defendants in non-capital cases), *Brady v. Maryland*, 373 U.S. 83 (1963) (establishing the prosecutor's obligation to turn over exculpatory evidence to the defense) and *Sherbert v. Verner*, 374 U.S. 398 (1963) (holding that state government cannot refuse unemployment compensation to those declining to work on the Sabbath). Other important cases on the docket followed from the *Brown* decision and the seismic shift that it caused.

Warren was very conscious at the time that *Brown* had caused a lot of controversy. How could he not be? Controversy erupted not only in the South but in academic circles and the mainstream press as well. As to the latter, the complaint was that the opinion was unsatisfactory. James Reston of the *New York*

*Times* had called it a "sociological decision."[23] Learned Hand delivered his Holmes Lecture at Harvard Law School in 1958, which I attended as a college student, and, in the context of the Fourteenth Amendment, Hand argued strongly for judicial restraint.[24] In the subsequent year's Holmes Lecture, "Toward Neutral Principles of Constitutional Law," Herbert Wechsler criticized *Brown* for its apparent lack of rigor.[25] These criticisms made the implementation of *Brown* even more difficult. The critics failed to appreciate that the price of unanimity in the *Brown* decision was the very lack of detailed reasoning that would suggest that *Plessy* had been wrong in the first instance, which some justices found to be a bridge too far.[26] Or, if the critics did understand this reality, they still hungered for a more detailed opinion justifying a result which they argued was unquestionably correct.

The public clamor over the Court's decisions, and the disparagement of Warren in particular, had grown considerably during the 1950s, and the criticism was not limited to *Brown*. Conservatives attacked the Warren Court's criminal procedure decisions, such as *Mapp v. Ohio*, 367 U.S. 643 (1961) (establishing that state courts were obligated to exclude evidence secured in violation of the Fourth Amendment). They viewed those decisions as interfering with the state's sovereign prerogatives and as undermining state criminal law enforcement. There were billboards across the country recommending "Impeach Earl Warren." The most well-known of the several groups campaigning to impeach Warren was Robert H. W. Welch's John Birch Society, which had an $8 million annual budget and membership close to 100,000.[27] Welch even sponsored an essay competition for college students on the question, "Why Chief Justice Warren should be impeached," to which Warren responded that his wife should enter as "she knows more of my faults than anyone else."[28] Warren became very gun-shy about talking to the press. He said that if he made himself available to the press, even a "no comment" would be used to create a headline: "Warren refuses to comment on" whatever subject. But Warren refused to be cowed. In the 1962 Term, he confronted the sit-in cases.

### The Sit-in Cases

Southern resistance to integration had continued for years after *Brown*, and the Court returned again and again to its implementation. But Southern whites were not the only ones made unhappy by the Court's approach. Southern Blacks were unhappy with the glacial pace of racial desegregation in the wake of *Brown* and the fact that segregation continued in private facilities otherwise open to the public. This anomaly led to the sit-in demonstrations at privately owned lunch counters. Lunch counter sit-ins to achieve racial integration went back as far as World War I and World War II when sit-ins occurred in

Washington, DC,[29] but what we think of as the sit-in movement started in 1960. The demonstrations were the focus of national attention, so much so that the Democratic Platform at the 1960 convention endorsed the sit-ins[30] and Johnson in his vice-presidential acceptance speech approved them.[31]

Unlike *Brown* and related desegregation litigation, the objective of the sit-in protesters was not to accomplish reform by litigation, and the demonstrations were not initiated or directed by the legal arm of the NAACP (National Association for the Advancement of Colored People) (which initially questioned the value of the movement). The litigation was a by-product of the demonstrations, and it resulted largely from trespass charges (and breach of the peace charges) brought against the demonstrators. Unbeknownst to me when I started clerking in August 1961, the sit-in cases would occupy a large part of my clerkship. The largest group of sit-in cases came before the Court in the 1962 Term.

*Brown* did not ban segregation unless there was "state action"—that is, where the discrimination could be traced directly back to the state government. The issue in the sit-in cases was whether there was state action or only private action.[32] The viability of the legal defenses to the sit-in convictions was open to question. The earlier version of public accommodations legislation from the post-Civil War period had been invalidated in the *Civil Rights Cases*, 109 U.S. 3 (1883), over the dissent of the first Justice Harlan (also the lone dissenter in *Plessy*). So, there was no statutory ground to rely on. The Commerce Clause, which ultimately formed the basis for the Civil Rights Act of 1964, could not provide a workable theory for there could be no serious claim that the Commerce Clause was self-executing in this context, as opposed to a source of government authority to regulate commerce. A constitutional defense to the trespass convictions would have to be framed in terms of state-action doctrine and the Equal Protection Clause—that is, that the state (or municipal government) was responsible for the lunch counter discrimination either through the action of the police or the courts. But there were problems. While both the police and the state court systems were involved in enforcing the private discrimination, typically neither the arrests by the police nor the convictions by the courts required knowledge or approval of the private discriminatory intent. In this respect the situation was unlike *Shelley v. Kraemer*, 334 U.S. 1 (1948), where the Supreme Court had held that it was unconstitutional for the courts to enforce racially restrictive housing covenants. A similar approach was reflected in *Pennsylvania v. Board of Directors of City Trusts*, 353 U.S. 230 (1957), where the Court held unconstitutional a limit on a charitable bequest for white orphans only. In those situations, the courts were aware of, and were directly enforcing, the private discrimination. Justice Black and other Justices were opposed to extending *Shelley* to reach ordinary trespass convictions.

One of the sit-in convictions came before the Court in the 1960 Term before I began my clerkship (*Burton v. Wilmington Parking Authority*, 365 U.S. 715 (1961)). The Court set aside the conviction because the incident occurred in a building that was government-owned and operated, providing the required state action. In the following term, the Court (with Warren writing the majority) decided *Garner v. Louisiana*, 368 U.S. 157 (1961), setting aside a breach of the peace conviction because of a complete lack of evidence (a due process violation). Still left for the future were the harder cases—trespass convictions where the facilities were privately owned and operated, and the evidence supported conviction under state law.

When appeals from the trespass convictions (and related breach of the peace convictions) came before the Court in the 1962 Term, the Court heard argument in seven of those cases: *Peterson v. City of Greenville*, 373 U.S. 244 (1963); *Shuttlesworth v. City of Birmingham*, 373 U.S. 262 (1963); *Lombard v. Louisiana*, 373 U.S. 267 (1963); *Wright v. Georgia*, 373 U.S. 284 (1963); *Gober v. City of Birmingham*, 373 U.S. 374 (1963); *Avent v. North Carolina*, 373 U.S. 375 (1963); and *Griffin v. Maryland*, 378 U.S. 130 (1964). The United States participated as *amicus* (friend of the Court). The concern within the Court was about the risk of going too far in expanding the state-action doctrine, and this concern was also shared by Solicitor General Cox.[33] The latter was no small matter because the Court depended for its legitimacy in part on the solicitor general's support. Eventually, Cox did support reversing the convictions, though on limited grounds.

The Supreme Court majority never doubted that it wanted to reverse the convictions in those cases. The Court was not going to let those convictions stand because the justices did not want the southern sheriffs and police departments to be able to arrest people for attempting to use public facilities or to peacefully demonstrate. As it turned out, the sit-in decisions by the Court proved to be a delaying action, which afforded some protection to the demonstrators pending the enactment of the Civil Rights Act of 1964. Yet when certiorari had been granted in those cases, I do not think the Court had a very clear idea of the path to follow or what the future would hold. What the Court had to do was to find sufficient state action to strike down the trespass convictions under the Equal Protection Clause without writing too broadly, and to strike down breach of the peace convictions as well.

I was assigned by Chief Justice Warren to work on those cases. My recollection is that the instructions were to avoid resting the decision on some grand principle and to draft the opinions narrowly, which is what I did. The drafts were successful in securing the vote of a majority of the Court. The changes suggested by other chambers were limited. In the trespass cases, one justice (Harlan) dissented, and one (Douglas) would have gone further. One of the cases, *Griffin v. Maryland*, was re-argued and then decided the following year with the same opinion that I had drafted for Chief Justice Warren the previous year. The cases established several propositions: (1) that government action in the form of public accommodation segregation ordinances turned private choice into government action (*Peterson*, 373 U.S. at 247–48); (2) that executive government action prohibiting sit-ins also turned private choice into government action (*Lombard*, 373 U.S. at 273); (3) that private directions by lunch-counter owners to a state officer to enforce racial segregation made the officer's action discriminatory state action (*Griffin*, 378 U.S. at 135); and (4) that private action encouraging sit-ins could not be punished if the sit-ins themselves were constitutionally protected activity (*Shuttlesworth*, 373 U.S. at 265). The Court decided one additional breach of the peace case, holding that disobedience to a police officer's order to disperse could not be punished when the order was based on the officer's desire to enforce segregation and the only disturbance was by counter-demonstrators (*Wright*, 373 U.S. at 291–92).

At the end of the term, Warren asked me to write a memorandum as to the status of the remaining sit-in cases on the Court's docket, which he distributed to the entire Court. In the following term, the Court set aside convictions in other sit-in cases, for example in *Bell v. Maryland*, 378 U.S. 226 (1964), finding that after the enactment of a Maryland public accommodations law, the sit-ins were no longer a crime, and remanding to the state courts to reconsider the convictions. The Court's conferences on *Bell* were among the longest in the Warren era.[34] Ultimately in *Hamm v. City of Rock Hill*, 379 U.S. 306 (1964), after enactment of the Civil Rights Act of 1964, the Court vacated the remaining sit-in convictions on the abatement theory, finding that the enactment of the Civil Rights Act abated the state convictions.[35] Some have been critical that the Court did not go further in affording constitutional protection to the sit-in demonstrators,[36] but I think that the Court wisely chose not to up-end the state-action doctrine, and Congress appropriately provided the necessary resolution.

## Gideon v. Wainwright

Another noteworthy case in my second year was *Gideon v. Wainwright*, 372 U.S. 335 (1963), holding that states were obligated to provide free counsel to indigent criminal defendants in noncapital cases. The case resulted in an opinion by Justice Black overruling *Betts v. Brady*, 316 U.S. 455 (1942). *Betts* had held that, while there was a right to court-appointed counsel in state capital cases, there was no right to appointed counsel in noncapital state cases absent special circumstances. *Gideon* was granted certiorari in my first term at the Court and argued and decided during my second term. The seminal work on *Gideon* is

Anthony Lewis's carefully researched *Gideon's Trumpet*.[37] But in some respects his work is incomplete, and the process was a good deal more complicated than Lewis depicted.

There were several oddities.

The first oddity lay in the background authority. The Sixth Amendment provides that "in all criminal prosecutions, the accused shall enjoy the right [...] to have the Assistance of Counsel for his defense." In 1938, the Supreme Court held in *Johnson v. Zerbst*, 304 U.S. 458, that the Sixth Amendment conferred a right to appointed counsel in federal criminal cases. This was a generous reading of the Amendment since its purpose was not to require appointed counsel. The government in the case conceded that the Sixth Amendment encompassed a right to appointed counsel if requested ("such right is specifically pledged by the Sixth Amendment")[38] and that question was not even addressed in the Court's opinion. So, one of the foundations of the *Gideon* opinion was open to question. Recently, Justice Thomas, joined by Justice Gorsuch, criticized that expansive reading of the Sixth Amendment, seeing it as designed primarily to reject an old English common-law rule that prohibited counsel, not as a guarantee that government must provide and appoint counsel.[39] Whatever the merits of reliance on the Sixth Amendment, it seemed to me then, and seems to me now, that there should be no question that the right to appointed counsel for accused indigents was a fundamental right by the middle of the twentieth century, protected by the Fourteenth Amendment's Due Process Clause if not the Sixth Amendment.

The second oddity was that conferring a right to appointed counsel was hardly an issue of major controversy in most states. Indeed, in *Gideon* an amicus brief by 23 states urged the Court to overrule *Betts* and hold that there was a right to appointed counsel in state cases.[40] Third, with a liberal majority on the Court, the outcome of the case was never in doubt; all the fine briefing and argument in the case by Abe Fortas (counsel for *Gideon*) and his team had no impact on the result, though it did perhaps convince other justices to join the opinion and enshrine Fortas as a legal legend.[41]

Finally, *Gideon* did not arrive at the Court by accident. Before cert in *Gideon* was granted, the Court had granted cert in the *Douglas* case (*Douglas v. California*, 372 U.S. 353 (1963)) which, among other things, involved the right to appointed counsel on appeal in state criminal cases. At the conference in *Douglas* after argument, the justices expressed concern about the anomaly of recognizing a right to counsel on appeal when no such right had yet been recognized at the trial level. At some point during the Court's deliberations about *Douglas*, the Court apparently decided (or the chief decided) that the Court needed a companion case involving the right to appointed counsel at trial, and the Warren clerks (responsible for the IFP docket) were told to find the right case.[42] *Gideon* was the result.

Gideon offered the promise that indigent defendants would finally be competently represented in criminal cases. In large part, that hope has not been fulfilled because of the unwillingness of the states to spend money on appointed counsel and because the Court has been largely unwilling to set aside convictions because of incompetent counsel.[43]

### Other Roles

One of my few responsibilities as chief clerk for Warren was to arrange lunches for the clerks with the justices and other prominent people in the clerks' own dining room near the Court cafeteria. The reason for the separate dining room was to ensure confidentiality—so that the clerks could talk about the work of the Court without being overheard. Each of the justices came and had lunch with the clerks in the dining room during the year. I remember Justice White, in particular, chewing ice from his iced tea and being taciturn. Others from outside the Court were also invited. Dean Acheson came; I remember picking him up at the Defense Department where he was consulting on some matter. McGeorge Bundy, the National Security Advisor to President Kennedy, was another guest.

Attorney General Robert Kennedy came to lunch with us during my second year. It was a bit embarrassing for me to invite the attorney general to lunch because he had also had lunch with the clerks the year before, and it had not gone well. That year, instead of coming to the Supreme Court, Kennedy had generously arranged to have the clerks come to his cavernous office at the Justice Department, where he had a beautiful, catered lunch with us, and then sat around afterwards to discuss anything that we wanted to bring up. One of the clerks, George Saunders, was quite liberal and was intimately familiar with Kennedy's work with Joe McCarthy and on the McClellan Committee (a Senate select committee studying alleged criminal and other improper practices in labor-management relations in the late 1950s).[44] George started questioning Kennedy in a very aggressive way about his past record as an anti-communist. I did not have the wit to interrupt or change the subject, nor did any of the other clerks. So, this went on for some time. Afterwards, Kennedy was quoted in an article for Esquire magazine about that lunch, describing us clerks as

> young men who made the best marks in law school, had all the best
> offers when they graduated, and went into these clerkships without any
> trouble. They've never seen a war or a depression, and everything's been

smooth for them. You should have heard the kind of questions they asked—a lot of complaints about little things—the secretary wasn't very good, or the elevator didn't work. They were things that people—that men—don't complain about.[45]

It was not clear to us what war and what depression Kennedy had personally experienced, or that quizzing Kennedy about McCarthy and McClellan constituted complaining about "little things," rude as that questioning may have been. After this incident, Warren insisted that the clerks were no longer to appear together outside of the Court as a group to avoid the appearance of being too cozy with litigants.

So, it was awkward for me to invite Kennedy for lunch the next year. But I did it, and he agreed to come. We had the lunch, and there was no unpleasant incident as there had been the first year. After lunch, I walked Kennedy back to his limousine that was parked in the Supreme Court garage. Kennedy was a very shy man, and I was both shy and intimidated. We walked down the hall in silence for a minute or two until Kennedy finally turned to me and asked, "What do you do for exercise?" and I responded "Nothing," once again giving the wrong answer to an important question. That was the end of our conversation and the end of my budding relationship with Kennedy.

Our contact with other justices was not limited to the formal lunches in the clerks' dining room. We also had lunch with some of the justices in the public cafeteria when, for example, they would be eating with their own clerks, and we would be asked to join them. I remember one lunch in particular with Justice Harlan. He told us of a case that he argued before Judge Learned Hand at the Second Circuit. My recollection is that it was a bankruptcy case. In those days there were no page or word limits on briefs, and Harlan had filed a brief in excess of 100 pages. The Second Circuit did not (strangely) read the briefs before argument but read them only after argument. At the argument Hand picked up the Harlan brief, tossed it aside, and complained that Harlan had abused the court by filing an unnecessarily long brief. Harlan was mortified. A few days later he received a call from Hand's secretary telling him to come to chambers because the judge wanted to see him. Fearing the worst, Harlan showed up, was ushered into Hand's office and stood there in front of Hand who was reading. Hand finally looked up and said simply, "Damn fine brief." Harlan treasured that.

During the time of my clerkship, there was only one occasion when I can remember meeting with one of the other justices on a Court matter. There was some question about a footnote in an opinion, and Warren asked me to join Justice Brennan and him to discuss it. But in general, all of our communication went through Chief Justice Warren, and there was no direct communication with any of the other justices about the work.

An important task of the chief clerk was to ensure that the IFP memos were done in a timely way and circulated to the other justices. Either because of my own negligence or the negligence of my co-clerks or the collective negligence of the three of us, we came toward the end of the term with a backlog of cases that had not been written up, and I went to the chief justice and asked if it would be okay if those were carried over to the next term, to which he said, "Absolutely not!" We spent nights and weekends writing the memos about those cases, much to the irritation of the other justices, who all of a sudden were flooded with memos at the end of the term, when they were busy trying to finish their work so they could leave for the summer.

One of the most interesting things clerks had to do was sit with the chief justice when he gave orders to the clerk of the Court after the conference of the justices. At the conference, the justices voted on the just-argued cases, and on cert petitions. When the conference concluded, the chief would sit down with the clerk of the Court and dictate the orders. So, we got a window into what had happened before anyone else. Then after the clerk of the Court left, Warren would give us the scoop on what happened at the conference.

October 1962, during my second year, was the time of the Cuban Missile Crisis. I think we were all convinced that there was a very good chance that we would be dead soon, but it did not affect business at the Court, or what we did. I do recall learning later that the chief justice had been approached by the Defense Department and told that if the Soviet missiles started coming in, they would have about 20 minutes notice. They could send a helicopter to pick him up from the Supreme Court and whisk him out of town. And Warren said, "Well, can I bring my wife?" And they said, "No, sir. There is not time." Warren said "Well, never mind then." There was no concern, we noticed, about getting the law clerks out.

I mentioned earlier that the chief justice had a limousine provided by the Court with a number 10 license plate and that other justices did not have Court cars, but had their messengers, people who delivered memos from their chambers to other chambers, drive their own cars. Almost all the messengers, and none of the other staff, were African-American, as best I can recall.[46] But the Court did not have the sort of imperial trappings that now exist, where the justices have a motor pool of cars available and routine security details. People could walk into the Supreme Court without going through metal detectors, which was also true at the Justice Department and other federal offices. There were brass gates that kept the public from going to the justices' chambers unannounced. The Supreme Court had a police force, but there was much less of a security-conscious atmosphere than there is today. Now if you go to the Court, the main doors are closed, and visitors have to go through a metal detector and have their bags inspected. If you drive into the Court garage, a bomb sniffing dog checks out your car.

Every year there was a dinner at the University Club where the chief and his current and former clerks would get together for the evening. Those dinners continued until Chief Justice Warren died. I remember those as remarkable occasions. President Kennedy had come to the dinner the year before I clerked. In a later year, President Johnson, with whom Warren was quite close, came to the dinner and had drinks with the chief justice and his law clerks. Thurgood Marshall was also an honored guest. I also remember meeting President Truman at the Court when he was being escorted around by Justice Clark. I was a great fan of President Truman, so it was a thrill to meet him. To my great regret, I did not keep a journal of my experiences as a clerk on the Court.

## Reflections on My Time at the Warren Court

The Warren Court era is undoubtedly one of the most discussed and most controversial periods in the Supreme Court's history: deified as profoundly transformative by liberals and vilified by conservatives for perceived improper activism. Neither of these positions really captures the artful way in which Warren managed the Court at a critical time for the country.[47]

With the perspective of more than fifty years I think I am able to assess the chief justice with some measure of objectivity that I lacked at the time that I clerked. This assessment no doubt differs from that of others who clerked for Warren in other terms. It also differs from the assessment of some of his biographers.

Despite his directness, candor, graciousness and his warm and smiling exterior (I remember, for example, several years after I left, his cooing over my infant daughter when she sat in his lap), there was an essential aloofness and lack of introspection about Warren, at least in the workplace setting. Certainly, his own feelings about the criticism he received over *Brown* and other cases rarely surfaced, hidden by a facade of sports banter. There was no window into his soul. And Warren seemed uninterested in the litigants and counsel who appeared before him. This even extended to his clerks. In my experience, he rarely asked about what we thought of the world beyond the Court or our personal lives or what our future plans were. With exceptions, he did not volunteer career advice or promote his clerks in their later lives. There was also an essential simplicity in his thinking. He did what he thought was right and moved on with unfailing integrity. Perhaps this approach was necessary for Warren to accomplish what he did as an elected official and as chief justice. After all, agonizing, introspection and complexity of thinking can lead to paralysis, as in the case of Whittaker. But Warren's essentially simple nature makes it difficult to write about him, presenting a challenge of the sort Edmund Morris faced when writing about another California political figure—Ronald Reagan.[48]

What was clear was that Warren made his own decisions. The clerks may have made recommendations in their bench memos as to disposition, but Warren provided little opportunity for lobbying by clerks thereafter. In my experience, after the bench memo was written, he never asked for advice as to how the case should be decided, much less did he assemble his clerks for discussion sessions as to how to decide cases. In my own case, I came to the clerkship with no agenda of my own; I was there to help Warren make his own decision. Nor did the clerks from the various chambers form cabals to help influence the justices to adopt what the clerks viewed as the right decision, a feature of some later years.

With the benefit of hindsight, I can offer some thoughts about why Warren was able to accomplish what he did, some of which appeared in a review I wrote for Law360 in 2020.[49] Many of his decisions were not models of legal craftsmanship—*Brown* being a primary example. But, as I mentioned, there were often good reasons for this—in the case of *Brown*, the need to achieve unanimity. Yet most of the Warren Court's significant decisions have stood the test of time, earning general acceptance in the legal community, and few have been overruled.

The Court accomplished a major expansion of civil liberties. And all this was done (some would argue, the right of privacy aside) with fidelity to and reliance on fundamental constitutional principles, though not enough to satisfy a strict originalist. For example, in *Brown*, the Fourteenth Amendment was not in its inception designed to outlaw school (and other) segregation, but the amendment enshrined the basic principle of legal equality for people of all races.

So too in *Gideon*, the Sixth Amendment (incorporated into the Fourteenth Amendment) was not designed to provide free counsel for indigents, but it was no stretch to find that legal representation in criminal proceedings was essential to a fair trial guaranteed by the Due Process Clause. It was not much of a leap to find that legal representation was effectively unavailable unless provided to indigents free of charge.

How and why did the Warren Court succeed? It was not just because the justices had the right moral compass. That was surely an important ingredient, but it is a good deal more complicated than that. Other factors I think played a critical role, factors that make a twenty-first-century Warren Court unlikely even with the "right" president and the "right" appointments.

First, there was Warren himself, sometimes seriously undervalued as the driving force behind the Warren Court. As a former public official, his approach was to identify and solve problems. Enormously self-confident, selfless and expert at wielding the few levers of power granted to a chief justice, his stature on the national stage gave him unique authority within the Court. One example was his ability to urge criminal procedure reform, drawing from his long prosecutorial experience to assure his colleagues that fair criminal procedure was not inconsistent with strong law enforcement. Also, his willingness to allow Justice Brennan to claim more than his fair share of credit contributed to an effective partnership.

Second, an important set of the nation's problems needed to be addressed. These problems were susceptible to a judicial solution and, in most instances, unlikely to be addressed by legislation without action first by the Court—segregation, criminal procedure, state legislature malapportionment, First Amendment rights and the like. To be sure, the Court could not solve all these problems alone. The country needed the Civil Rights Act of 1964 to eradicate state-sponsored and private segregation. The country needed (but did not get) adequate legislative appropriations at the state level to provide indigents with counsel in criminal cases. But the Court lit the fire.

While the current Court has been faulted by some for shying away from issues that could and should be addressed, such as political gerrymandering, many of the country's central problems—including immigration, income inequality and relations with China and other countries—are evidently not susceptible to judicial solutions. On the other hand, police misconduct at the center of the Black Lives Matter movement is in part a judicial problem.

Third, most members of the Warren Court were politicians, by nature eager to address and solve problems, willing to broker compromise attuned to the public mood, and inured to conflict and occasional failure. At the beginning of the Warren Court (in *Brown*), there was Warren himself, former governor of California, and experienced at many levels of state government. Hugo Black, Harold Burton and Sherman Minton had been US senators. Stanley Reed, William Douglas, Robert Jackson and Tom Clark had served in high positions in the executive branch. Felix Frankfurter was the perpetual adviser to Franklin D. Roosevelt.

By the time Warren retired, others who had political experience had joined the Court—William Brennan (the son of a politician and active in crafting legislation),[50] Byron White (deputy attorney general), Arthur Goldberg (secretary of labor), Abe Fortas (gadfly on the Frankfurter model), Potter Stewart (who had been elected to the Cincinnati city council) and Thurgood Marshall (solicitor general and general of the civil rights movement). Only John Harlan and Charles Whittaker did not have political experience.

And even if the Court was not liberal enough for some—doing too little and too slowly for school desegregation, postponing a decision on interracial marriage until *Loving v. Virginia*, 388 U.S. 1 (1967), sustaining punishment for symbolic speech (draft card burning in *United States v. O'Brien*, 391 U.S. 367 (1968)) and sustaining opt-out for women in jury service (*Hoyt v. Florida*, 368 U.S. 57 (1961))—it was because of the Court's political sense that the country was not yet ready for more. Claims that the Warren Court was too constitutionally conservative miss this point.[51] The political caste has been largely excluded from the Supreme Court in recent times. Former public officials with their problem-solving pragmatism have, by and large, not been appointed. If you think that has not made a difference, compare Sandra Day O'Connor's pragmatic views to those of her nonpolitical peers.

Fourth, despite the "Impeach Earl Warren" signs and conservative opposition to some of the Court's decisions, the general public at the time was receptive to, or at least tolerant of, many of the Warren Court reforms. Many in the South violently resisted *Brown*, but the rest of the country was on board—until busing became an issue. As noted, 23 states filed an amicus brief supporting the result in *Gideon*. In various other cases, there was little or no amicus opposition by the states to the decisions reached by the Court. That was true, for example, of *Mapp v. Ohio*, 367 U.S. 643 (1961) (exclusion of illegally obtained evidence), *Griswold v. Connecticut*, 381 U.S. 479 (1965) (the right of married couples to buy contraception), *Loving v. Virginia*, 388 U.S. 1 (1967) (interracial marriage) and *Katz v. United States*, 389 U.S. 347 (1967) (search and seizure). Significant amicus opposition was voiced only in *Engel v. Vitale*, 370 U.S. 421 (1962) (on school prayer), *Miranda v. Arizona*, 384 U.S. 436 (1966) (limits on police interrogations) and *Shapiro v. Thompson*, 394 U.S. 618 (1969) (the fundamental right to travel).

The country's support of the Civil Rights Act of 1964, the Voting Rights Act of 1965 and the Great Society programs demonstrated a generosity of spirit necessary to the Warren Court's accomplishments. The support of a strong and liberal press (the Greenhouse effect, as named by conservatives after the Pulitzer Prize-winning *New York Times* Supreme Court reporter Linda Greenhouse) was important as well. If you think that the public plays no role in shaping the Court's jurisprudence, the role of public opinion is clear from the long road between *Bowers v. Hardwick*, 478 U.S. 186 (1986) (sustaining prosecutions for sodomy) and *Obergefell v. Hodges*, 576 U.S. 644 (2015) (recognizing the right to same-sex marriage).

Finally, the members of the Warren Court were not, by and large, subscribers to the Holmes creed of judicial restraint: When Judge Learned Hand urged Justice Oliver Holmes to "do justice" on the bench, the justice demurred—"That is not my job. My job is to play the game according to the rules."[52] For the members of the Warren Court, their job was not just to decide cases according to the rules but to also do justice. Like it or not, that was the way it was. Warren was an essential figure in the development of jurisprudence that led the country into the modern era. I do not have Warren's political background. As a judge, I fit more into the Harvard mold. Yet, I learned from the chief justice that there is more to judging than the careful analysis of cases, statutes and regulations that characterized my education at the Harvard Law School.

## Notes

1   "Earl Warren (1891–1974)," *Biography of Earl Warren*, Earl Warren College, UC San Diego, https://warren.ucsd.edu/about/biography.html.

2   John A. Farrell, "The Inside Story of Richard Nixon's Ugly, 30-Year Feud with Earl Warren," March 21, 2017, https://www.smithsonianmag.com/history/inside-story-richard-nixons-ugly-30-year-feud-earl-warren-180962614/.

3   A history of the *Brown* decision can be found in Richard Kluger, *Simple Justice, the History of Brown v. Board of Education and Black America's Struggle for Equality* (New York: Knopf Doubleday, 2011).

4   Richard Brust, "The Court Comes Together," *American Bar Association Journal*, April 1, 2004, https://www.abajournal.com/magazine/article/the_court_comes_together.

5   Michael O'Donnell, "Commander vs. Chief," *The Atlantic*, April 2018, https://www.theatlantic.com/magazine/archive/2018/04/commander-v-chief/554045/.

6   "Reed, Stanley Forman," Federal Judicial Center, https://www.fjc.gov/history/jud ges/reed-stanley-forman.

7   "Burton, Harold Hitz," Federal Judicial Center, https://www.fjc.gov/history/judges/burton-harold-hitz.

8   Many of the law clerks of Chief Justice Warren participated in recording oral histories of their experiences in and around 2014 to commemorate 50 years since the *Brown* ruling. The Oral History Center project is housed at the Bancroft Library, University of California, Berkeley. See Laura McCreery, "The Law Clerks of Chief Justice Earl Warren: R. Gordon Gooch," Oral History Office, The Bancroft Library (University of California, Berkeley, 2014), 22 and 401–2; also, Laura McCreery, "The Law Clerks of Chief Justice Earl Warren: Peter Ehrenhaft," Regional Oral History Office, The Bancroft Library (University of California, Berkeley, 2014), 12.

9   Laura McCreery, "The Law Clerks of Chief Justice Earl Warren: Peter Ehrenhaft," Regional Oral History Office, The Bancroft Library (University of California, Berkeley, 2014), 12.

10  Laura McCreery, "The Law Clerks of Chief Justice Earl Warren: R. Gordon Gooch," Oral History Office, The Bancroft Library (University of California, Berkeley, 2014), 22; and Ed Cray, *Chief Justice: A Biography of Earl Warren* (New York: Simon & Schuster, 1997), 402.

11  Paul C. Bartholomew, "The Supreme Court of the United States, 1961–1962," *The Western Political Quarterly* 15, no. 4 (December 1962): 652.

12  Paul C. Bartholomew, "The Supreme Court of the United States, 1962–1963," *The Western Political Quarterly* 16, no. 4 (Decemer 1963): 757.

13  Adam Feldman, *Final Stat Pack for October Term 2019 (updated)*, SCOTUSblog (July 10, 2020, 7:36 p.m.), https://www.scotusblog.com/2020/07/final-stat-pack-for-october-term-2019/.

14  Gregory A. Caldeira and John R. Wright, "The Discuss List: Agenda Building in the Supreme Court," *Law & Society Review* 24, no. 3 (1990): 810; and Richard A. Posner, *Reflections on Judging* (Cambridge, MA: Harvard University Press, 2013), 47.

15  J. Roger Wollenberg, interview by Jeffrey F. Liss, *Oral History Project*, The Historical Society of the District of Columbia Circuit (1997), 19–20.

16  Patricia Sullivan "Old Angler's Inn Proprietor Olympia Reges Dies", *The Washington Post*, September 4, 2005, https://www-washingtonpost.com/archive/local/2005/09/04/old-anglers-inn-proprietor-olympia-reges-dies/.

17  Earl Warren, *The Memoirs of Chief Justice Earl Warren* (Garden City, NY: Doubleday & Company, 1977), 149.

18  Earl Warren, The Bill of Rights and the Military, *New York University Law Review* 37, no. 181 (1962): 181–85.

19  Ken Gormley, *Archibald Cox: Conscience of a Nation* (Reading, MA: Addison-Wesley, 1997), 153.

20  Linda Kerber, *No Constitutional Right to Be Ladies* (New York: Hill & Wang, 1999), 177–81.

21  Laura McCreery, "The Law Clerks of Chief Justice Earl Warren: Peter R. Taft," Regional Oral History Office, The Bancroft Library (University of California, Berkeley, 2014).

22  Laura McCreery, "The Law Clerks of Chief Justice Earl Warren: Stuart R. Pollak," Regional Oral History Office, The Bancroft Library (University of California, Berkeley, 2013).

23  James Reston, "A Sociological Decision: Court Founded Its Segregation Ruling on Hearts and Minds Rather than Laws," *The New York Times*, May 18, 1954, 14, https://www.nytimes.com/1954/05/18/archives/a-sociological-decision-court-founded-its-segregation-ruling-on.html.

24  Learned Hand, *The Bill of Rights* (Cambridge, MA: Harvard University Press, 1958).

25  Herbert Wechsler, "Toward Neutral Principles of Constitutional Law," *Harvard Law Review* 73, no. 1 (1959): 20–22.

26  Richard Kluger, *Simple Justice, the History of Brown v. Board of Education and Black America's Struggle for Equality* (New York: Knopf Doubleday, 2011).

27  Cray, *Chief Justice: A Biography of Earl Warren*, 389.

28  Ibid., 390–92.

29  David Brinkley, *Washington Goes to War* (New York: Alfred A. Knopf, 1988), 250; and Gilbert Ware, *William Hastie: Grace under Pressure* (Oxford: Oxford University Press, 1985), 9.

30  Thomas Oliphant and Curtis Wilkie, *The Road to Camelot: Inside JFK's Five-Year Campaign* (New York: Simon & Schuster, 2017), 251.

31  Ibid., 272.

32  The sit-in cases have become the focus of much scholarship in recent years, not least through the efforts of Christopher Schmidt. See "Divided by Law: The Sit-Ins and the Role of the Courts in the Civil Rights Movement," *Law and History Review* 33, no. 1 (2015): 93; and *The Sit-Ins: Protest and Legal Change in the Civil Rights Era* (Chicago: University of Chicago Press, 2018).

33  Gormley, *Archibald Cox*, 156–57.

34    Ryan C. Black and Timothy R. Johnson, "Behind the Velvet Curtain: Understanding Supreme Court Conference Discussions through Justices' Personal Conference Notes," *Journal of Appellate Practice and Process* 19, no. 2 (Fall 2018): 241–42.

35    Years later in *Adickes v. Kress & Co.*, 398 US 144 (1970), the Supreme Court held that state involvement in lunch counter segregation supported a claim for civil damages under 42 USC 1983.

36    Cristopher W. Schmidt, *The Sit-Ins: Protest & Legal Change in the Civil Rights Era* (Chicago: University of Chicago Press, 2018), 147–51.

37    Anthony Lewis, *Gideon's Trumpet* (New York: Random House, 1964).

38    Brief for the United States at 10.

39    See *Garza v. Idaho*, 586 U. S. ——, 139 S. Ct. 738, 756–58 (2019) (Thomas, J., dissenting).

40    Bruce A. Green, "Gideon's Amici: Why Do Prosecutors so Rarely Defend the Rights of the Accused?" *Yale Law Journal* 122, no. 8 (2013): 2336.

41    Laura Kalman, *Abe Fortas: A Biography* (New Haven, CT: Yale University Press, 1990), 182–83.

42    Laura Kalman, *Abe Fortas: A Biography* (New Haven, CT: Yale University Press, 1990), 181.

43    On the limits of Gideon, see Stephen B. Bright and Sia M. Sanneh, "Fifty Years of Defiance and Resistance after *Gideon v. Wainwright*," *Yale Law Journal* 122, no. 8 (2013): 2150–74; and Andrew Cohen, "How Americans Lost the Right to Counsel, 50 Years after 'Gideon,'" *The Atlantic*, March 13, 2013, https://www.theatlantic.com/national/archive/2013/03/how-americans-lost-the-right-to-counsel-50-years-after-gideon/273433/.

44    Robert F. Kennedy, *The Enemy Within: The McClellan Committee's Crusade against Jimmy Hoffa and Corrupt Labor Unions* (Boston, MA: Da Capo Press, 1994).

45    Dan Wakefield, "Bobby," *Esquire Magazine*, April 1, 1962, 128.

46    An article on the history of the Supreme Court Messengers was published not long ago in the *Journal of Supreme Court History*. See Matthew Hofsteft, "Afterword: A Brief History of Supreme Court Messengers," *Journal of Supreme Court History* 39, no. 2 (2014): 259–63.

47    The classic liberal interpretation in M. J. Horwitz, *The Warren Court and the Pursuit of Justice* (New York: Hill and Wang, 2018), compared with the conservative critique of Robert H. Bork, *The Tempting of America: The Political Seduction of the Law* (New York: Simon & Schuster, 1990), esp. chapter 3.

48    Edmund Morris, *Dutch—a Memoir of Ronald Reagan* (New York: Random House, 1999). See also Andrew Ferguson, "The Tragedy of Edmund Morris," *The Atlantic*, May 28, 2019, https://www.theatlantic.com/ideas/archive/2019/05/why-edmund-morris-couldnt-capture-reagan/590353/.

49    Timothy Dyk, "Judging a Book: Dyk Reviews 'Democracy and Equality'," *Law360*, January 13, 2020, https://www.law360.com/articles/1231233.

50    Seth Stern, Stephen Wermiel, *Justice Brennan: Liberal Champion* (New York: Houghton Mifflin Harcourt, 2010).

51    See Driver's claim that "Absent from the scholarly debate about the Warren Court thus far, however, is a sustained liberal argument contending that it made significant mistakes-not for going too far, but for not going far enough in its judicial reforms," in Justin Driver, "The Constitutional Conservatism of the Warren Court," *California Law Review* 100, no. 5 (2012): 1101–68.

52  Learned Hand, "A Personal Confession," in *The Spirit of Liberty*, 3rd ed. (New York: Irving Dilliard, 1960), 302, 306–7. See also the opening paragraph of my dissent in *Beer v. United States*, 696 F.3d 1174, 1187 (Fed. Cir. 2012) (Dyk, J., dissenting), discussed in subsequent chapters.

# Chapter 5

# THE TAX DIVISION, 1963–64

## Special Assistant to Louis Oberdorfer

In the spring of 1963, finishing my second year clerking on the Supreme Court, I turned to the question of what I would do next. The other clerks and I were anxious to get out into the real world—to go to the government or to a firm, which is very much contrary to the attitude of many of the clerks that I see now at our court. Today many look at their clerkships as the high point of their lives. Things are never going to be that good again, and they are not looking forward to private practice, though the academy or government service still appeal.

I assumed that I would finally join the large firm in New York, whose offer I had previously accepted twice and postponed for my clerkships. I again interviewed with the firm, and one of the firm's older and most distinguished partners (by dint of his ancestry and well-publicized public service) was my contact. We will call him Garrett. At the time I was earning almost $10,000 a year as the chief clerk ($1,000 more than the other clerks for no good reason). Garrett offered me $11,000, and I agreed to start in the fall. Two weeks later, Garrett wrote to say that the firm could only pay $9800 (about the same as I was then earning) because that was the set salary for lawyers two years out. He was clearly embarrassed. I declined, my thought being that a deal was a deal. My impression was that the firm was reluctant to depart from the agreed salary scale followed by the New York firms (an agreement broken some years later by Cravath). I do not mean to suggest that it was not a fine firm. It was, and is, and I think things turned out for the best. Interestingly, Justice Stevens apparently earned less in his first year of private practice than he did as a clerk.[1]

This left me without a job but with a new attitude toward my professional life. Until then, my approach toward my professional career was that things would work out, that the world would take care of me, and that very little effort was required by me to shape the future. That now changed.

The Kennedy Administration had enormous appeal for young lawyers. We all envied Richard Goodwin, former president of the *Harvard Law*

*Review*, who had joined the administration and at the time was assistant special counsel to President Kennedy. I learned that there was an open position as special assistant to Louis F. Oberdorfer, the assistant attorney general (AAG) in charge of the Tax Division at Justice, a position previously filled successfully by Frank Michelmen and Dan Mayers, both of whom had been in the class ahead of me at Harvard Law School. I interviewed, and I was offered the job. I accepted for a one-year period from July 1963 to July 1964. The salary was $11,000 a year, the same as the New York firm's original offer. Gone now are the days when a lawyer could earn more in government service than in a firm. John Jones, who had been a partner at Covington & Burling, was the first assistant to the AAG, and Ed Smith was the second assistant. Ironically, Smith later became a judge on the Federal Circuit. So, I briefly overlapped with him, both at the Department of Justice and as a Federal Circuit judge.

Being a special assistant was in some ways a bit awkward because you had a special relationship with the AAG that line attorneys did not have, and a special assistant was treated better than most young lawyers. I tried not to exacerbate the natural tensions. The lawyers in the department, with a few exceptions, were excellent. They took their jobs very seriously and regarded it as an honor to work for the government.

My office at the Tax Division was small, but was part of the Oberdorfer suite. My recollection is that I worked pretty hard at the department. My duties were not well defined. My primary job was to serve Oberdorfer. One of my tasks was to review recommendations for the prosecution of people who failed to file income tax returns or evaded taxes. In those days, the Tax Division frequently prosecuted people who failed to comply with their tax obligations, something that is a good deal less common today. Edmund Wilson was prosecuted and convicted for failure to file income tax returns for nine years, which he unconvincingly claimed was an act of protest because his money was being used to develop nuclear, chemical and biological weapons. He later wrote a book about the experience, *The Cold War and the Income Tax: A Protest*, seeking to exonerate himself from the criminal charge.[2] My review of the prosecution recommendations did not take much time and probably was not useful to anyone.

In the early months at the department, the majority of my workload was dependent on what Oberdorfer was doing. From July to November 22, 1963, when President Kennedy was assassinated, Oberdorfer focused both on civil rights and tax issues. My recollection is that he was not involved in the work to enforce *Brown* in school desegregation, but he was involved with efforts to voluntarily desegregate public accommodations. The Kennedy Administration sought to bring about the end of discrimination in public accommodations by encouraging voluntary action by business owners. This was before the Civil Rights Act of 1964 banned such discrimination.

For Oberdorfer, who had grown up in Alabama, it was natural for him to be part of that effort, though my sense was that he was not as much a part of it as he might have liked. Often during the fall of 1963, he would tell me that he was going to take a trip to someplace in the South to work on civil rights issues. He would say to me, "Tim, pack your bag. Bring it in tomorrow, and we are going to go to Birmingham, Alabama" or wherever it was, and I would pack my bag and bring it in the next morning. But we never went anywhere. I watched, but did not participate in the march on Washington in August 1963, thinking that as a Justice Department employee, it was not appropriate. Oberdorfer became even more involved in civil rights once he had left the department, becoming co-chairman of the Lawyers Committee for Civil Rights Under Law.[3]

## Kennedy Assassination

In November 1963, President Kennedy was assassinated. I vividly recall the moment when I learned the news. I had gone to lunch with Peter Edelman, who was then serving as the special assistant to John Douglas, the head of the Civil Division. We came back from lunch, and there was a lot of commotion. People were listening to the radio, and that is how I learned that President Kennedy had been shot, and later that he had died. And, of course, everyone was shocked. In the next few days, over the weekend, we spent every waking hour sitting in front of the television set at home at 35th Street in Georgetown with Peter and other friends watching the events unfold in the aftermath of the assassination. Later I went to witness the funeral procession on Pennsylvania Avenue in front of the White House with the riderless black horse and a train of dignitaries including such disparate figures as Charles De Gaulle, the French president, and Haile Selassie, the Ethiopian emperor.

After the assassination, the Kennedy family was trying to collect material for a Presidential Library. My assignment was either a joke or a pointless exercise. The assignment was to collect material from the FBI for inclusion in the library. The FBI had a great deal of material that related to President Kennedy's accomplishments, problems and activities. I met with someone at the FBI, I cannot remember who it was, and asked him for material to include in the library. The response was to give me copies of a couple of J. Edgar Hoover's books, which I sent to the Presidential Library, and that was that. Nothing else.

Hoover was not a great fan of Robert Kennedy, as they had often fought over control of the FBI. Hoover was not going to cooperate with the Presidential

Library. Hoover regarded everyone as having a secret that he could turn to his advantage and kept file cabinets with dirt on every politician and on other people in Washington. After Hoover's death in 1972, there was a question of what should be done with his files. Many were destroyed on Hoover's posthumous orders by his secretary Helen Gandy.[4] Those that remained were transferred to Mark Felt, then associate director in the FBI and much later revealed as "Deep Throat," the confidential source at the heart of the Watergate affair.[5] Eventually, the files were transferred to a congressional committee, and many disappeared. In 2005, a number of Hoover's "Official and Confidential" files were transferred to the National Archives. It is not clear how much of Hoover's original collection survived.[6] So far as I know, they never made their way to the Kennedy Library.

One of the things that was different about the Justice Department in 1963 and 1964, compared to now, was the level of security. You could walk into the Department off the street without going through a metal detector or identifying yourself and wander around the building. Today the security is extremely tight. You have to show an ID and go through a metal detector, even if you are a federal judge. For years there was a sign at the entrance which told of Attorney General Ramsey Clark, who did not show his identification to get into the building, and the guard said in response "I do not care if you are J. Edgar Hoover, you are not allowed in without showing your ID," revealing the guard's view as to the relative importance of the attorney general and the FBI director. Maybe the sign is still there.

Even though I had met Attorney General Kennedy on two occasions when I was clerking at the Supreme Court, I never saw Kennedy during the time that I was at the department. I can only recall two projects of mine in which Kennedy was involved. One was the effort to collect JFK material from the FBI after the Kennedy assassination. The other was helping on a Kennedy speech. I came up with some boring topic, and instead the attorney general chose to talk about the Kitty Genovese murder in Queens in New York, an example of the so-called bystander effect, where the dying screams of 28-year-old Genovese were reportedly ignored by multiple witnesses, though the accuracy of the reporting of the case has recently been doubted.[7] Kennedy gave his speech about the murder and the reported "bystander effect," which of course was much more relevant and interesting than what I had proposed.

## Work on Tax Issues

With the assassination of President Kennedy, the department's focus shifted away from voluntary desegregation to the passing of the Civil Rights Act. With

Johnson as president, Attorney General Kennedy had much less authority and influence, and Oberdorfer worked primarily on tax issues. While in the Tax Division, I was fortunate to argue nine tax cases in various circuits around the country. In some I briefed the case, and in others I did not. I recall three incidents in connection with those arguments.

The first argument that I had was in *Estate of Hull v. Commissioner*, 325 F. 2d. 367 (3d Cir. 1963), at the Third Circuit in Philadelphia. The presiding judge on the panel was the iconic Judge William H. Hastie, the first Black federal appellate judge. I was scheduled to fly to Philadelphia on the morning of the argument. It was a short flight, probably about 40 minutes. I cut it very close in terms of making the flight, and, in fact, I missed the plane, which of course caused me a good deal of anxiety. There were many flights at that time, and I was able to get on the next one and arrive well before the oral argument not much the worse for wear. Unhappily, I lost the case, but the Department of Justice thought enough about the position that I was arguing that they authorized a petition for rehearing, which was denied. Hastie was earlier considered by Kennedy for appointment to the Supreme Court, but Warren and Douglas advised Kennedy against this because Hastie was too conservative.[8] Justice White was appointed instead.

A second experience involved a trip to the Ninth Circuit in San Francisco. At that time, I stayed with one of my mother's cousins, Don Owen, who was a patent lawyer in San Francisco. He had a house at the top of Belvedere Island in San Francisco Bay. He had a commercial fishing boat, which he used as a pleasure boat. He also had a classic yacht (appropriately named Pat Pending). He had a couple of Rolls Royces and a couple of Land Rovers, one of which he lent to me for my use when I was there. He was obviously doing very well. When I was there, he asked if I would be interested in seeing his office, which was in downtown San Francisco. I said that I would be very much interested. We went to see his office, which was extremely spare. It had bare wooden furniture and linoleum on the floor. It struck me that he was trying to convince his clients that he ran a no-frills operation and was a very good bargain as a patent lawyer. I had no sense at the time that patent law would become a focus of mine many years later.

The third incident that I recall was when I went to the Fourth Circuit to argue a criminal tax case, and my then-wife Inga came with me to the argument. The tradition in those days (and I think still is in non-COVID times) was that after the argument the judges come off the bench to shake hands with the counsel. When they did, one of the judges pointed to my wife and asked if she was the criminal defendant. This was, I guess, a joke. I very much enjoyed those cases and the opportunity to argue in appellate courts the year after finishing my clerkship.

### First National City Bank Case

Another notable project was working on the *First National City Bank* case (*United States v. First National City Bank*, 325 F. 2d 1020 (2d Cir. 1964) (en banc)), which ultimately went to the Supreme Court (*United States v. First National City Bank*, 379 U.S. 378 (1965)). It involved the question of whether a district court could enjoin a US bank with foreign branches from transferring assets held at one of the foreign branches. The foreign branch in this case held assets of the US taxpayer, and the Tax Division was trying to prevent the foreign branch from transferring those assets to the taxpayer.

The case had started before I began at the Tax Division. By the time I arrived, the district court had decided that it had the authority to issue the injunction. The Second Circuit, by a two to one vote, had reversed, rejecting the Tax Division's argument that the injunction was permissible (*United States v. First National City Bank*, 321 F.2d 14 (2d Cir. 1963)). The case was being briefed en banc before the full Second Circuit, and the Tax Division was working on the brief for the United States.

The en banc brief was drafted initially by the US Attorney's Office in the Southern District of New York. There was, and is, a well-known strained relationship between the Southern District and the main Justice Department in Washington, DC. My recollection is that at the time the Department of Justice lawyers referred to the Southern District lawyers as the "Sovereign State of the Southern District of New York" or something on that order.

In those days before e-mail, communicating about briefs involved sending a hard copy of the brief from one place to another, and then discussing the brief on the telephone. That is what happened in this case. The Southern District draft brief had been sent to Oberdorfer for his review. He had asked me to read the draft and to give him comments, which I did. Oberdorfer was convinced that changes were necessary. Oberdorfer and I got on the telephone with the lawyer in the Southern District to discuss the necessary revisions.

The lawyer in the Southern District was Bob Arum, a Harvard Law School graduate who later became famous as a boxing promoter. Arum's interest in boxing had come about through his work for the department, having been assigned in 1962 to confiscate the proceeds from the Sonny Liston-Floyd Patterson fight.[9] Arum had what were seen as the usual characteristics of a lawyer in the US Attorney's Office in the Southern District—that is, he was quite arrogant. In the telephone call, Oberdorfer gave Arum extensive changes in the brief. Oberdorfer went on for probably a half-hour giving detailed comments, such as, page three, line six, add the additional sentence such and such and such and such. After about half an hour of this, Oberdorfer asked Arum to read back the last change, and Arum said he could not do it. When

Oberdorfer asked why, Arum said, "Because I have not been taking down any of your changes."

This absolutely infuriated Oberdorfer, who had quite a temper. In fact, one of my tasks as special assistant was to suggest sometimes that he ought to follow Lincoln's practice of thinking about things before he dashed off a letter to someone expressing his anger and outrage. Sometimes he would listen to me and wait until the next day when he would abandon the diatribe. In this instance, Oberdorfer did not wait and told Arum that this was unacceptable and that I would be sent to New York to rewrite the brief on the premises, which I did. This was during the Chinese New Year. I remember hearing the sounds of fireworks outside as I reworked the brief. So, there were fireworks both inside and outside.

The argument on rehearing took place in October 1963. Oberdorfer argued the case. I do not recall going to the argument, but the decision came down in January 1964 and it continued to reverse the district court's injunction (*United States v. First National City Bank*, 325 F.2d 1020 (2d Cir. 1964)). Ultimately the United States petitioned for certiorari. The Supreme Court granted certiorari and heard the case in November 1964 after I had left the department. Oberdorfer again argued the case. The Supreme Court reversed the court of appeals and held that the injunction could be properly issued (*United States v. First National City Bank*, 379 U.S. 378 (1965)).

While the case was pending in the Supreme Court, the Office of the Solicitor General was working on the merits brief. Even though I had left the Department, Oberdorfer asked me to comment on the draft brief. I called the deputy or assistant in the solicitor general's office who was working on this and offered some comments, which were rejected because I was no longer in a position of authority. I learned a valuable lesson from that: when you are gone, you are gone. And that is the end of it.

Oberdorfer was always very generous to me, and I continued to keep up with him after he left the department. He thought well of me, and I thought very well of him. Within a couple of years of my leaving to join Wilmer Cutler (described below), Oberdorfer came to Wilmer Cutler as a partner. Oberdorfer had no joy in being a tax lawyer. His motto was "I don't mind what I do as long as I don't do the same thing twice." Another of his favorite sayings (one that I have appropriated) is "Don't kick an open door"—meaning stop arguing when you have won the point. After some years at Wilmer Cutler, he became a federal district judge in the District of Columbia. I recall vividly years later then-judge Oberdorfer's telling me that he had been excited about becoming a district judge because he was going to help to right wrongs in the civil rights area which had always been his passion. But what he found was that many of the cases (e.g., involving employment discrimination) had no merit—they involved a plaintiff who was paranoid and was complaining about things that never happened. I think he was a bit disappointed that his role as a district judge did not enable him to redress wrongs as often as he would have liked. I have heard similar complaints from other district judges.

The experience of district judges in some individual cases is hardly a measure of the importance of the Civil Rights Act of 1964. The main impact of the law was on companies and employees who never came to court. In other words, most employers would tailor their conduct to fit the demands of the law. When they did have a problem, they would often settle meritorious cases, so many meritorious cases did not end up in court. The law had a tremendous impact, but it was not an impact that was manifested as much at the district court level on a daily basis. Landmark Title VII cases or not, Oberdorfer was a distinguished judge and he made substantial contributions to the administration of justice. I am so grateful I had an opportunity to work closely with him.

## Notes

1   John Paul Stevens, *Five Chiefs: A Supreme Court Memoir* (New York: Little, Brown, 2011), 138.
2   Edmund Wilson, *The Cold War and the Income Tax: A Protest* (New York: Farrar, Straus and Giroux, 1963).
3   "Legends in the Law: Louis F. Oberdorfer," Bar Report, https://www.dcbar.org/bar-resources/publications/washington-lawyer/articles/legend-oberdorfer.cfm.
4   Greg Bradsher, "Thank You Very, Very Much J. Edgar Hoover," National Archives, September 10, 2012, https://text-message.blogs.archives.gov/2012/09/10/thank-you-very-very-much-j-edgar-hoover/.
5   "Hoover's Official and Confidential Files to Be Transferred to the National Archives from the FBI," Press Release, National Archives, August 1, 2005, https://www.archives.gov/press/press-releases/2005/nr05-89.html.
6   Ibid.
7   Robert D. McFadden, "Winston Moseley, 81, Killer of Kitty Genovese, Dies in Prison," *The New York Times*, April 4, 2016, https://www.nytimes.com/2016/04/05/nyregion/winston-moseley-81-killer-of-kitty-genovese-dies-in-prison.html.
8   J. N. Giglio, *Presidency of John F. Kennedy* (Kansas: University Press of Kansas, 1991), 41–42.
9   "Bob Arum," International Boxing Hall of Fame, accessed June 9, 2021, http://www.ibhof.com/pages/about/inductees/nonparticipant/arum.html.

# Chapter 6

# WILMER CUTLER, 1964–90

## Moving into Private Practice

My time at the Department of Justice had been a source of great satisfaction, but my appointment as a special assistant was only for one year. In spring 1964, I began to look for another job in private practice. I made a mistake by not accepting the opportunity to serve as an assistant US attorney in the US attorney's office in Washington, DC, something that was then available to people who had served as special assistants at justice. You could sign up for a six-month tour of duty, but I did not do that. What I missed was the valuable opportunity to try jury cases, something that I never had in private practice.

I felt some urgency about getting started in private practice. By that time, I had caught the Washington bug and did not consider returning to New York. Among the appeals of Washington was the revolving door. I could join a firm, leave for a period to serve in the executive branch and then return to the firm, the Washington firms' often being tolerant and even encouraging of such detours. In my case it never happened, but that prospect was a major factor in my decision to stay in Washington.

At that time, there was no such thing as a clerkship bonus for those who had served as Supreme Court law clerks (as evidenced by my New York firm experience), and there was not any great rush by the firms to hire people who had clerked. So, I had to find a firm rather than waiting for a firm to find me. Washington was not then the vibrant center of national practice that it became in later years. Federal regulatory practice at the law firms in Washington in the early 1960s was limited. Since regulatory practice was what I wanted, my choices were similarly limited. In my mind, it boiled down to Covington & Burling, Arnold, Fortas & Porter (A, F & P) and Wilmer, Cutler & Pickering.

Covington had 100 lawyers in 1960 and was growing.[1] A, F & P had 31 and Wilmer 22 by the end of 1963.[2] From the outset, I did not seriously consider Covington for the simple reason that I wanted to join a firm where I was likely to become a partner. A large number of my Harvard Law Review classmates had gone there; despite a liberal partnership policy, the chances of advancing to partnership seemed uncertain. This narrowed it down to A, F & P or Wilmer, though I interviewed at a number of other firms to see if I was missing something.

I remember the interview at A, F & P. I met with one of the partners, who, following their usual practice, said: "if we invite you for a full set of interviews here, we will of course want a commitment from you in advance that you will accept a job if we offer it." And I said, "Well, that is very nice, but I do not think I can agree to that condition." And he said, "Well, okay, we will make an exception in your case and will allow you to interview without having such a commitment." I did the interviews, which included going to a Friday end-of-the-week cocktail party. It struck me that there was more than a little self-satisfaction in the firm, which I found to be a bit off-putting, and eventually I decided instead to go to Wilmer Cutler whose culture I found more congenial. Both were excellent firms, and A, F & P (now Arnold & Porter) can count many distinguished alums, including Attorney General Merrick Garland.

Wilmer Cutler was a new entity. In 1962, Lloyd Cutler and others broke off from Cox, Langford, Stoddard & Cutler and combined with the former Cravath Washington outpost called Wilmer and Broun.[3] The breakup of Cox, Langford, Stoddard & Cutler was precipitated by Cox's refusal to take Sam Stern as a partner. Stern was a protégé of Cutler, and I guess that was the last straw in a rocky relationship. I believe that I was the sixth associate at Wilmer Cutler. Two of the other associates were people I knew from the Harvard Law Review in the class above me: Dan Mayers and Arthur Gardiner. My recollection is, that having earned $11,000 a year as a lawyer at the Justice Department, I was offered $12,000 a year (about $106,000 in today's money) to begin work as an associate. I began in September 1964 as the only associate in my law school class. When I was hired, it was agreed that I would receive credit toward partnership for the three years I had spent clerking and working at Justice. Eventually, I became a partner on January 1, 1969.

After being at Wilmer Cutler for a couple of years, as with other young associates at that time, it seemed sensible to buy a house in the District of Columbia. Previously Inga and I had rented, first on Columbia Pike in Virginia, and then on 35th Street in Georgetown. After joining Wilmer Cutler, we had rented a house on Newark Street in Cleveland Park. Housing has become very, very expensive in the inner cities of Washington and New York and other metropolitan areas, and most associates starting at a law firm now would not be in a financial position to purchase a large house in Northwest Washington (unless the associate had other income or assets). But in those days, I could afford to buy a house in Cleveland Park in the same area where some of the firm's partners lived. My daughter Caitlin (fondly known as Miss Ethicality because of her high standards) was born while we lived there.

One collateral benefit of buying in Cleveland Park was that I could carpool to work with another associate and a couple of the partners who also lived in Cleveland Park. This fostered a connection with the partners in the firm that was not immediately work related. The carpool probably did not increase my prospects with the firm because I was usually late for the pickup. Early in my time at Wilmer Cutler, John Jones, the deputy assistant attorney general at the Tax Division at Justice, asked me if I would like to be the tax assistant in the Office of the Solicitor General. I regretfully declined. Working in the Office of the Solicitor General would have been an exciting and valuable experience, but if I had done that, it was almost certain that I would have missed the even more valuable CBS experience that I describe below.

In the beginning at Wilmer Cutler, Cutler was the firm's primary rain-maker, attracting business from a variety of sources. The notion of organized business development was not initially on the firm's radar. Cutler brought in a sufficient amount of business that the firm was operating at capacity and sometimes beyond capacity. Cutler was brilliant, complicated and the very opposite of warm and cuddly. He was liberal in the context of the time, and, when attacked by those further to the left, defensive. He shared a remarkable number of traits in common with Abe Fortas (founding partner of A, F & P and later Supreme Court justice). Both were secular Jews and youthful prod-igies, attended Yale Law School, had continued strong ties to the school, loved classical music, were great rainmakers for their firms, and were charming to clients and government officials. Like Fortas, Cutler was not generally a mentor to the younger lawyers. Cutler certainly was not a mentor to me. He viewed me perhaps as insufficiently deferential. My strained relationship with the primary rainmaker in the firm was not beneficial.

But there were differences between Fortas and Cutler. Fortas was all-in on client representation; Cutler was more comfortable when he could play the role of counsel to the situation. While both were demeaning to those who worked for them, Cutler demeaned more by neglect than by outright humili-ation (which Fortas often did).[4] At a going-away party for a young associate at Wilmer Cutler, one of the partners read a mock telegram from Cutler, saying that he had often considered talking to the departing associate when they were in the elevator together. Both Cutler and Fortas projected enormous self-con-fidence, but there was something endearing in the fact that Cutler's hands shook so much when he was giving an oral argument that he had to clasp his hands behind his back to conceal it. And Cutler, unlike Fortas, would never do anything remotely unethical.

Anyone who has read the comprehensive history of the Cravath firm knows how deadly dull recitation of firm work can be.[5] I hope what follows does not fit into that category.

## CBS Litigation

I was fortunate to do interesting work at Wilmer Cutler right from the beginning. At about the time that I joined the firm, CBS had hired Wilmer Cutler
to work on a Federal Communications Commission (FCC) rulemaking known
as the Prime Time Access proceeding. Cutler had earlier represented Times-
Mirror Broadcasting in bringing regulatory proceedings against CBS and
other networks with some success. CBS had been impressed by Cutler and the
quality of his work. Wilmer Cutler had another attraction and that was Roger
Wollenberg, who was a venerated communications lawyer. So, CBS decided to
bring its regulatory business to Wilmer Cutler, and the relationship continued
for over twenty years.

### *The Broadcasting Regulatory Structure*

Necessary to an understanding of the CBS work is an appreciation of the
then regulatory structure. In some respects broadcasters do not enjoy the same
First Amendment protections as the print media. Primarily on the theory that
spectrum scarcity warranted regulation of broadcasting in the public interest,
Congress had enacted several relevant statutes regulating broadcast programming. These statutes included, first, the Equal Time provision (Section 315 of
the Communications Act) requiring broadcasters that provided time to a political candidate (with some exceptions) to provide free equal time to opposing
political candidates. This provision was a serious concern to broadcasters.
For them, it was essential to avoid equal time obligations because of the
expense and disruption to popular entertainment programs. The scope of the
exemptions was much litigated. One significant example of an equal time
problem arose in connection with the famous Roger Mudd interview with Ted
Kennedy that doomed Kennedy's run for the 1980 nomination.[6] CBS management almost nixed the broadcast because of equal time concerns and ran
it only after one of the CBS lawyers, Ralph Goldberg, convinced management
that the broadcast was exempt from Equal Time obligations.

Second, there was also a provision requiring broadcasters to sell advertising and program time to federal political candidates (Section 312(a)(7) of
the Communications Act), a requirement that ultimately proved to be very
profitable to the broadcasters. Third, there was a provision barring indecency
(defined to be broader than obscenity) (Section 1464 of the Criminal Code).
Fourth, and most significant, was the statute giving the FCC the authority
to license broadcasters and to regulate broadcasters in the "public conveni-
ence, interest, or necessity."[7] The FCC exercised this authority to require
that broadcasters provide substantial amounts of news and informational

programming and provide opposing views in such coverage (the so-called fairness doctrine).These obligations (none of which would be valid against the print press under the First Amendment) were enforced by the FCC by individual rulings, and, most concerning, were considered in broadcast license renewal proceedings. Renewal of a license could be denied for failure to abide by the programming requirements or for other violations of law. The potential for license denial was greatly feared. The broadcast networks themselves were not licensed, but each held licenses for stations in major markets. The loss of such a license would be catastrophic because of the value of the license and the role the network stations played in the overall enterprise. The system lent itself to jawboning and threats not only by FCC commissioners but also by presidents. Nixon famously schemed to deny renewal of the broadcast licenses of the *Washington Post* using broadcast-related threats to affect print press coverage.[8]

CBS was intent on resisting additional program regulation. The FCC, on the other hand, for years had been obsessed with the supposed oligopic power of the three television networks (then, CBS, NBC and ABC), which FCC Chairman Newton Minow once claimed created a "vast wasteland" of mediocre programming.[9]

During that time, CBS was a great institution, flawed to be sure, but dedicated to excellence in broadcast journalism and to protecting the news and other programming from FCC and other government intrusion. While the old CBS lasted, it was a privilege to represent it on some matters of major significance. CBS thought of itself as a journalistic entity entitled to virtually the same protections as the print press. William Paley, the CEO of CBS, and Frank Stanton, the CBS president and later vice-chairman, cared deeply about broadcasters' First Amendment rights, though not always as much as the news staff thought they should. Stanton was the industry leader in this respect. CBS itself was the leader in television news and the anchor on the *CBS Evening News*, Walter Cronkite, became famously "the most trusted man in America." CBS News' renown served as an antidote to whatever regulatory problems might arise in other areas (the quiz show scandals—the fixing of game shows by CBS and others—being an example).

CBS was willing to pay lawyers to defend it from program regulation, even though the bottom-line impact of such regulation in most instances was not large. The concerns with a network oligopoly and the FCC regulation that it spawned now seem quaint in light of the competition from cable, satellite and streaming. But, at the time, when broadcast television, radio and print publishing were the prime sources of news and information, broadcasters' First Amendment rights and the scope of FCC regulation mattered a great deal.

During the early years, Paley and Stanton selected excellent presidents of the news division and talented broadcast executives. We worked with many of them. At the news division, first was Richard Salant, whose tenure was interrupted by Fred Friendly, before Salant resumed in 1966. In his past life, Salant had been in the Office of the Solicitor General and ironically had worked on the first Supreme Court case sustaining network regulation (*NBC v. United States*, 319 U.S. 190 (1943)). As the head of the news division, he had prominently displayed in his office a quote from Shakespeare: "The first thing we do, let's kill all the lawyers."[10] Of course, the quote from Shakespeare was misleading. Shakespeare's point was that the anarchists wanted to kill the lawyers precisely because the lawyers represented stability and fairness. Salant displayed the quote because, not having been a news reporter, he felt that he had to prove that he was not a lawyer anymore and did not like lawyers. Salant was succeeded by the able Bill Leonard and then by the less able Van Gordon Sauter.[11]

CBS also had a series of really distinguished general counsels and other outstanding lawyers in its general counsel's office. When Wilmer Cutler was first retained, Leon Brooks was the general counsel. He died from a heart attack at the Harvard-Yale football game and was succeeded by Richard Jencks, and then Bob Evans. John Appel was the deputy and Ralph Goldberg eventually became associate general counsel. Others of significant ability were Eleanor Appelwhaite and Howard Jaeckel in New York and Joe DeFranco in Washington. All of them were excellent and valued the Wilmer Cutler relationship. In later years, Jim Hill was general counsel for a time, succeeded by the mercurial Jim Parker and then by George Vradenburg, formerly with Cravath. These later general counsels were less friendly to our firm, even though Cutler himself had unwisely recommended Parker for general counsel.

For most of the relationship, it was a great pleasure working with CBS lawyers, with those in the news division and with the network management. The lawyers were thoughtful and sensible. They did not take themselves too seriously, and they valued outside counsel. I do not remember any disputes about legal fees in the early days, something which has become an unhappy part of the relationship today between clients and law firms. Many of the CBS lawyers became friends as well as professional colleagues of mine. For many years, CBS broadcast the US Open tennis tournament, and Ralph Goldberg would get tickets to the semifinals and finals and invite Sally, my children and me to join his family for the finals weekend. John Appel was also a friend and a great repository of funny stories, each of which had a particular point. One involved a rope. Abdul approached his friend Hamad who was sitting in front of his tent. Abdul asked to borrow Hamad's rope that was coiled next to the tent. Hamad refused. Abdul asked why not, and Hamad said that he was using the rope to hold down the sand. Abdul: "That's ridiculous. A rope can't hold the sand in place." Hamad: "When you don't want to do something, one reason is as good as another." John must have seen the face of Hamad in CBS management at various times.

From about 1964 to the early 1980s, Wilmer Cutler was CBS's regulatory counsel for almost all significant matters at the FCC, and we also did additional work for CBS outside the regulatory area. I was fortunate to work on most of the CBS projects that the firm handled. Even in the beginning, Cutler would often bring me and other associates along to meetings with the client or meetings with the consultants, which was possible because the fees were not considered to be extravagant. I remember being called aside by one of the partners, Sam Stern, because I tended to speak up at the meetings and occasionally would disagree with what Cutler had said. Stern said that I had to tone this down because it was not appropriate. But he added, "The worst part of it is when you speak up, you are always right." It was a very gentle way of telling me to cool it. My outspokenness on another occasion on another client led one of the junior partners (Max Truitt) to bring a gun with him (as a joke) to sessions in which he edited my work. I guess the threat was that I would be shot if I disputed too much. Later, as a young partner, I went to New York to meet alone with Paley and/or Stanton on some regulatory matters. Eventually I argued many of the firm's cases on behalf of CBS.

As noted, CBS first retained the firm to work on the Prime Time Access proceeding, which involved a proposed FCC regulation that would limit the amount of programming that the networks could broadcast in the first hour of prime time, generally between 7:00 p.m. and 8:00 p.m. The purpose of this regulation was to foster programming by local stations often purchased from nonnetwork program suppliers. Another piece of the proposed regulation would bar the networks from engaging in the business of syndication, which is selling programs to local stations after the network run, and a related provision would bar networks from acquiring financial interests in programs produced by nonnetwork producers. The networks saw the Prime Time Access Rule as undermining their First Amendment rights and detrimental to their core business and, in the case of the other proposed rules, as undermining their ability to make money in the related business of syndication.

The proposed rules were the brainchild of Ashbrook Bryant, chief of the Office of Network Study at the FCC. There was a good deal of liberal sentiment at the FCC in those days. Bryant had written in 1969 that "the maximum possible number of independent diversified sources of ideas to foster the development and continuity of our open competitive society and the evolution of its free institutions has been established as the conceptual base for the operation of our broadcast structure," citing Jefferson and

Mill as his inspiration.[12] As mentioned earlier, there were only three broadcast networks at the time: ABC, CBS and NBC (PBS was created in 1969 and began operations in 1970),[13] and no competitors of any significance. The networks were viewed as oligopolists that threatened program diversity, though to me they seemed to be more oligopolies of virtue than evil. One of the goals of the FCC was to encourage the development of a fourth broadcast network, which years later became the Fox Network. Another was to keep the networks out of cable ownership (the subject of an earlier rule). There was little awareness or concern that increased competition in programming would lead to the demise of network news as a unifying national institution. Nor was there any awareness that new technologies—cable, satellite and streaming—on their own would bring the diverse entertainment programming that the FCC sought to achieve by regulation.

CBS hired Cutler and the firm to mount the opposition to the proposed Prime Time Access Rule and other rules. I was fortunate to work on that with Cutler, Wollenberg and Sam Stern. NBC hired Schnader Harrison in Philadelphia. Bernie Segal was their senior lawyer. Jerry Shestak was next in line, and the third lawyer was Harvey Levin. ABC at that time was not a particularly profitable network, and it largely tagged along with what the other networks did or stayed on the sidelines. In the case of the Prime Time Access proceedings, it tagged along.

The FCC had issued a notice of proposed rulemaking and invited comments from interested parties and the public as to whether the proposed rules should be adopted.[14] CBS and the other networks prepared comments in an effort to dissuade the FCC from issuing rules and to create a record for a later court challenge. Arthur D. Little (ADL) in Cambridge was hired to prepare an economic analysis for use in the comments. We met with them frequently. In those days you could fly to Boston, get off the plane, board a helicopter on the tarmac and be at ADL in a few minutes. Eventually, ADL finished its report with generous help from us in the drafting. I told Cutler that I thought some of the material was less than convincing. This view was rejected. After the report was filed, one of the opposing parties found an error in the data that turned out to be significant. The Second Circuit later held that, "though the original data had showed a slight increase in the amount of non-network programming carried by affiliates in the 50 largest markets, the corrected data indicated that quite the reverse was true"—a result useful to the other side's argument (*Mt. Mansfield Television Inc. v. FCC*, 442 F.2d 470 (2d Cir. 1971)). I displayed some *schadenfreude* when the error was later discovered and was roundly and appropriately chastised by Cutler.

When the case was argued before the FCC, the parties supporting the rule went first. They were encouraged by Commissioner Nick Johnson, who argued that the proposed rules were necessary to prevent monopoly control. He painted the existing networks as censors of free speech. That led to one of the oddest opening argument lines I ever heard, with Cutler saying, "I am almost embarrassed to be here today." Perhaps we would have had more success if we had adopted the suggestion of the CBS deputy general counsel, John Appel, that the network would have to shoot Lassie (the canine star of a CBS entertainment program) if the rules were adopted. The FCC went ahead and adopted the rules.[15] Lassie survived. The Second Circuit affirmed the FCC in *Mt. Mansfield Television Inc. v. FCC*, 442 F.2d 470 (2d Cir. 1971).

When the Prime Time Access Rule was being reconsidered years later, I was the counsel for CBS in arguing before the FCC. CBS's position was that the rule should be repealed. I remember that Jerry Shestack argued for NBC. He started to talk about the minutiae of the rule, the exceptions, and suggested that maybe there should be other exceptions. After 10–15 minutes, one of the commissioners said, "Mr. Shestack you have not mentioned yet whether you want the rule repealed in its entirety." Shestack responded: "Funny you should ask. We have changed our position," which was somewhat of a shock to us, and a very odd way of announcing that our partner had bailed on us. The rule was not formally repealed until 1996.[16]

Other CBS litigation that I worked on involved various claims for access to broadcast time, and this became a staple of our CBS work. The first of these access cases involved challenges to new rules expanding the FCC's fairness doctrine. As noted earlier, that doctrine required that free time be devoted to persons with opposing views on controversial issues when the broadcaster had given time to one side. The networks and other broadcasters had lived with the doctrine for a long time. In fact, Paley and CBS had themselves originated the concept of the fairness doctrine many years earlier as a feature of CBS News policy, implemented not by the government, but by its own news staff.[17] However, the new proposed rules expanded the doctrine and made it more mechanical by requiring free time to respond to personal attacks and political editorials—that is, free time for the person attacked in the program or the candidate opposed in the editorial. CBS and others viewed this as too much FCC intrusion into editorial policy and decided to challenge the rules in court. CBS, together with NBC and the Radio and Television News Directors Association (RTNDA), decided to file in the Seventh Circuit, but the lawyers spent so much time dithering about the one-page petition for review that Red Lion Broadcasting—a small local broadcaster that challenged the application of the personal attack feature of the fairness doctrine in an individual case—filed first in the D.C. Circuit. That case was argued and decided in favor of the FCC before the Seventh Circuit got around to hearing the RTNDA case (*Red Lion Broadcasting Co. v. FCC*, 381 F 2d 908 (D.C. Cir.1967)).

Red Lion petitioned for Supreme Court review, which was granted (*Red Lion Broadcasting Co. v. FCC*, 389 U.S. 968 (1967)). CBS and the others feared that they would be relegated to the role of amicus. I suggested that we file for cert before judgment in the Seventh Circuit, a rarely used procedure allowing Supreme Court cases to bypass the courts of appeals. CBS agreed. Cert before judgment had never been used when the case originated in an administrative agency. On the day the petition was to be decided by the Supreme Court, I checked the order list. The petition for cert before judgment had been denied (*RTNDA v. United States*, 390 U.S. 922 (1968)), but when I turned the page, I discovered that the *Red Lion* case had been stayed pending a decision of the Seventh Circuit (*Red Lion Broadcasting Co. v. FCC*, 390 U.S. 916 (1968)), which was just as good. After the Seventh Circuit decision (*RTNDA v. United States*, 400 F.2d 1002 (7th Cir. 1968)) invalidating the rules, the Supreme Court granted cert in the Seventh Circuit case, and the two cases were heard together. Roger Robb (later a judge on the D.C. Circuit) briefed and argued the *Red Lion* case for Red Lion, the local broadcaster. In the *RTNDA* case, there was much jockeying by the clients to retain high-profile lawyers to appear on the briefs. CBS hired Herbert Wechsler, a distinguished law professor at Columbia. I drafted the CBS brief that was sent to Wechsler for comment. His comment came back: "boring but powerful."

There was also a good deal of competition among the lawyers hired by CBS, NBC and RTNDA as to who would represent the aggregated clients in oral argument before the Supreme Court because the Court would not allow more than one person on each side to argue. Eventually it was decided that RTNDA's lawyer, Archibald Cox, the former solicitor general, would argue. Erwin Griswold, as solicitor general, argued for the United States. When the Supreme Court's adverse *Red Lion* decision was handed down, I was on vacation. We lost, and the expanded fairness doctrine was upheld (*Red Lion Broadcasting Co.* v. *FCC*, 395 U.S. 367 (1969)). Wollenberg sent me a book: *A Fairly Honorable Defeat*.[18]

Another significant access case was the *Democratic National Committee (DNC)* case. It involved the question of whether networks and other broadcasters could be forced to sell time for issue advertising. The theory was that the First Amendment and the statute compelled the FCC to adopt a rule requiring such sales. The FCC ruling refusing to impose such a requirement was appealed to the D.C. Circuit. Because of my work in the Tax Division, I could credibly claim to be a somewhat experienced appellate advocate. The firm suggested to CBS that I argue in the D.C. Circuit. The client was happy to have me argue a case, but thought that maybe the *DNC* case was too important to begin my career as an advocate for the company. Wollenberg argued the case instead and lost, through no fault in his advocacy (*DNC v. FCC*, 450 F.2d 642 (D.C. Cir.

1971)). The *DNC* case eventually went to the Supreme Court. CBS was not the only party. Since the Supreme Court would only allow one counsel per side to argue, the best way to resolve the question of who was going to argue was to flip a coin. We won the flip, with the result that Wollenberg got to argue the case in the Supreme Court and won (*CBS v. DNC*, 412 U.S. 94 (1973)).

Coin flips and card cutting to determine who would argue in multiparty Supreme Court cases became a feature of our practice, as it was in other firms with Supreme Court cases. In a separate coin-flipping episode (not involving the firm or me), one client had hired a new specialist advocate to argue the case, replacing their original, less experienced lawyer. However, other clients continued with the original lawyer, who refused to stand aside. The Supreme Court Clerk had to flip a coin to decide who would argue the case. The less experienced lawyer won the flip but lost the case after making arguments before the Court that have been described as "strange at best."[19] It ended with a messy situation of lawsuits and counter claims.[20] In another recent case, the Supreme Court itself pulled the name of a lawyer from a box when the two lawyers involved in the case could not agree who would argue.[21]

My consolation prize for losing the opportunity to argue the *DNC* case was the argument in the *Republican National Committee (RNC)* case (*CBS v. FCC*, 454 F.2d 1018 (D.C. Cir. 1971)), which CBS was happy for me to argue. The case involved a CBS challenge to an FCC order requiring CBS to provide free time to the RNC to respond to a DNC broadcast that, in turn, responded to broadcasts by Nixon (*CBS*, 454 F.2d at 1020). The D.C. Circuit decided that that was a bit too much and reversed, so I won my first CBS case and my first appellate argument in private practice. The case, while not of major legal significance, was of some significance to Paley and Stanton.[22]

Over time, I was fortunate as a young lawyer in my late 30s and early 40s to argue a number of court of appeals cases involving equal time and the obligation to sell political advertisements. Then, in 1981, I argued a CBS case before the Supreme Court involving the refusal of the FCC to regulate radio formats (*FCC v. WNCN Listeners Guild*, 450 U.S. 582 (1981)). We won. These were opportunities that were unusual for young lawyers, even then.

There were later efforts to get the FCC to repeal the fairness doctrine upheld by the Supreme Court in *Red Lion*. By the mid-1980s, the regulatory tide seemed to be turning. These efforts followed a tortuous course. In 1984, the Supreme Court ruled in *FCC v. League of Women Voters*, 468 U.S. 364 (1984), that a ban on editorializing by stations receiving grants from the Corporation for Public Broadcasting violated the First Amendment (we had supported the result in an amicus brief for CBS and others). The following year, the FCC itself declared that the fairness doctrine disserved the public interest.[23] I represented CBS in the court cases that resulted. Floyd Abrams, representing NBC, was active in these cases as well. Though the FCC declined to decide whether the doctrine was constitutional, on review of the FCC decision, the D.C. Circuit ordered the Commission to consider the constitutional question (*Meredith Corp. v. FCC*, 809 F.2d 863 (D.C. Cir. 1987)). On remand, the FCC concluded that the doctrine was unconstitutional and that it did not serve the public interest. The decision eliminating the doctrine was sustained by the D.C. Circuit in *Syracuse Peace Council v. FCC*, 867 F.2d 654 (D.C. Cir. 1989), without reaching the constitutional question. In later litigation in the Eighth Circuit, petitioners claimed that the doctrine could not be eliminated by the FCC because it was required by statute. The Eighth Circuit agreed with our position that the doctrine was not statutorily required (*Arkansas AFL-CIO v. FCC*, 980 F.2d 1190 (8th Cir. 1992), *vacated and aff'd en banc*, 11 F.3d 1430 (8th Cir. 1993)). Another long-running FCC issue was regulation of indecent material—that is, material that appealed to the prurient interest but that was not obscene. I discuss this in a later chapter.

A significant CBS case involved tobacco. During the time I was there, Wilmer Cutler refused to represent tobacco companies. The tobacco companies thought that they almost always lost no matter how good a job the lawyers did because there was so much hostility to them. It was referred to as "tobacco law." In this case, we and CBS benefited from tobacco law. The tobacco companies, including Philip Morris, American Brands and Reynolds, sued CBS and the other television networks, which had refused to broadcast some cigarette commercials, relying on a newly adopted National Association of Broadcasters (NAB) code provision concerning nicotine claims in cigarette advertising. The networks thought the advertisements were misleading. The tobacco companies claimed an antitrust conspiracy in restraint of trade. The tobacco companies were represented by Arnold & Porter, Philip Morris' regular counsel. Abe Krash was the lead lawyer.

I was told that, before the case started, there had been a meeting between the Arnold & Porter lawyers and the CBS general counsel, at that time Bob Evans. Krash asked CBS whether it would back down and agree to run the commercials. Evans told them no. Then Krash said that they were going to sue. As the tobacco company lawyers were leaving, Evans said to them, "When you do bring suit, please do me one favor?" Krash asked, "What is that?" Evans said, "Name us first in the complaint." So Krash did name CBS first in the complaint, and to inflict maximum discomfort, he brought the suit immediately before Christmas in the District Court for the District of Columbia.

I did not argue the case in the district court, but was charged with conducting discovery and writing the brief. I remember that Joseph Cullman, who was the CEO of Philip Morris, was one of the witnesses that I deposed, and I caught him in what he argued was a misstatement in his affidavit. I do not think it had great consequence for the suit, but it was satisfying.

We were on such a rushed schedule that we were taking depositions and writing the brief at the same time. Ray Clevenger, who is now a colleague of mine on the Federal Circuit, and Sally Katzen were working on the brief, and we got it done before Christmas. It was a close call because the clerk's office at the court was closing early for its office party, and the copying machine at Wilmer Cutler lost the capacity to collate the documents. On top of that, it was snowing in Washington. We collated the brief in the cab to the courthouse and used the clerk's stapler while they partied on. Years later, when I was sworn in as a judge at the Federal Circuit with Clevenger and other judges in attendance, I said: "Ray you have achieved every associate's dream: to be senior to a partner that you worked for." Ultimately, the District Court ruled against the tobacco companies (*American Brands, Inc. v. NAB*, 308 F. Supp. 1166 (1969)). After losing in the lower court, Krash continued the breakneck pace by appealing immediately before New Year's, but the appeal was later withdrawn. Nobody was going to force the television networks to run tobacco commercials that were thought to be misleading.

## Reporter's Privilege

CBS and other news outlets often received subpoenas in court cases for unpublished material that had been gathered but not used in the published version of the story (known as outtakes). They objected that producing such material would chill newsgathering and, hence, impair their First Amendment rights. Here, the broadcasters could claim equal First Amendment rights with the print press since FCC regulation was not involved. The problem was that the Supreme Court appeared to have generally rejected a reporter's privilege in *Branzburg v. Hayes*, 408 U.S. 665 (1972). But Justice Powell's pivotal concurring opinion (*Branzburg*, 408 U.S. at 709–10) left some room for a qualified privilege, which many circuits recognized. Based on that circuit authority, CBS and other news organizations resisted such subpoenas. I was fortunate to litigate some of those cases.

One was a contempt case in the District of New Jersey, where the district judge was Judge Herbert Jay Stern, who was both unpredictable and irascible. He had been the US Attorney for the District of New Jersey and had gained a reputation for taking on the mob and corrupt politicians. CBS was the target of a defense subpoena in a criminal case seeking outtakes, as well as broadcast material for a *60 Minutes* segment entitled "From Burgers to Bankruptcy." Judge Stern ordered the materials produced for in-camera inspection. When CBS refused, it was held in contempt, and Judge Stern threatened the network with a "terribly large" contempt fine.[24] On appeal to the Third Circuit, the court, while recognizing a reporter's privilege, ordered the material produced for in-camera inspection (*United States v. Cuthbertson*, 630 F.2d 139 (3d Cir. 1980)). At that point I became CBS's counsel. The opposing counsel representing one of the criminal defendants was a man named John Barry. Very oddly to us, the prosecutor in the case supported the defendant's request. One of the prosecutors in the case was President Donald Trump's sister, then Maryanne Trump, who later became a district judge and then a court of appeals judge. She married Mr. Barry a year after this incident.[25]

There was a hearing in the case in which I presented Mike Wallace, the lead reporter of the *60 Minutes* broadcast, as one of our witnesses. This was one of my first district court appearances and, being green, I strayed from the podium during the examination, only to be admonished by Judge Stern. It was clear that we were going to lose before Judge Stern, and the question was: Could we win at the Third Circuit on appeal? Ultimately, I concluded that the CBS position was going to be difficult to defend in the Third Circuit, in that we were resisting the production of material that had actually been broadcast as well as outtakes (material not broadcast). So, in the middle of the proceedings, I went to New York one night to meet with Bill Small, then an executive in the CBS News Division, to tell him that I thought we needed to moderate our position a little to do better on appeal. He agreed, and I went back and told the court that we were giving up on material that had been broadcast. Nonetheless, Judge Stern ordered that the outtakes be provided to the defense (*United States v. Cuthbertson*, 511 F. Supp. 375 (D.N.J. 1981)), and we sought review of the district court order without going into contempt. Eventually we succeeded with our more limited position. The Third Circuit held that the outtakes were admissible only for impeachment, and that the defense had failed to establish that "the only practical access to the information is through the media source" (*United States v. Cuthbertson*, 651 F.2d 189 (3d Cir.1981)).

There was another CBS case in New Orleans that involved an order to produce a broadcast script. In a criminal case, the district court (expressing concerns about a fair trial) had enjoined CBS from broadcasting an account of the events and required production of the script. While the injunction against the broadcast had been stayed, CBS did not comply with the script production order. The district court then hired special prosecutors to go after CBS for contempt. We moved to disqualify all the district judges in the district (the Eastern District of Louisiana, which included New Orleans) because the judges had employed the prosecutor. They did disqualify themselves from hearing the contempt proceeding, and a district judge was brought in from out of state. We were successful in convincing him that CBS should not be held in contempt (*In re CBS*, 570 F. Supp. 578 (E.D. La. 1983)). The Fifth Circuit held that the prosecutors, not being part of the Justice Department, could not represent the United States and lacked standing to appeal (*United States v. McKenzie*, 735 F.2d 907 (1984)).

There was one significant CBS outtakes case where I was not involved. This was Cutler's successful effort to resist a contempt finding by the House of Representatives for failure to produce outtakes in response to a committee subpoena relating to the CBS broadcast titled "The Selling of the Pentagon."

## Watergate Litigation

My most notable outtakes case was not a CBS case. It was in the Watergate case before Judge John Sirica, involving the break-in at the Democratic National Headquarters at the Watergate Complex in Washington. By June 1972, the discovery of a team of burglars at the hotel, as well as their connections to the Nixon Administration, was being widely reported. The *Los Angeles Times'* reporting duo of Jack Nelson and Ronald Ostrow had conducted interviews with Alfred C. Baldwin, an alleged conspirator, who had been a look-out at the Howard Johnson motel across the street from the Watergate, and had alerted the burglars that a watchman was heading their way. Gordon Liddy, one of the Watergate defendants, had subpoenaed those outtakes (the interview tapes). The *Los Angeles Times* refused to produce them since they had not been publicly disseminated. The *Times* was hauled up before Judge Sirica. And again, even though I was a fairly young partner, I was fortunate to represent the *Times*.

Our immediate client was John Lawrence, the Washington bureau chief of *The Los Angeles Times*, who was the *Times'* representative. He was threatened with jail for contempt for refusing to produce the outtakes. This all happened shortly before Christmas. I remember making an emotional plea to Judge Sirica that Lawrence should be allowed to spend Christmas with his wife and children instead of being locked up in jail. Sirica was having none of it. He held Lawrence in contempt and told the marshals to take Lawrence away, making him the first person sent to jail in the Watergate case (*United States v. Liddy*, 354 F. Supp. 208 (D.D.C. 1972)). Sirica was sending a signal to the defendants. He showed what was going to be his general approach—to intimidate everyone through the threat of harsh sentences to force disclosure of what happened.

I do not think that Lawrence's time in the DC jail was particularly trying. He had brought the tapes to court and had given them to his wife, Bunny. My now wife Sally, still an associate at the firm, hustled Bunny (and the tapes) out of the courtroom and then went to the basement to visit Lawrence in the jail of the courthouse to get any valuables he had in his possession in case he was taken off to another jail. Sally knew the court staff from having clerked on the D.C. Circuit. She was allowed into the jail, where the door of the cell was open, and Lawrence was sitting with his feet on the table, talking baseball with the marshals. John Pickering (a named partner at the firm), who was also involved in the case, tried to visit Lawrence in his cell (this being the first paying client of the firm to go to jail), but he was told that he could not go in because Lawrence was busy with his lawyer (Sally).

We took the case to the court of appeals right away, seeking a stay, and Lawrence was released from custody after a few hours pending a decision on the merits (*United States v. Liddy*, 478 F.2d 586 (D.C. Cir. 1972)). Roger Wollenberg argued in the court of appeals, and he ultimately encouraged the client to settle the case by getting a release from the interviewee (Baldwin). The *Los Angeles Times* followed the advice, got a release, turned over the material, and the contempt proceeding became moot.

The *Los Angeles Times* case was not the only Watergate-related outtakes case that we handled. We also represented *Time Magazine* in connection with the criminal prosecution brought against Spiro Agnew, who was then the vice president. The Agnew case was a very big deal since no one wanted Agnew (because of his likely criminal conduct) to succeed Nixon as president if Nixon were impeached or resigned. By October 1973, when the Agnew case was pending, Nixon was in serious jeopardy, having just been ordered to hand over some of the White House tape recordings to Judge Sirica for review. After Agnew was indicted, *Time* and other news organizations were subpoenaed by the Agnew defense for their outtakes (a delaying tactic). We filed a brief on *Time's* behalf seeking to quash the subpoena. I was in district court in Baltimore ready to argue for reporter's privilege, when it was announced that Agnew was pleading *nolo contendere* (no contest) to a criminal charge of tax evasion for the year 1967 (*United States v. Agnew*, 428 F. Supp. 1293 (D. Md. 1977)). This was absolutely astonishing. Part of the plea deal was that he would resign as vice president. I vividly recall sitting in the courtroom after the brief proceeding was over. The courtroom deputy called "all rise!" as is customary when a judge gets up to leave the bench, and the secret service agents, still protecting Agnew, said "Everybody remain seated until the Vice President leaves." Everybody stood. I thought that was an example of the triumph of the judiciary. Shortly afterward, Agnew resigned, and Nixon selected Gerald Ford as the new vice president, which in turn led to Ford's becoming president in 1974 after Nixon's resignation.[26]

Sometimes we represented broadcasters in cases that were 180-degree opposite of the reporter's privilege cases. In these cases, the press was seeking access on First Amendment grounds to materials that the government sought to keep confidential. In *CNN v. United States*, 824 F 2d 1046 (D.C. Cir. 1987), we established a right of access to jury *voir dire* proceedings in the high-profile *Deaver* case (*United States v. Deaver*, Crim. No. 87–096, 1987 WL 13366 (D.D.C. June 22, 1987)). Another was an effort by the *New York Times* to secure access to the cockpit voice recorder from the Challenger disaster, where Pat Carome in our firm was the lead lawyer. The *New York Times* sued NASA to release the recordings, and we were initially successful at the D.C. District Court, but the firm was eventually unsuccessful on appeal and on remand in the district court.[27]

We occasionally did libel work. A Vietnam War–related libel case involved Anthony Herbert, the author of *Soldier*.[28] Herbert's book suggested that the US military was guilty of war crimes in Vietnam. The book was published by Holt, Rinehart and Winston, a CBS subsidiary. One of those accused in the book sued CBS and Herbert for libel, and I represented CBS in the lawsuit. Later Herbert himself sued CBS for libel based on a *60 Minutes* episode titled "The Selling of Colonel Herbert," claiming that Herbert's war crimes allegations were false. It was thought unwise for me to represent CBS in both Herbert suits, one in which he was a defendant together with CBS and the other in which he was a plaintiff suing CBS. The Herbert case against CBS ultimately went to the Supreme Court (*Herbert v. Lando*, 441 U.S. 153 (1979)) (holding that in libel cases there is no First Amendment privilege barring inquiry into the editorial process). One significant piece of CBS libel business that got away was the representation of CBS in the Westmoreland libel case, eventually handled by David Boies of Cravath, a firm that already had a long relationship with CBS. General William Westmoreland, the US commander in Vietnam, sued CBS for broadcasting a *CBS Reports* program called "The Uncounted Enemy: A Vietnam Deception." The case was eventually settled before verdict, but the trial was front-page news.[29]

## License Renewal Proceedings

Another significant source of communications work in those days was license renewal proceedings. Every broadcaster had to apply for a license renewal every three years. When the license came up for renewal, it could be challenged by another applicant seeking to secure the license for itself. The existing licensee would defend itself by showing that it had done an outstanding job, particularly in presenting news and information programming. The chances were nonexistent that a challenger would succeed by arguing it would do a better job than the existing license holder. So, the approach of these challengers was to argue that the existing licensee had engaged in misconduct, particularly a lack of candor with the FCC, and should therefore be disqualified. Then the challenger would be the only one left standing and would get this very valuable broadcast license. It was a long shot, but there were some occasions when the challenge was able to succeed, the RKO Boston case, discussed below, being an example. The D.C. Circuit appeared to be on the side of the challengers, encouraging the FCC to revoke licenses. After several cases where the D.C. Circuit suggested that the FCC take away licenses, the FCC did revoke the license of a classical music FM station on the ground that the station broadcast too little news programming (*In re Applications of Simon Geller Gloucester, Massachusetts for Renewal of License*, 90 FCC 2d 250 (1982)). The D.C. Circuit reversed saying this is not what we meant (*Committee for Community Access v. FCC*, 737 F.2d 74 (D.C. Cir. 1984)).

These license challenges were not to be dismissed as frivolous. There would be a hearing before an administrative law judge, at which the existing licensee would present evidence about what a wonderful job it had done, and the challenger would seek to establish that the broadcaster had not been candid with the FCC or had engaged in other kinds of misconduct.

In the early 1970s, the CBS license in Philadelphia (WCAU-TV) was challenged by a group seeking to disqualify CBS, so that it could secure the license itself. In the WCAU proceedings, I was the lead lawyer for CBS, with overall supervision from Roger Wollenberg and the very able assistance of Bob McCaw, Dan Marcus, Sally Katzen, Steve Hut and many others. The matter was set for hearing before an FCC administrative law judge. We brought CBS executives to testify about the excellent job CBS had done during the previous three-year license period. One of the executives was William Paley, CEO of CBS. Paley had a special affection for WCAU, having bought a piece of the station even before acquiring the predecessor of the CBS network.[30] We met him in New York and rode to Washington in his Gulfstream, the first time that I had been in a private jet. The night before his testimony, I had dinner with him alone at a Washington restaurant. Paley appreciated good food. At the dinner I broached the subject of my then former father-in-law Bill Shirer. Shirer had been a long-time fixture at CBS starting with his radio broadcasts from Berlin on the eve of World War II. But, in 1947, he had been forced out, leading to a break with Murrow that was never healed. Shirer's version was that he had been sacked for being too liberal. I asked Paley if that was true. Paley said no, Shirer had been fired for spending too much time running after women and not enough time working. Which version should I credit? Both perhaps. Perhaps neither. The next day Paley was scheduled to testify after lunch. A catered lunch was arranged at the CBS Washington office near the FCC. Paley wanted wine with lunch. I told him that he should not drink before testifying. He drank anyway. His testimony was routine and uneventful.

The challenge to the CBS license in Philadelphia (*In re Applications of CBS etc.*, 39 FR 15158, (1974)) was bankrolled by a plaintiff's antitrust lawyer named Harold E. Kohn, who had a firm in Philadelphia. The challenger had retained the Washington firm of Welch & Morgan to represent it in the FCC proceeding. Ed Morgan was the lead lawyer. Morgan had an interesting background, having been a chief inspector of the FBI and chief counsel to Joseph McCarthy's subcommittee during McCarthy's witch-hunt in the early 1950s.[31] Michael S. Yaroschuk was a young lawyer with the Morgan firm with day-to-day responsibility for the case.

Morgan was a stockholder of the challenger as well as its lawyer. During the course of the proceeding, we asked that an issue be added to determine whether Morgan had made a misrepresentation to the FCC in another proceeding. As a result, Morgan was asked to withdraw from the stockholder group. But the challenger represented to the FCC that the withdrawal was Morgan's "unilateral decision." Morgan also withdrew as counsel, and Yaroschuk moved to the Kohn firm. Morgan nonetheless appeared as a witness for the group before the administrative law judge on November 14, 1975. In my cross-examination of Morgan, nothing much happened until it was almost over. I noticed, in response to what I had called my last question, that he had moved his hand toward the inside of his jacket. I then said I had one more question of this witness. There was a strong objection from the other side, saying that my cross-examination was over and that I should not be allowed to ask any more questions. I recollect that the judge said: "Oh well just, you know, let him, let him ask another question or two." I asked: "Mr. Morgan, why did you move your hand toward the inside pocket of your jacket?" He said: "Because I was going to pull out this piece of paper from my pocket." And I asked: "What is that piece of paper?" He said: "It is a document concerning the challenge." And I asked: "Could I see it?" He gave me the piece of paper. The document was an April 7, 1975, letter from Morgan to Kohn.

While I looked at the document, there were strong objections from Yaroschuk to my line of questions. I said: "That is odd. I have a copy of this document produced in discovery, but my copy of the document has two paragraphs. This has three." The missing third paragraph stated that "I have heretofore accepted your proposal that I cease to be a stockholder [...]" thus appearing to contradict the earlier statements and testimony of others in the challenge group that the withdrawal had been Morgan's unilateral decision.

I asked: "Can you explain to me why the two versions of the documents are different?" This questioning went on for a while and eventually the challenger had to admit that Yaroschuk had doctored the document to take out the last paragraph and had produced it in discovery in the altered form without disclosing the alteration. The whole thing unraveled: there were other document alterations and false testimony by principals of the challenger. Eventually I think Yaroschuk may have ceased being a lawyer as a result of this episode. It appears that he later bought a country inn in Vermont, using proceeds from the sale of a dry cleaners that had been given to him in lieu of settling a legal bill.[32] He died in 1985. Happily, CBS's license was renewed when the challenger withdrew. That was my one Perry Mason moment in private practice.

Some years later, in the 1980s, I represented RKO in its Los Angeles license challenge. RKO had lost its Boston television license (WNAC) to the challenger on grounds of misconduct (*RKO General v. FCC*, No. 81–1545 (1980)). The Los Angeles TV license had also been challenged, and there was a hearing before an FCC administrative law judge. Unhappily for RKO, while the case was pending, there had been another episode of misconduct at RKO that involved overcharging for television advertising. RKO again risked losing a valuable TV license as a result of misconduct. Some of the executives in the TV division had been deeply involved in this, and RKO had made the mistake of not firing those people. RKO had authorized us to disclose the misconduct to the FCC, which we did, but nonetheless this became a huge problem. Ultimately, after a lengthy hearing, the administrative law judge recommended that RKO lose its license. I argued the case on appeal before the full FCC, which was one of my first experiences arguing in front of TV cameras. The FCC never decided the case. Rather, RKO settled with the Los Angeles challengers and with the challengers to all their other TV and radio licenses. Their licenses went to the challengers, but they had to compensate RKO. The O'Neill family had long owned RKO, and the loss was emotional as well as financial. It turned out not to be terrible for RKO as they salvaged a good portion of the value of their stations as a result of this settlement. This experience led to my being retained years later by opposing counsel in the RKO case in another renewal proceeding, as discussed in a later chapter.

Now decades later, much has changed in broadcast regulation. The fairness doctrine, as noted earlier, and the personal attack and political editorial rules have been repealed. This has had the unintended consequence of fostering right-wing radio, such as the Rush Limbaugh program, because the stations no longer need to present opposing views or time to respond to personal attacks. The license renewal rules have also been changed so that if a license challenger succeeds, it does not get the license, but the proceeding is opened to new applicants, thus eliminating most of the incentive to challenge licenses.[33] The FCC's refusal to repeal the syndication and financial interest rules was set aside by the Seventh Circuit in an opinion by Judge Posner (*Schurz Communications, Inc. v. FCC*, 982 F. 2d 1043 (7th Cir. 1992)). As noted earlier, the Prime Time Access Rule was repealed in 1996, but indecency regulation remains a thorn in the side of broadcasters. A new regulatory debate has emerged related to Section 230 of the Communications Decency Act of 1996 (47 U.S.C. § 230), which protects Facebook and others from liability for the content they transmit.

More than 30 years after these events, it seems to me that government regulation and assaults on the press have had the counterintuitive effect of making the press stronger as an institution. Deregulation of the broadcast press has not made for better journalism, and the government-assisted fragmentation of the television press has eliminated the unifying force that the old CBS and the broadcast press in general had provided to the nation.

## Other Litigation

In addition to cases asserting that government action violated the First Amendment rights of broadcasters, I worked on some cases arguing against First Amendment claims. The *CBS v. DNC* case discussed above, 412 U.S. 94 (1973), rejecting the argument that the First Amendment compelled broadcasters to sell issue advertising time, was one of those. Another was the *Writers Guild* case. There, the Writers Guild and others in the business of producing programs for television sued the three networks and the FCC, claiming that FCC's jawboning of the networks to adopt the so-called family viewing hour violated the First Amendment. The networks' own actions in adopting and enforcing the policy was also said to be unconstitutional. On appeal, I successfully urged that we change the approach from defense to offense, arguing that enlisting the courts to regulate network editorial decisions would itself violate the First Amendment. The court punted, holding that the claim had to be brought to the FCC as a matter of primary jurisdiction (*Writers Guild of America v. ABC*, 609 F.2d 355 (9th Cir. 1979)).

In *Lloyd Corp. v. Tanner*, 407 U.S. 551 (1972), we represented a shopping center that had been taken to court for restricting leafletting on its property. This was a problem because the Supreme Court, in *Amalgamated Food Employees Union Local 590 v. Logan Valley Plaza, Inc.*, 391 U.S. 308 (1968), had held that such restrictions violated the First Amendment because the shopping center was like a company town subject to First Amendment requirements. I suggested that we distinguish *Logan Valley* on the theory that here there were opportunities for leafletting on the public streets and sidewalks leading into the shopping center where there was a red light. The original shopping center counsel who had involved Wilmer Cutler in briefing the case insisted on arguing the case himself. He began by describing the factual differences between the two cases. When the Court broke for lunch (which happened in those days), the chief justice said that he hoped counsel would turn from the facts to the law after lunch. After lunch, counsel kept arguing the facts. We won 5–4, with the Court distinguishing *Logan Valley* in large part on its facts (*Lloyd Corp.*, 407 U.S. at 563–66, 570). In a later case, the Supreme Court held that *Lloyd* had overruled *Logan Valley* (*Hudgens v. NLRB*, 424 U.S. 507 (1976)). This was my one experience in getting the Supreme Court to overrule itself.

The CBS work and related First Amendment and FCC regulatory work for other clients was not enough to keep me busy, and I worked on quite a wide variety of other projects. As I noted, Wilmer Cutler, at least in the early days, was not a large firm. Simply because of economic conditions or chance, there were times when there was too much work to do and other times when there was not enough work to do. In the times of too much work, somehow or other, we got it all done, but when there was not enough work, it was really stressful. You would wonder where the next case was coming from. I remember that we were thrilled with victories, but then about two hours later became concerned about the potential lack of work. If we lost, it was worse. In the law business, the wins are less gratifying than the losses are painful. In the CBS work, we were very fortunate over the years to win most of the cases.

One example of a non-FCC or First Amendment–related case that I worked on, when I was still an associate, was the *General Motors Wheels* case with Boyden Gray and Chuck Hill (*U.S. v. General Motors Corp.*, 518 F.2d 420 (D.C. Cir. 1975)). The firm was retained to represent General Motors (GM) in a highway safety proceeding involving Kelsey Hayes wheels installed on GM trucks. The wheels had the unfortunate habit of exploding. There were issues as to whether GM had properly reported the failures.

Years before, Ralph Nader had published an exposé called *Unsafe at Any Speed*, where he highlighted the apparent danger of GM's Chevrolet Corvair.[34] In response, GM hired a private detective to tail Nader and had even hired prostitutes to try and discredit him. Nader sued, and GM was forced to pay a significant settlement. Ross Malone, former president of the American Bar Association, was brought in as the GM general counsel after that debacle.[35]

Malone was an impressive general counsel. Less impressive was the quality of the GM products. On my many trips to GM headquarters in Detroit to meet with GM engineers, I was regaled with stories of the assembly line. They recounted that the quality of vehicles coming off the line was so poor that GM executives would not buy the standard issue. Instead, the executives insisted on vehicles that were specially monitored by quality control inspectors as they were assembled. The line workers had other ideas. They would sabotage the executives' cars by, for example, placing dead rats in the door panels. The engineers were particularly amused by GM's inability to figure out a way to prevent the GM Mark of Excellence badge from often falling off the vehicles. One could see trouble coming. The wonder is that it was so many years in the future.

Another project is memorable for a mistake in litigation judgment. In the late 1970s, when I was a partner, we represented Kaiser Aluminum in litigation and arbitration concerning the construction of liquified natural gas (LNG) ships pursuant to a contract between Kaiser and another entity. Kaiser's subcontractor had done a very poor job in the construction of the tankers, and the ships had to be scrapped. The subcontractor was terminated. The subcontractor sought arbitration and compensation from Kaiser. Kaiser sued the subcontractor for damages for breach of contract in district court. There was a dispute about what claims belonged in arbitration and what claims belonged in court. We succeeded in getting a favorable ruling at the outset from District Judge John H. Pratt, which was reversed on a small point on appeal. But Judge Pratt did not like being reversed under any circumstances, and suddenly he turned against us and insisted that the whole thing go forward in arbitration.

The arbitration went on for quite a while. The selection of the arbitrators involved the opposite side's picking one arbitrator and our side's picking one arbitrator, and then the two of them picking a neutral. In the course of this proceeding, there were quite a variety of associates and partners working on this very big project, including Steve Hut, Jamie Kilbraith and Carolyn Cox. In these days, a project like that would be much valued by the firm, but in those days, some at the firm thought we should not be handling large cases like this, and there were associates who disliked the drudge work that is part of such cases. So, there was some hostility toward the case, and toward me, the lead lawyer on the case.

The neutral arbitrator on the panel was Gilbert Cuneo, who was a distinguished government contract lawyer. Unhappily in April 1978, midway through the proceedings, he died.[36] Under the American Arbitration Association rules, either party had the right to ask that the proceedings start over again with new arbitrators, or, by agreement, the parties could proceed with the two existing arbitrators. I remember agonizing about it, and in the end, I made a mistake. It was not just my mistake—I did it in consultation with a lot of other people. We decided to go forward with the two arbitrators. That did not turn out well. Cuneo had been skeptical of the other side's case, but the other arbitrators were not. We lost the case before the arbitrators, and the client lacked the stomach for a court challenge to the award. Every bad event seems to be outweighed by a good one. During the arbitration, our son, Abe, was born on April 2, 1982.

## Pro Bono Work

When I was at Wilmer Cutler, the firm was quite receptive to pro bono work by both partners and associates. Cutler and Pickering led by example. This was due in part to the fact that the firm was basically a firm of liberal Democrats. While at Wilmer, I did pro bono work that fell into several different categories: teaching, criminal defense, civil rights cases and public-interest board memberships. In addition, the firm allowed me to take a leave of absence to work on the Eugene McCarthy presidential campaign in 1968 for a greatly reduced salary paid by the campaign.

### The McCarthy Campaign

This leave of absence occurred in 1968, shortly before I became a partner. The main focus of the McCarthy campaign was ending US participation in the Vietnam War. The United States had entered Vietnam in the 1950s, but under Presidents Kennedy and Johnson, the US presence had been significantly ramped up. In 1964, after the Gulf of Tonkin incident, in which the Johnson administration claimed that the North Vietnamese had attacked US warships, Congress had given President Johnson full congressional leeway in undertaking military action in Vietnam. It did not go well. Despite troop escalations and a campaign of strategic air bombing, little progress seemed to be occurring on the ground amid mounting casualties, while in the meantime the population of Vietnam endured the effects of military action from both sides. Senator Eugene McCarthy decided to challenge Johnson for the Democratic nomination on an anti-war platform. Then, notwithstanding reassurances from President Johnson and General William Westmoreland that the war would soon be won, the Viet Cong and their North Vietnamese sponsors launched a major, country-wide offensive coinciding with the January 1968 Tet holiday. In the aftermath of Tet and with the growing stalemate in Vietnam being much in the evening news and in the papers,[37] McCarthy's campaign gathered momentum.

In March 1968, McCarthy ran surprisingly close to Johnson in the New Hampshire primary, falling just a few percentage points short of actually beating him. It was a shock. A few days later, Robert Kennedy announced his run for the Democratic nomination.[38] Johnson announced two weeks later that he would not run for a second term.[39] Vice President Humphrey became Johnson's pick for the Democratic nomination. The race for the Democratic nomination was among Humphrey, Kennedy and McCarthy.[40]

I joined the McCarthy campaign in Washington, DC, where the headquarters was located. This was after the New Hampshire primary but before Kennedy entered the race. At that time, the nominal campaign manager was Blair Clark (formerly of CBS), but the real campaign manager was a man named Thomas Finney. Finney was a formidable figure in the Democratic establishment, who had advised Presidents Johnson and Kennedy and had previously represented billionaire Howard Hughes.[41] Howard Hughes was a big donor to the McCarthy campaign because he was interested in eliminating nuclear bomb testing in Nevada, which adversely affected his various interests there. It was expected that McCarthy would take a position opposed to the bomb testing, which McCarthy was slow in doing.

I had responsibility for some fundraising and for position papers, and eventually for organizing a rally at Constitution Hall. Because of the opposition to Johnson, various distinguished people were willing to work on position papers for McCarthy. The problem was that McCarthy had relatively little interest in issuing any position papers. This was very frustrating to people like John Kenneth Galbraith, who helped with an economics paper on McCarthy's behalf, and to Bernard Wolfman, a preeminent tax law scholar, who wrote a position paper on tax policy. So while the position papers were well done, they never had any impact because most were never issued. This was evidence of a fatal flaw in McCarthy's quest for the presidency—he wanted to be president, but he had very limited interest in campaigning for the position.

On the fundraising side, part of my job was to telephone previous donors to the McCarthy campaign to ask them to give more. That was an extraordinary experience. At the time, there was, I think, a $3,000 limit for donations to each political committee. The candidates got around that rule by setting up different committees, so that an individual donor could give $3,000 each to more than one committee. I recall telephoning previous contributors asking them to give another $3000 to a different committee. And on more than one occasion, the reaction was, "Are you sure $3,000 is enough?" They were actually eager to give more than they were being asked to give. I had some sense of guilt associated with this because, from inside the campaign, it was clear to me that the money was not being particularly well spent, and the candidate was sufficiently aloof from his own campaign that his chances of securing the nomination were not great. In those days, the campaign contributions, some in the form of cash, were mailed to the campaign headquarters. One of my jobs was to supervise the opening of the mail, which was done by volunteers, and to do my best to prevent the volunteers from stealing the cash that came in.

One of my last assignments for the campaign was organizing a rally at Constitution Hall for McCarthy on August 15, 1968, one of many rallies scheduled for that day across the country. McCarthy was not going to make a personal appearance at Constitution Hall (a venue owned by the Daughters of the American Revolution (DAR)), as he was speaking to a crowd of 19,000 at Madison Square Garden that evening.[42] He was going to appear by video, and there was some concern that it would be difficult to fill the Hall by selling tickets. I was able to paper the hall. Not only was the hall filled, but there were hundreds of people on the outside trying to get in who were blocked from entry by the fire marshals, which made for a good story in the paper the next day.[43]

After the rally, I held a party at my home for some of the musicians and others who had appeared at the rally. That turned out to be a mistake because a lot of our household silver went missing. I invited the DAR official who was in charge of Constitution Hall to the party. He became incredibly drunk and unfit to drive himself home. I was only able to convince him to let me drive him home by claiming to have been a parking lot attendant and knowing how to drive different cars. Eventually, someone else did the driving. The official got home safely without killing either himself or anybody else.

After a few months in the campaign, it became apparent to me that the McCarthy campaign was a lost cause. While I felt that I did some things that were useful, ultimately my work and the work of many others was wasted. I found it significant that McCarthy, always casual about his campaign, was never at campaign headquarters in Washington. It became a point of personal pride that I never met him during the campaign. Interestingly, I think some of the people who ran the McCarthy campaign became convinced that McCarthy was going to fail, and vast amounts that had been contributed to the campaign were reportedly shifted to future use for other Democratic candidates.

The McCarthy experience did not entirely sour me on politics. When George McGovern was running for president in 1972, I was considered for the position of general counsel to the McGovern campaign. I remember having a lunch appointment with the campaign manager, who showed up an hour late for the lunch, which convinced me that the campaign was not particularly well organized. I decided to take a pass. That was pretty much the end of my participation in partisan politics. Ironically, that is an area in which my son Abe eventually became very active and engaged.

### *Teaching*

Shortly after I joined Wilmer Cutler, I got an offer from Roy Schotland, then associate dean at the Georgetown Law Center and member of the *Harvard Law Review* in the class ahead of me, to teach the Federal Courts course. I declined because I did not think that I was really ready to teach Federal Courts. Also, it would have been an enormous amount of work to prepare, and I was just starting out as an associate. I thought that I did not have the time that was needed. In retrospect, I regret not doing it. It would have been a good way to become expert in federal practice and procedure.

After I became a partner at Wilmer Cutler, I did teach at three different law schools: Georgetown, the University of Virginia (UVA) and Yale. Initially the courses that I taught at all three schools were Communications Law or

First Amendment Law. Georgetown was a cab ride across town. UVA was harder. I would drive down to Charlottesville on Friday afternoon, teach for two hours on Friday night, teach again on Saturday morning, and then drive back to Washington. In those days, you could get from Washington to UVA in a reasonable amount of time on a Friday afternoon. It was a pleasure because the students were always very interested. There was a self-selection process at work. Anyone who signed up for a seminar that started on Friday evening and ended early on Saturday morning was definitely going to be dedicated.

Then, in 1985, as part of the Wilmer Cutler sabbatical program, I was enti-tled to a six-month sabbatical, which I took in two three-month increments. For the first segment, UVA invited me to serve as a visiting professor. In the fall term I taught the introductory Constitutional Law course and a seminar on First Amendment and the Press. In my courses, I had students who later became quite successful: One was Nancy McFadden, who became the general counsel of the Department of Transportation during the Clinton administra-tion, and then the chief of staff to Governor Brown in California. Tragically, she died several years ago.

When I was teaching as a visiting professor at UVA, Chief Justice Warren Burger came to visit the school, and I was asked to host him in my Constitutional Law class. The chief justice had written the opinion of the Supreme Court in *Chandler v. Florida*, 449 U.S. 560 (1981), which held that it was not a denial of due process to have cameras broadcast a criminal trial. As it turned out, on the day of Chief Justice Burger's visit, the subject of the class was cameras in the courts. One of the students asked him whether he thought that having cameras in criminal trials was a good idea. He said that he did not, which was consistent with the position that he had taken earlier. But then the student asked a second question—whether having cameras in criminal trials was unconstitutional. To the surprise of both the class and me, Burger opined that it was clearly unconstitutional, contrary to his own opinion in the *Chandler* case. We were too polite to tax him with the contradiction. That evening, I was seated next to the chief justice at a dinner held in the Rotunda. A good deal of our conversation was occupied by his tale of troubles with an architect who was designing a new home for him. Unhappily, we did not get to larger subjects.

I enjoyed teaching. It was satisfying to help the students understand legal analysis, and it gave me a window into the thinking of a new generation of lawyers and law school professors. I thought a bit about becoming a full-time academic, but ultimately I was convinced that I did not want to do that. I was particularly struck by the hostility of the regular faculty toward practitioners who taught courses as adjuncts and, even more to the point, the regular faculty's heightened hostility to former practitioners who joined the regular faculty. The knock on the practitioners was that they would only tell war stories and not be interested in the theory of the courses. They were kind enough to say that this was not true of me, but it seemed to me that making the transition from private practice to the academy would not be easy. Another disincentive was the requirement to churn out articles. I did end up writing a few law review articles, a couple of which were published in the *Stanford Law Review*,[44] but writing articles was not my favorite pastime. A final discouragement was the super sensitivity of the students. This was manifest in the bitter arguments between liberals and conservatives, and also in increasing resistance to the intense give-and-take of the Socratic method.

As noted, in addition to teaching at Georgetown and Virginia, I also taught Communications Law at Yale, which required flying in the morning to Hartford, renting a car, driving to New Haven, teaching the course and then, typically, flying back that evening. It was quite an effort. It was interesting to me how different the atmosphere of the Yale Law School was to what I had experienced at Harvard. Students at Yale were very friendly toward the faculty. They would ask you to lunch (or dinner if I was staying over). It was a much warmer place than Harvard Law School. Yet despite the image of Yale as promoting a noncompetitive atmosphere, the students were still stressed. Another anomaly was the competition among the faculty. I was puzzled by the fact that, at one of the faculty lunches that I attended, the faculty members compared their LSAT scores to see who had done the best. This remarkably successful group seemed insecure, as though they had to prove that they belonged with the elite.

Toward the end of my time teaching, I taught a course at Georgetown on leveraged buyouts and creditors rights. I had become convinced that leveraged buyouts were vulnerable to being challenged on a fraudulent transfer theory because, as a result of borrowing to fund the stock buybacks, some companies were rendered insolvent. Many companies eventually went bankrupt. This seemed likely to become a great source of law business. I thought the best way to learn this area of the law was to teach it. So, I suggested the course to Georgetown, and they agreed to let me do it. I was right that there were a lot of problems with the leveraged buyouts, but, ironically, the amount of money involved in these transactions was so great and the consequences of losing so significant that few wanted to litigate the issues, and, with some exceptions, they were resolved by settlement.

### Criminal Defense and Civil Rights Cases

In addition to teaching, another type of pro bono activity at Wilmer Cutler was in criminal defense cases. As a result of the Supreme Court's decision in *Gideon v. Wainwright*, discussed in Chapter 4, the States and the District of Columbia were obligated to provide free counsel to defendants in criminal cases. The District's solution was to have the cases handled by the private bar. Eventually, in 1970, Congress did establish a Legal Aid Agency for the District of Columbia (which later became the D.C. Public Defender Service).[45] Even then, however, the private bar handled roughly 40 percent of the cases.

While in theory the big firms would be compensated through the Criminal Justice Act of 1964, most of those firms waived the compensation.[46] The involvement of the big firms caused a certain amount of hostility. The first source of hostility was from the judges in the General Sessions Court (then the local trial court), which had the responsibility for these cases. They thought that the big law firms did too good a job representing these criminal defendants and mucked up the system by rejecting plea deals, so that the cases had to go to trial. The other source of hostility came from what was known as the "Fifth Street Bar"— the lawyers who made their living by representing criminal defendants for a few hundred dollars a case. These lawyers thought the big firms were taking bread from their mouths by doing this work on a pro bono basis.

Over the course of my time at Wilmer Cutler, I represented several indigent criminal defendants. I represented a man named Willis Cherry, who was accused of armed robbery of a gas station and illegal possession of a firearm. I began the representation shortly after he was arrested. The Bail Reform Act of 1984[47] had not yet been enacted, so it was difficult for indigent criminal defendants to get out on bail because they did not have the money to pay for a bail bond. Mr. Cherry was married and had a child and was the source of support for his family. The only way I could convince the judge to release Cherry was on the condition that he call me every day. This put me in a difficult position as his lawyer. If he did not make the required call, what was I supposed to do? Was I supposed to call the court and advise it that my client had violated the conditions of his release? The issue never came up because Mr. Cherry faithfully called me every night to report in. He was not satisfied with just reporting in—he wanted to talk on the phone. We had conversations lasting anywhere from 5 minutes to 20 minutes every evening. I also arranged to get him a job, which he had while he awaited trial.

Before Cherry's pretrial release, there was a preliminary hearing at which I examined the police officers about the information they had gathered. Because there was a gun charge in addition to the robbery charges, the examination included asking the officers about where they found the gun in Mr. Cherry's car. Some while later, before Cherry's robbery trial was scheduled, the gas station attendant, who had allegedly been held up at gunpoint by Cherry, apparently decided that crime did pay, and he (allegedly) embezzled money from the gas station and fled town. So, the government was missing its star witness in the robbery case and dismissed the armed robbery charges, electing to pursue Cherry only on the charge of illegal possession of a handgun.

At that point, I had never tried a criminal case. Indeed, I had never tried any kind of case. So, I was paired with an experienced criminal lawyer for the trial. My recollection was that he let me handle most of the witnesses. The government's case rested on the testimony of the officers. Based on the preliminary hearing transcript, I was able to impeach the police officer's testimony that the gun had been found in the car next to Cherry. Of course, these police officers were busy, and they could not remember what had happened in an individual case several months earlier. I guess the prosecutor also did not have the time to refresh their recollection using the preliminary hearing transcript. At the trial it looked as though they had made up their testimony. This was a bench trial, rather than a jury trial, and my client was acquitted. I never heard from Willis Cherry after the acquittal, and I wondered whether he had grasped his chance for redemption. Judging from his later long criminal record, things did not go so well.

A second criminal case that I handled was an appeal of a murder case for a man named Warren Jefferson. Mr. Jefferson was out on bail, and he would visit me at the office, visits that made me a little apprehensive. I briefed and argued the appeal before the D.C. Court of Appeals, which agreed with my arguments and granted Mr. Jefferson a new trial (*Jefferson v. United States*, 463 A.2d 681 (D.C. 1983)). He was represented at trial by my then-partner Art Matthews who got him acquitted.

A third criminal case that I recall involved a gentleman who was charged with embezzling about $10,000. I worked out a plea agreement whereby he would pay the total amount that he had actually embezzled, which was about $20,000. I remember appearing before Judge Barrington Parker, who was presiding over the case, and asking him to approve the plea agreement. Parker refused to require that my client pay back $20,000 because he was only charged with embezzling $10,000. I felt a little foolish, but this was a good result for the client.

Some of the other criminal cases that I took while at the firm involved the 1968 riots in the District of Columbia in the aftermath of Martin Luther King's assassination. I vividly recall the pall of smoke hanging over the city, the broken windows and store fronts, and the unease of the population. Clients were mostly accused of looting, and I remember calling one of my clients to tell him that he had a court date, and he answered the phone with "Sam's Swap Shop" or something like that, implying that maybe he had been trying to unload the proceeds of ill-gotten gains.

It has been suggested that the involvement of the uptown bar with the criminal justice system and the acquired knowledge of the deficiencies of the system spurred important reforms in later years. Robert Tobin's 1999 book

*Creating the Judicial Branch: The Unfinished Reform* describes the clash of cultures that took place as a result of corporate lawyers' working pro bono in the D.C. criminal justice system in the wake of the 1968 riots and their encountering what he characterizes as the "sleazy" general sessions courtrooms and "seedy" Fifth Street Bar practices.[48] He contends that it was the exposure to this that led to a reform campaign, which resulted in the change from the general sessions court to the D.C. Superior Court in 1970.[49]

I also represented pro bono a man named Rafeedie, who was a resident alien in the United States and who had then gone abroad and was refused readmission to the United States. The government's refusal to readmit him was based on evidence that the then Immigration and Naturalization Service refused to disclose. One of the associates at Wilmer Cutler, Kerry Kircher, represented Rafeedie. Kerry asked me to be the supervising partner, which I agreed to do. I probably spent fewer than 25 hours on the case. Kerry wrote the briefs and argued in the D.C. Circuit. The court held that secret evidence could not be used, and that Rafeedie was entitled to due process. It set aside the exclusion order (*Rafeedie v. INS*, 880 F. 2d 506 (D.C. Cir. 1989)). Kerry deserved the credit, not me. He later became counsel to the House of Representatives. Curiously, this representation came back to bite me during my confirmation hearings for the Federal Circuit.

### Migrant Workers

Another pro bono activity that I undertook while at Wilmer Cutler involved the Migrant Legal Action Program, which was a Legal Services Corporation–funded program that litigated migrant issues. One of the things that has happened since then, as a result of Republican dissatisfaction, is that the Legal Services Corporation has been largely limited to funding individual representation. In other words, legal service–funded organizations now must avoid broadly based challenges, which has made them less effective. At the time I was involved, the constraints were looser, and the issues were important. The abuse of migrant farm workers, a subject first made prominent in 1960 by Edward R. Murrow in his documentary for CBS, *Harvest of Shame*, continued.[50]

I was on the board of the Migrant Legal Action Program and a related privately funded organization for several years. I handled a few cases for them in federal court involving, for example, access to the camps where the migrants lived (*Peterson v. Talisman Sugar Corp.*, 478 F. 2d 73 (5th Cir. 1973)) and, later at Jones Day, the failure of employers to pay workers as required by the Fair Labor Standards Act (*Aimable v. Long & Scott Farms*, 20 F.3d 434 (11th Cir. 1994)). Unhappily, our executive director misappropriated funds from the program and used them for lavish entertainment. I remember that he once bought elk steaks for everybody at a dinner. When this was discovered, we discharged the executive director, but the Legal Services Corporation proposed to defund the Migrant Legal Action Program. I had to testify before an administrative law judge at the Legal Services Corporation to show how we rectified the situation by firing the executive director and putting various controls in place. Ultimately, the program was not defunded.

This was not my first experience testifying. In the early 1970s, when I was getting divorced from Inga, one of the parties had to come to court to get approval of the divorce, which was based on voluntary separation for six months. I remember sitting in the D.C. General Sessions courtroom waiting to be called before the judge, who was Black. Most of the couples who were getting divorced were also Black, and the judge seemed to have a prurient interest in the sex lives of the people who were appearing before him. He would ask them questions about their sex lives during their marriage and in any extramarital affairs. It was shockingly inappropriate, and I wondered, as I waited for my turn, how I was going to answer these questions. But lo and behold, presumably because I was white and a lawyer, he did not ask me any questions, and just granted the divorce.

## Mozert v. Hawkins County

The most significant pro bono work that I did while I was at Wilmer Cutler involved a case called *Mozert v. Hawkins County*, which received a considerable amount of national attention during the summer of 1986. The suit arose in the context of a long-standing battle by religious fundamentalists to eliminate secular humanism, as they called it, from the public schools. The result was litigation about the teaching of evolution and other subjects, schoolbooks and the school curriculum. *Mozert* involved a suit by a group of parents against the Hawkins County Tennessee school board, asserting that the public school's requirement that the students participate in the reading program violated the students' Free Exercise rights under the First Amendment, given their religious objections to some of the materials.

I was brought into the *Mozert* case by People for the American Way, which was then deeply involved in defending public school curricula from charges of secular humanism. Tony Podesta, later a well-known and influential lobbyist in Washington, was at that time the executive director of People for the American Way. Tony got me involved in the *Mozert* case, with People for the American Way paying litigation costs and arranging for my pro-bono representation of the school board.

The assigned materials to which the parents and students objected included, for example, *The Wizard of Oz* (because it included a "good" witch),

*The Diary of Anne Frank* (because she questioned how God could permit what was happening) and Archibald MacLeish's anthology of poems in *Riders on the Earth* (*Mozert* parent Robert Frost: "This book is part of the Antichrist system. It calls God our Father a liar. [...] The Book relates to the worship of the Zodiac, Astrology, Greek gods, Hinduism, evolution. [...] It teaches children to be Rebellious.").[51] The parents, led by Vicki Frost and Bob Mozert, formed an organization called Citizens Organized for Better Schools (COBS) and arranged a series of protests in 1983. Vicki Frost attempted to have her two children excused from reading the books and protected from overhearing other children reading the books. The school principal suspended both children. Frost attempted to return her children to the school in the following days and was ultimately arrested for being on the school premises without permission.

Beverly LaHaye, the founder of Concerned Women for America (CWA), and Michael Farris took up the plaintiffs' case. Farris and CWA had a history of supporting conservative and Christian legal causes, and Farris had successfully argued at the Supreme Court in the *Larry Witters* case to enable Witters to secure state funding to attend Bible camp (*Witters v. Washington Department of Services for the Blind*, 474 U.S. 481 (1986)). Farris filed suit in December 1983 in federal district court in Tennessee, arguing that the students' First Amendment Free Exercise rights were infringed by the requirement to read the assigned reading material. They sought an injunction to stop students' having to read the materials and an undetermined amount of damages. In an initial ruling in March 1984, the district court dismissed the case (*Mozert v. Hawkins County Public Schools*, 582 F. Supp. 201 (E.D.Tenn.1984)). However, this ruling was reversed by the Sixth Circuit in June 1985, and the case was returned to the district court for trial (*Mozert v. Hawkins County Public Schools*, 765 F.2d 75 (6th Cir.1985)).

It was at this point, in the fall of 1985, that Tony Podesta asked me to represent the school board. The school board agreed. I recall going to the first deposition in Tennessee where Michael Farris was representing one of the parents being deposed. Farris was extremely hostile. Fortunately, over the course of time we developed a pretty good relationship and managed to litigate the case in a civil manner. The case was heard as a bench trial before Judge Hull in the Eastern District of Tennessee. In addition to me, there were two other Wilmer Cutler lawyers representing the School Board at the trial: John Payton, a partner, who later became the head of the NAACP Legal Defense Fund and tragically died at a relatively early age, and Judith Wish, who was an associate at Wilmer Cutler and later a lawyer in the Office of Professional Responsibility of the Department of Justice. The district for this trial was a fairly rural area. We stayed at a B&B. My bed had a beautiful wood frame with, unfortunately, a foot board. The bed was 6 feet long. I was 6 feet 4 inches. I never got a good night's sleep while I was there.

Our local counsel, Nat Coleman, understanding that John Payton, who was Black, was not going to be well received in that community, was kind enough to ask us over to dinner fairly frequently. Interestingly, John was treated civilly by the judge in court, but outside of court, there was still a great deal of racial prejudice. This happened even in the courtroom sometimes—not on the record and not by the judge. I remember one time that John told me that the lawyers sitting in the back row were whispering racial slurs. I had not been as conscious of what was going on, but I did talk to them about it, and they stopped. With Judith Wish, it was the opposite: Outside of court, she was treated with Southern courtesy, but in court she was treated dismissively by the judge. Both John and Judith did outstanding work.

The trial went on for quite a few days and made front page news in the *New York Times* and the *Washington Post* and was covered by the television networks.[52] The *Mozert* case had some echoes of the earlier *Scopes* case (*Scopes v. State*, 278 S.W. 57 (Tenn. 1925)). The *Scopes* case was famously dramatized in the movie *Inherit the Wind*. Clarence Darrow represented the teacher accused of unlawfully teaching evolution, and William Jennings Bryant represented the state. The media enjoyed calling the *Mozert* case the *Scopes II* case, though any resemblances between Clarence Darrow and me and between Bryant and Farris were tenuous at best. There was no camera coverage of the actual trial. At the end of each day's proceedings, the lawyers for each side would appear on the courthouse steps and give their version of what happened inside to the assembled press corps and particularly to the television cameras. You can imagine that the versions of what happened inside the courtroom were quite different, depending on which side's lawyers were describing the events. This suggested to me that there was value to having cameras in the courts to give an accurate picture of what was going on, even though reporters were present in the courtroom.

At trial, the plaintiffs took the stand to describe their objections. My strategy early in the trial was to try to minimize the objections, to show that the parents actually objected to very few books, and that there was no need for their children to be excused from the entire reading program just because of a few objections. Perhaps their objections could be accommodated by not making the students read particular books.

But lo and behold, when the plaintiffs got on the stand, their objections were not limited to a few books but extended to almost all books in the reading program and in the social sciences program as well. Having been given this gift, I ran with it, and got the parents to admit that they objected to practically everything in the school reading and social sciences curriculum, which suggested that maybe they did not really belong in the public schools at all.

Our argument was that the Free Exercise Clause was not violated by simply exposing children to ideas because Tennessee permitted homeschooling. If the parents did not like the public school program, the solution was not to treat the public schools like a cafeteria, where they could choose one thing and reject another, but simply to homeschool their children. We lost the case at the district court (*Mozert v. Hawkins County Public Schools*, 647 F. Supp. 1194 (1986)). I recall that Judge Hull reported that he had agonized about the decision. Later, Judge Hull sought to be nominated to the Sixth Circuit and asked for my support. I wrote a letter for him saying that I did not think he had been unfair. He was not nominated.

We appealed to the Sixth Circuit, where I argued. At oral argument, one of the judges articulated a theory of the case which was somewhat different from the position that we were taking. I remember saying at the oral argument "Well, yes that is exactly our position!" Whether embracing the court's idea was the reason, we won unanimously in the Sixth Circuit (*Mozert v. Hawkins County Board of Education*, 827 F.2d 1058 (6th Cir. 1989)), with the court holding that mere exposure to objectionable material had not violated any Free Exercise rights. Showing the difference between media coverage of the trial courts and the appellate courts, our victory was not featured anywhere nearly as prominently as was the loss in the district court. The *Mozert* case is frequently cited and is significant in the field. Garry Trudeau penned a Doonesbury strip about it, and I have a signed copy. Interestingly, many years later in a FCC license renewal proceeding, I represented the same interests that I had opposed in the *Mozert* case, which I describe in a later chapter.

Having been successful in the *Mozert* case, I was asked to join the Board of People for the American Way. The Board consisted of a large number of people. Other than getting to know Norman Lear and sitting next to Alec Baldwin at board meetings, the meetings were not notable, and my efforts to pour cold water on some of the organization's more aggressive ideas fell on deaf ears.

In the aftermath of the *Mozert* case, there was a book about the case—*Battleground*[53]—and someone had the bright idea of making a movie—in the lingo of Hollywood "based on a true story." I participated in a telephone script conference. I was dubious that the experience would translate into a blockbuster film—which it did not. My one memory of the conference was that one of the promoters asked me whether I would agree to be portrayed as having Christian fundamentalist in-laws, who violently objected to my litigating on the other side. I said that I thought this was stretching things a bit. My in-laws may not have been overly fond of my religious views, but they were moderate Jews, not Christian fundamentalists, and they did not support the plaintiffs. Ironically, years later when I sat on the Delaware district court, Netflix made a movie about one of my cases titled *The Billion Dollar Case*.

The press was friendly to our side in *Mozert* and cases involving freedom of the press, but the press was not always my friend. In the 1970s, Sally and I, though not yet married, were living together in my house in Dupont Circle—an arrangement that was less common and less accepted then than now. Sally became my law partner in 1975. I had the idea of hiring a college student to cook meals for us and for my children when they visited. We advertised at several local college student employment offices. Expecting perhaps a female French student, we were surprised when the sole applicant turned out to be a Tunisian man named Tahar Amar (known as Tony). He worked for a couple of years and was succeeded by his brother Farhat Amar (known as Fred). In 1978, Fred met someone from the *Washington Post* Style section, and to his delight and at his urging, the *Post* decided that it would do a piece on Fred and his employers. We naively consented. The result was a front-page article in the *Post*'s Style section, pictured in Image 4, that included the lines "Sally Katzen and Tim Dyk are not rich. Or famous, but they just happen to have a cook."[54] The predictable ribbing that ensued was widespread. (An irony was that another front-page story in the *Post* Style Section on that date was headed

**Image 4.** *Washington Post* headline

(The *Washington Post* (1974–Current file); Washington, D.C. [Washington, D.C] February 16, 1978: E1.)

"Silencing the Chorus of Yuks."). I learned a lesson: Do not invite the press to write of stories about your personal life.

Three years later, Sally and I were married. More than a few other partners at Wilmer Cutler also married firm associates or former associates.

## Notes

1   "Firm History," About, Covington & Burling LLP, last accessed June 9, 2021, https://www.cov.com/en/about/firm-history.
2   Daniel J. Cantor, "Law Firms Are Getting Bigger ... and More Complex," *American Bar Association Journal* 64, no. 2 (1978): 218.
3   Siobhan Roth, "The Public Lawyer: John Pickering Looks Back," *Legal Times*, August 2, 1999, 16.
4   Laura Kalman, *Abe Fortas: A Biography* (New Haven, CT: Yale University Press, 1990), 190.
5   R. T. Swaine, *The Cravath Firm and Its Predecessors, 1819–1948* (New York: Lawbook Exchange, 2007).
6   For a recent recollection of the events surrounding the Mudd–Kennedy interview, see Jonathan Martin, "Mudd: Kennedy Recollection a 'Fantasy,'" *Politico*, September 18, 2009, https://www.politico.com/story/2009/09/mudd-kennedy-recollection-a-fantasy-027316.
7   47 U.S.C. § 303; see also, the FCC's detailed manual of regulations concerning broadcast licenses on its website at "The Public and Broadcasting," *Federal Communications Commission*, August 2019, https://www.fcc.gov/media/radio/public-and-broadcasting.
8   Aaron Blake, "Trump's Threat to NBC's License Is the Very Definition of Nixonian," *The Washington Post*, October 11, 2017, https://www-washingtonpost.com/news/the-fix/wp/2017/10/11/trumps-threat-to-nbc-license-is-exactly-what-nixon-did.
9   For an audio file and transcript of the "vast wasteland" speech, see "Newton N. Minow," American Rhetoric: Online Speech Bank, May 2, 2019, https://www.americanrhetoric.com/speeches/newtonminow.htm.
10  William Shakespeare, *Henry VI, Part Two*, (Oxford: Oxford University Press), 4.2.
11  Peter J. Boyer, *Who Killed CBS? The Undoing of America's Number One News Network* (New York: Random House, 1988), 95.
12  Ashbrook P. Bryant, "Historical and Social Aspects of Concentration of Program Control in Television," *Law and Contemporary Problems* 34, no. 3 (1969): 610.
13  "Public Broadcasting Service," *Encyclopedia Britannica*, last revised April 2012, https://www.britannica.com/topic/Public-Broadcasting-Service.
14  *Competition and Responsibility in Network Television Broadcasting: Notice of Proposed Rulemaking*, 30 Fed. Reg. 4065 (March 27, 1965).
15  *In re Amendment of Part 73 of the Commission's Rules and Regulations with Respect to Competition and Responsibility in Network Television Broadcasting*, 23 FCC2d 382, 1970 FCC LEXIS 1339, 18 Rad. Reg. 2d (P & F) 1825.
16  "FCC Repeals PTAR Rule," Press Release, FCC, July 28, 1995, https://transition.fcc.gov/Bureaus/Mass_Media/News_Releases/nrmm5085.txt.
17  Lewis J. Paper, *Empire: William S. Paley and the Making of CBS* (New York: St. Martin's Press, 1987), 64.
18  Iris Murdoch, *A Fairly Honorable Defeat* (London: Chatto and Windus, 1970).
19  Tony Mauro, "Fruit Fight!", *New Jersey Law Journal*, 29 September 1997: 67.

20    Krista M. Enns, "Can a California Litigant Prevail in an Action for Legal Malpractice Based on an Attorney's Oral Argument before the United States Supreme Court," *Duke Law Journal* 48, no. 1 (October 1998): 122–24.

21    Marcia Coyle, "SCOTUS Picked Lawyer for Key Argument to Resolve Stalemate," *The Legal Intelligencer*, April 23, 2021, 4.

22    Paper, *Empire: William S. Paley and the Making of CBS*, 283.

23    *General Fairness Doctrine Obligations of Broadcast Licensees*, 50 Fed. Reg. 35, 418 (Aug. 30, 1985).

24    Anna Quindlen, "CBS News, Relenting, Gives Judge '60 Minutes' Material," *The New York Times*, March 25, 1981, https://www.nytimes.com/1981/03/25/nyregion/cbs-news-relenting-gives-judge-60-minutes-material.html.

25    "Maryanne Desmond Weds John Barry," *The New York Times*, December 27, 1982, https://www.nytimes.com/1982/12/27/style/maryanne-desmond-weds-john-barry.html.

26    "Vice President Agnew Resigns," This Day in History, History.com, *A&E Television Networks*, last revised Oct. 8, 2020, https://www.history.com/this-day-in-history/vice-president-agnew-resigns.

27    *New York Times Co. v. NASA*, 679 F. Supp. 33, 37 (D.D.C. 1987); and, on appeal, *New York Times Co. v. NASA*, 852 F.2d 602, 603 (D.C. Cir. 1988). The same court reversed its decision shortly after in an en banc decision in *New York Times Co. v. NASA*, 920 F.2d 1002, 1004 (D.C. Cir. 1990). Both parties then sought summary judgment in the District Court, which found in favor of NASA (*New York Times Co. v. NASA*, 782 F. Supp. 628, 629 (D.D.C. 1991)).

28    Anthony B. Herbert, *Soldier* (New York: Holt, Rinehart and Winston, 1973)

29    M.A. Farber, "Suit Against CBS Is Being Dropped by Westmoreland," *The New York Times*, February 18, 1985, https://www.nytimes.com/1985/02/18/movies/suit-against-cbs-is-being-dropped-by-westmoreland.html.

30    Paper, *Empire: William S. Paley and the Making of CBS*, 22.

31    Joseph D. Whitaker, "Edward Morgan Dies at Age 72," *The Washington Post*, March 5, 1986, https://www.washingtonpost.com/archive/local/1986/03/05/edward-morgan-dies-at-age-72/b2aa02e0-5852-4d7f-816b-74487a5fc825/.

32    Deborah Doyle-Schechtman, "Home and Hearth, Field and Plow: A Brief History of the Quechee Inn at Marshland Farm," The Quechee Inn, last updated 2016, http://www.quecheeinn.com/wp-content/uploads/2016/03/History-of-The-Quechee-Inn-at-Marshland-Farm.pdf.

33    "License Renewal Applications for Broadcast Television," Broadcast License Renewal Information, FCC, March 25, 2020, https://www.fcc.gov/media/television/broadcast-television-license-renewal.

34    Ralph Nader, *Unsafe at Any Speed: The Designed-In Dangers of the American Automobile* (New York: Grossman, 1965).

35    "Ross Malone, Lawyer, Is Dead; President of the A.B.A. in 1958," *The New York Times*, August 14, 1974, https://www.nytimes.com/1974/08/14/archives/ross-malone-lawyer-is-dead-president-of-the-aba-in-1958-counsel-for.html.

36    "Gilbert Cuneo, Expert in Contract Law," *The Washington Post*, April 13, 1978, https://www.washingtonpost.com/archive/local/1978/04/13/gilbert-cuneo-expert-in-contract-law/d41626cf-7f07-48e3-a03c-cb5cb75d283b/.

37    Joel Achenbach, "Did the News Media, Led by Walter Cronkite, Lose the War in Vietnam?," *The Washington Post*, May 25, 2018, https://www.washingtonpost.com/national/did-the-news-media-led-by-walter-cronkite-lose-the-war-in-vietnam/2018/05/25/a5b3e098-495e-11e8-827e-190efaf1f1ee_story.html.

38    "Robert F. Kennedy and the 1968 Campaign," John F. Kennedy Presidential Library and Museum, March 16, 2008, https://www.jfklibrary.org/events-and-awards/for ums/past-forums/transcripts/robert-f-kennedy-and-the-1968-campaign.

39    Ron Elving, "Remembering 1968: LBJ Surprises Nation with Announcement He Won't Seek Re-Election," *NPR*, March 25, 2018, https://www.npr.org/2018/03/25/596805375/president-johnson-made-a-bombshell-announcement-50-years-ago.

40    "The Election of 1968," PBS, last accessed June 9, 2021, https://www.pbs.org/john gardner/chapters/5a.html.

41    "Thomas Finney, Lawyer, Political Strategist, Dies," *The Washington Post*, February 1, 1978, https://www-washingtonpost.com/archive/local/1978/02/01/thomas-finney-lawyer-political-strategist-dies/dd8ecb8a-a8c7-4e66-bec0-32d4dd33c73a/; Michael Drosnin and Howard Hughes, *Citizen Hughes* (New York: Broadway Books, 1985), 208–9.

42    Homer Bigart, "McCarthy Talks at Garden; 19,000 Hail Candidate," *The New York Times*, August 16, 1968, https://www.nytimes.com/1968/08/16/archives/mccarthy-talks-at-garden-19000-hail-candidate.html.

43    Shirley Elder, "They Filled the Hall for Gene," *Evening Star* (Washington, DC), August 16, 1968: 39.

44    Timothy Dyk, "Supreme Court Review of Interlocutory State-Court Decisions: 'The Twilight Zone of Finality,'" *Stanford Law Review* 19, no. 5 (1967): 907–46; Timothy Dyk, "Newsgathering, Press Access, and the First Amendment," *Stanford Law Review* 44, no. 5 (1992): 927–60.

45    Home Page, Federal Public Defender for the District of Columbia, last accessed June 3, 2021, https://dc.fd.org.

46    "PDS Historical Timeline," About Us, The Public Defender Service for the District of Columbia, last accessed June 3, 2021, https://www.pdsdc.org/about-us/historical-timeline.

47    Pub. L. No. 98–473, §§202-03, 98 Stat. 1976–85 (codified as amended at 18 U.S.C. §§ 3141–56).

48    Robert W. Tobin, *Creating the Judicial Branch: The Unfinished Reform* (Williamsburg, VA: National Center for States Courts, 1999), 101.

49    Ibid.

50    For the stories published on the 50th anniversary of the documentary's broadcast, see Byron Pitts, "'Harvest of Shame' 50 Years Later," *CBS News*, November 24, 2010, https://www.cbsnews.com/news/harvest-of-shame-50-years-later/; and Elizabeth Blair, "In Confronting Poverty, 'Harvest of Shame' Reaped Praise and Criticism," *NPR*, May 31, 2014, https://www.npr.org/2014/05/31/317364146/in-confronting-poverty-harvest-of-shame-reaped-praise-and-criticism.

51    Quoted in Stephen Bates, *Battleground. One Mother's Crusade, the Religious Right, and the Struggle for Control of Our Classrooms* (New York: Poseidon Press, 1993), 22.

52    For example, see Dudley Clendinen, "Fundamentalists Win a Federal Suit over Schoolbooks," *The New York Times*, October 25, 1986, https://www.nytimes.com/1986/10/25/us/fundamentalists-win-a-federal-suit-over-schoolbooks.html.

53    Bates, *Battleground*.

54    *The Washington Post* (1974–Current file); Washington, D.C. [Washington, DC] February 16, 1978: E1.

# Chapter 7

# JONES DAY, 1990–2000

## Making the Switch

Wilmer Cutler's relationship with CBS and the broadcast business generally, which had been so important to me over the years, began to peter out in the mid-1980s. The reasons for this were several. The first factor was FCC deregulation (as a result of the election of President Ronald Reagan), which substantially eliminated the threat of license challenges and other FCC regulations. This meant less legal business defending against the FCC. There was also management turnover at CBS. Those who fostered the relationship with Wilmer Cutler left the company or were demoted to lesser positions and were replaced by others less favorably inclined. This process began as early as 1969 when Jack Schneider and Dick Jencks (the latter a strong supporter of the firm) were scheduled to assume the positions of CEO and president, replacing Paley and Stanton, only to find at the board meeting to finalize the scheduled change that Paley had changed his mind.[1] Schneider reverted to president of the Broadcast Group, and Jencks became the Washington representative, with far less influence over the legal work. Stanton, a champion of broadcasters' First Amendment rights, retired in 1973, pushed out by Paley. Paley's ultimate failing was his inability to turn the reins over to Stanton and, thereafter, his unwillingness to plan for an orderly succession. At his core, he did not want to surrender his role as CEO. After a series of designated replacements either died or were fired, the control of the company passed to the Tisch family in 1986 with unhappy consequences for the company.[2]

Even before Tisch took over, the new CBS management decided that the FCC was no longer a threat, and CBS News needed to stand on its own. In other words, CBS did not need to have an impressive news service as a defense to license challengers and other FCC regulation. Cost cutting became the order of the day—cost cutting that extended to CBS News' outside legal fees. As a result of this emphasis on profit and belt tightening,[3] there was a drastic turnover in CBS personnel, and my friends in management at the company departed, the last being Ralph Goldberg. When Tisch took over from Paley in 1985–86, it became clear that Tisch was also unwilling to spend money on defending the First Amendment (to Paley's own distress). [4] My work for CBS was a shadow of its former self. The Wilmer Cutler communications practice was not limited to CBS, but the firm had resisted representing cable and other new media, just as the new media were becoming major players. There was, to be sure, money to be made in broadcast deregulation, but that money often went to firms with Republican connections such as the Wiley Rein firm, founded in 1983, which was better connected to the Republican FCC.

The larger difficulty was that Wilmer Cutler needed to reinvent itself for a different and now highly competitive world. This was a problem that other Washington firms, such as Covington and Arnold & Porter, confronted as well. At Wilmer Cutler, other practice areas in addition to communications, such as antitrust, were also suffering from deregulation. To the extent that corporate America had problems with government, they were less likely to work with a Democratic firm when the White House was controlled by Republicans. Beginning in 1980, the Republicans had a 12-year period of White House control, and Cutler's and the firm's influence in government was diminished. Cutler's support for the Bork nomination in 1987 seemed to some like a misplaced effort to ingratiate himself with a new breed of Republican conservatives. By the time I left Wilmer in 1990, Cutler had ceased to be a partner (being instead counsel) and was not the rainmaker he once was. He was 72 years old, and his contemporaries were no longer corporate CEOs or the movers and shakers in government. To be sure, Cutler's time in the sun was not over. He served with distinction as Clinton's White House Counsel in 1994.[5] Cutler's prominence in the political scene, however, did not translate into firm business. Cutler himself took virtually no interest in the administration of the firm and had shown little interest in succession—that is, in planning for a future Wilmer without Cutler. To be sure, Cutler had earlier brought in Manny Cohen, former head of the SEC, Art Matthews and, later, Ted Levine to create a securities enforcement practice. Even though Cohen had died shortly after joining the firm (having a heart attack on the elevator on the way back from a firm lunch), the practice thrived. But Cutler's efforts to bring in other laterals had typically been nixed by the firm because they did not seem likely to contribute meaningfully to the firm's business. There were other successes, such as the European practice, bankruptcy and banking. But the latter two were the result of individual partner effort, not the firm's strategic planning.

The firm had done little to replace the loss of the Cutler business engine and, with some exceptions, had no significant organized approach to developing new practice areas by bringing in significant lateral entrants from government or other firms, encouraging partners to write their way into expertise in a new practice area or merging with other firms. The firm to some extent resisted acquiring new areas of practice, for example rejecting until much later the idea of starting a legislative practice or, as mentioned earlier, representing new media. There were other lost opportunities. For example, it certainly was foreseeable in 1982, when the Federal Circuit was created, that there would be an increasing amount of patent litigation. Wilmer Cutler seemed unaware of this until many years later. Eventually, in 2004, Wilmer Cutler merged with Hale and Dorr, largely to secure the Hale and Dorr patent litigation practice, and took other steps to reinvent itself, for example, bringing in Jamie Gorelick to start a legislation and investigations practice.

There were other problems when I was at the firm. Many of the partners were talented at writing very good appellate briefs, but they were not entrepreneurial, and they were resistant to change. The view of many partners was that they should be generalists rather than specialists at a time of increasing lawyer specialization. With all that said, the firm attracted over time a remarkably talented group. But much of the talent left relatively early in their careers, certainly before retirement age. Wilmer kept an alumni list; recently I reviewed the list, 147 pages in length, from 2003, the year before the merger with Hale and Dorr, and supplemented the list with my own recollection. The firm produced four judges for the DC district court (Oberdorfer, Robertson, Moss and Engelmayer), two for the Federal Circuit (Clevenger and myself), one for the DC Court of Appeals (Kramer); general counsels of some of the country's leading corporations (Helfer at Citigroup, Melamed at Intel, Weiswasser, Westin and Braverman at ABC, for example); law school deans and law professors; partners at other leading firms; and countless high government officials. The questions are: why was the firm unsuccessful in keeping more of this talent, and why was the firm unable to make better use of the talent it did retain? There are no easy answers.

I experienced a keen sense of loss that a special relationship with a long-term client (CBS) and an entire practice area had come to an end. But, as with other setbacks in my life, I looked forward, recognizing that I had to retool. As previously mentioned, I became involved in bankruptcy work. This was both interesting and promising, but it was difficult to move to an entirely new area. At the time, developing a more general appellate practice (beyond broadcasting and First Amendment representation) was appealing to me. I thought that it was not possible to develop such a practice at Wilmer Cutler because so many of the partners viewed themselves as appellate lawyers, and some had a claim to appellate experience at least as good as mine. My relationship with Cutler was sufficiently strained that he was unlikely to promote me for such a position. There was another reason for considering leaving Wilmer Cutler. It was awkward to be married to one of my partners in the firm (Sally and

I having married in 1981). Even though I think we and the firm handled that fairly well, there were a few partners who objected to our relationship. So, I began to look elsewhere. Partners had left to become judges or to join the government or corporate law departments, but no partner had left Wilmer Cutler to join another firm. I began to look in that direction.

As a result of Sally's friendship with one of the partners at Jones Day through the Administrative Law Section of the American Bar Association, I was interviewed to be head of that firm's Issues and Appeals practice, a new practice, as its name suggests, that was both appellate and involved in other firm legal work. That position had first been held by Don Ayer. He had been deputy solicitor general, joined Jones Day as the head of the Issues and Appeals practice, and then went back into the government as the deputy attorney general, creating a vacancy at Issues and Appeals.

I met with Steve Brogan, who was the head of the Jones Day Washington office, and with the managing partner of the firm, Dick Pogue, and I was offered the Issues and Appeals position. I was entitled under the partnership agreement at Wilmer Cutler to payments over a period of 10 years. The firm was about to change that policy for the future. I thought that it would be fair to leave some of the money on the table, and I proposed to take only half of what I was entitled to. I was very careful also to talk to each of the partners in the firm and tell them how much I enjoyed Wilmer Cutler, how much I valued the firm and the reason I was leaving. I left the firm on good terms and began at Jones Day in 1990. Sally remained at Wilmer Cutler as a partner, but later left to join the Clinton Administration in 1993, never to return.

The announcement of my departure from Wilmer Cutler to join Jones Day received some attention in the legal press.[6] It was not huge news, but it was definitely noted because it was unusual. Today, the switching from one firm to another is very common. Shortly after I joined Jones Day, Don Ayer had a public falling out with the attorney general and decided to leave the department. He returned to Jones Day not as the head of Issues and Appeals, but as the number two. That created an awkward situation, but Don was very good about it.[7]

Jones Day's culture was quite different from Wilmer Cutler's. It was very much a top-down system. The managing partner of the firm had the ultimate authority to fix compensation for all partners and make decisions about the direction and administration of the firm and who would hold the firm's other leadership positions. Partners were not supposed to know what other partners earned, which had its advantages. In my experience, people were fairly faithful to the nondisclosure rule. In 1993, after I had been at Jones Day for a couple of years, Dick Pogue stepped down as managing partner and Pat McCartan took his place. Pat had clerked for Justice Whitaker during the 1959

Term,[8] and the Issues and Appeals practice had been his idea. He continued to support it. In fact, he wanted the Issues and Appeals practice to get him involved in appeals, which we never did successfully.

Joining Jones Day presented challenges. The primary challenge was that Issues and Appeals was a relatively new practice area. The Issues and Appeals practice had only been in existence for a couple of years, and its role in the firm was not well defined. To what extent was the Issues and Appeals practice going to help other practice areas of the firm with the cases they were handling? To what extent was it expected to develop new business independently? It was obviously supposed to do both, and to succeed it needed help from other partners in the firm.

The receptivity of other partners to involving the Issues and Appeals practice in their cases and in helping the practice develop its own cases was variable. Some of the partners were very receptive (Andy Kramer[9] and Herb Hansell[10] being prime examples.) Others were not. It was frustrating at times being sidelined when we had something to contribute. I remember one case that had potentially significant financial consequences for the firm. It was handled by partners who wanted no input from the Issues and Appeals practice. They had won a huge verdict in the trial court. On appeal, they thought that the appellant had raised a new argument in the reply brief. Instead of downplaying the significance of this new argument and addressing it in oral argument, they moved to strike the reply brief on the ground that it was a new argument that should have been raised in the opening brief, thus giving the argument great prominence. That is not something that an experienced appellate lawyer would have done. Ultimately, they lost the case on appeal based on the new argument. Could Issues and Appeals have made a difference? Perhaps or perhaps not.

One of the costs of switching from one firm to another is that long-term friendships are generally terminated as a result of your leaving the firm, but that was not entirely true for me. I maintained some of the friendships that I had had, and I still see some of my former Wilmer Cutler colleagues socially. However, when you go to a new firm, you are confronted with having to establish a whole new set of friendships. I was very fortunate to find people at Jones Day who became friends as well as colleagues.

More important than friendship is past work experience. When you change firms, the working relationships that you had with your partners based on long years of work together is gone, and you must establish new working relationships. You have to convince your new partners that you have something to contribute. The size of Jones Day (then hundreds of lawyers)[11] made this particularly difficult. It meant that a lateral partner would likely never know the whole partnership. I remember early in my tenure at Jones Day flying to

Cleveland on Continental Airlines in first class. I found that a gentleman was sitting in my seat. When I pointed this out to him and we had moved seats, we talked and it turned out he was one of my partners, and I did not even know it.

The difficulty in establishing working relationships with new colleagues was exacerbated by geography as well as by size. When I was at Wilmer Cutler, the firm was almost exclusively located in Washington, DC. It did have London and Brussels offices, but those were very small. Jones Day had multiple significant offices. I worked closely with lawyers in Cleveland, Chicago, Columbus and Pittsburgh, and so I found myself working with people whom I had never met face to face. It was easier once you had a face-to-face meeting, then you could work on the phone together. The lack of personal contact is a problem now with very large firms and modern technology. The personal relationships that used to exist and used to be the bedrock of the practice do not exist so much anymore.

I was very fortunate that we had quite a talented group of lawyers in the Issues and Appeals practice and that we were able to hire new talent, many of whom had been Supreme Court law clerks. Firms in Washington had become very eager to hire Supreme Court law clerks. This was a change from the 1960s.

At Issues and Appeals, we pursued hiring Supreme Court law clerks with some success. We were not always successful, sometimes because of the firm's culture. I remember a Supreme Court law clerk who we interviewed, and I had dinner with her and Pat McCartan. She asked if the firm was receptive to maternity leave for associates and partners. To my distress, McCartan threw cold water on that, with the result that we were unsuccessful in hiring her. The attitude has changed. I notice that the Issues and Appeals practice, until recently chaired by Beth Heifetz, has been strikingly successful in hiring clerks.

During my time with Jones Day, we had a number of excellent lawyers in our section. Many who were Supreme Court law clerks ultimately left the firm.[12] Jeff Sutton became a judge on the Sixth Circuit, Richard Cordray became head of the Consumer Financial Protection Bureau, Greg Katsas became a judge on the D.C. Circuit, Paul Capuccio became general counsel of Time Warner. Lee Liberman Otis did important work in Congress, in the executive branch and at the Federalist Society. Barbara McDowell, who left the firm and started a distinguished career in public service, tragically died. She was a close friend as well as a colleague. Others left too. Bob Klonoff became a law school dean at Lewis & Clark. Tom Fisher went on to be the solicitor general for Indiana and was almost appointed to the Seventh Circuit. John Nalbandian became a judge on the Sixth Circuit. Dan Bromberg joined the California State government. I was also fortunate to have hired some people who have become very successful in the firm, such as Greg Castanias and Beth Heifitz, and worked with other able lawyers who stayed, such as Glen Nager. Glen would have made a fine judge, but his desires were thwarted; though he was a Republican, he was deemed not sufficiently conservative.

## Cameras in the Courtroom

When I joined Jones Day in 1990, I did not bring with me many clients from Wilmer Cutler. I did bring some coalition business. One coalition was a group of news organizations whose objective was to get cameras in the federal courts. Our coalition included almost everybody in the news media except for the Courtroom Television Network, which was founded by Steve Brill in 1989 and had come to be known commonly as "Court TV." Steve Brill wanted to promote his own Court TV, and there was competition between Brill and our coalition. PBS (Nancy Hendry) was an important member of the coalition.

The camera project was not merely a client representation. I was personally very much in favor of allowing cameras in the courts, and the project was a labor of love. I had had experience arguing before cameras. I had done that in the New York Court of Appeals. I also argued before the FCC in the *RKO* case in front of cameras. As a result of those experiences, I was convinced that having cameras in court, if managed properly, had clear benefits in terms of public access and did not really alter lawyers' behavior, which was one of the primary concerns with cameras. I also thought that the cameras did not make the proceedings more newsworthy. The request for cameras in the courts came only in cases that were already significant and were already going to be covered by the news media. The camera coverage would enhance the coverage that was already going to take place. The concern about intruding into the privacy of judges, jurors and trial participants seemed misplaced. The whole point of a public trial, guaranteed by both the First and Sixth Amendments (*Globe Newspaper Co. v. Superior Court*, 457 U.S. 596 (1982)), was to expose the trial participants to public scrutiny.

There was an additional concern among the judges skeptical of camera coverage—that is, the camera coverage might result in distorted 30-second excerpts from the court proceedings, excerpts that would not be representative of what had happened. Judges were more favorably disposed to camera coverage that would be gavel to gavel, but that was not going to be the norm. The news media were always going to be selective, and editing was a necessary aspect of good journalism anyway. Selectivity would occur with or without camera coverage. Television demanded visuals, and the absence of cameras inside the court encouraged television to rely on interviews with lawyers, who would tell different versions of events, as was true in the Tennessee textbook case. As I mentioned earlier, the lawyers appeared on the courthouse steps and gave their own versions of what happened inside. This is not to suggest that I gave an inaccurate version of what happened inside, but obviously anyone in those circumstances is selective. In short, there was a tendency of the news media, particularly television, to rely on the lawyers' version of events if cameras were not present in the courtroom. It is better to have a selective and first-hand portrayal of what happened in the courtroom than a selective second-hand portrayal. Better to have journalists being selective than trial participants. Like the privacy concern, the concern with editing seemed contrary to trust in the First Amendment.

For many years the Judicial Conference, the governing body of the federal court system, had opposed allowing cameras in federal court proceedings.[13] In civil proceedings, the Judicial Conference had adopted a ban in 1972 applicable to both civil trials and appeals.[14] The ban on cameras in criminal trials under the Federal Rules of Criminal Procedure was adopted even earlier in 1946.[15] The criminal trial ban resulted from the 1935 Bruno Hauptmann trial. Hauptman had been accused and ultimately convicted of participation in the abduction and murder of Charles Lindbergh Jr., the infant son of famous aviator Charles Lindbergh. Cameras were allowed in the courtroom, and the result was a great media circus. The hearing was quickly dubbed "the trial of the century," and H. L. Mencken called it "the greatest story since the Resurrection."[16] It was generally thought that the uncontrolled media coverage denied Hauptmann a fair trial.[17] Many of the concerns were related to the way that the judge, Thomas Trenchard, had handled the media presence. Other concerns related to the technology itself, because the movie cameras at that time required very bright lighting and the cameras themselves were bulky and intrusive.[18]

When I began working on the cameras issue in the 1980s, the technology had changed significantly: no special lighting was required, and the cameras were small and unobtrusive. Many state courts had already changed the rules banning cameras.[19] Having cameras in state criminal proceedings was made possible in 1981 by a Supreme Court case mentioned earlier (*Chandler v. Florida*, 449 U.S. 560 (1981)), which held that having cameras in criminal trials was not unconstitutional. That made it possible to have criminal trial coverage in state courts. Nonetheless at the federal level, the ban persisted, as did the concerns with lawyers' grandstanding, the loss of privacy for judges and jurors and distorted reporting of proceedings.

In September 1990, after my move to Jones Day, our coalition was successful in securing a pilot program experiment allowing cameras in both federal district courts and federal appellate courts. The three-year program began in July 1991 and involved the US Courts of Appeals for the Second and Ninth Circuits and the US District Courts for the Southern District of

Indiana, District of Massachusetts, Eastern District of Michigan, Southern District of New York, Eastern District of Pennsylvania and Western District of Washington.[20] By December 1994, the experiment was complete. The Judicial Conference appointed a committee headed by Howard Markey, who was the chief judge of the Federal Circuit at that time, to consider the matter. Although Markey was hostile to cameras in the courts, we seemed to be on track to have the experimental rules made permanent. Then came the O. J. Simpson trial in 1995, and the failure of Judge Lance Ito, the state trial judge in that proceeding, to control the camera presence. It was generally agreed that Ito had allowed a circus atmosphere to develop again, like the Lindberg case. Eventually the Judicial Conference decided not to allow cameras in the trial courts, although cameras would now be allowed in the courts of appeals if the circuit approved.[21]

An important goal of the camera project was to have cameras in the Supreme Court—an issue not under the jurisdiction of the Judicial Conference Committee. C-SPAN, a member of our coalition, even promised gavel-to-gavel coverage. The Supreme Court was skeptical of cameras in the courts both then and now. Various justices, such as Thomas, Ginsburg and Kagan, stated that they did not object or favored cameras in the Supreme Court at their confirmation hearings. Once on the Court, they had second thoughts. [22] Justice Kennedy called the presence of cameras "insidious."[23] Justice Souter, always opposed to camera coverage, went as far as to announce in 1996 that cameras would only appear in the Supreme Court "over [his] dead body."[24]

In November 1988, we did a demonstration at the Supreme Court, which three justices attended. We tried to show what it would be like to have camera coverage of the Court.[25] I remember Justice White's asking if it would be possible to make the images of the bench smaller so that people could not identify the justices who were speaking, which was the exact opposite of what the media sought to achieve. Since then, the only progress at the Supreme Court has been in the area of audio, which is now available nearly contemporaneously for Supreme Court arguments and during COVID has been streamed live. Although Justice Kennedy in 1990 said that he thought cameras in the Court were "inevitable," it still has not happened.[26]

Legislation has been introduced opening the Supreme Court and other federal courts to cameras, but none of it has been enacted. In 2011, another three-year pilot program in civil cases in 14 district courts was launched by the Judicial Conference. In 2016, the Judicial Conference decided not to amend its policy further.[27] At the circuit level, where the policy change allowed cameras, the Third Circuit has joined the Second and the Ninth Circuit in allowing cameras in the courts. Before COVID, the federal courts started another pilot program in the district courts—this for livestreaming of audio.[28]

But the Judicial Conference continues to oppose legislation to admit cameras to the federal courts on the theory that the "intimidating effects of cameras on litigants, witnesses, and jurors has a profoundly negative impact on the trial process."[29] This seems to ignore that a purpose of the public trial requirement is to expose the trial participants to public scrutiny. In my own court, there is a lack of enthusiasm for camera coverage and we have not allowed cameras, though requests for such coverage have been rare. During COVID, live streamed audio has been the norm in all circuits and district courts, though recording of the live stream is prohibited.[30] I do not think that any problems resulted.

## Indecency Regulation

Other coalition work that I took from Wilmer Cutler to Jones Day involved federal indecency regulation. Obscenity is, of course, not protected by the First Amendment (*Miller v. California*, 413 U.S. 15 (1973)). Indecent speech is protected, and print, motion pictures, cable, satellite and streaming services are free to disseminate indecent material. Indecent over-the-air broadcasts, on the other hand, have been prohibited by statute for many years. The ban, though in a criminal statute, was not criminally enforced but rather was enforced by FCC rulings on complaints brought by members of the public. The ban was first challenged in *FCC v. Pacifica Foundation*, 438 U.S. 726 (1978), a case involving the broadcast of George Carlin's *Seven Dirty Words* monologue.[31] While at Wilmer Cutler, I worked on an amicus brief for the networks and others, and later a petition for rehearing. We were unsuccessful. The Court reasoned that broadcasting was unique, and that the FCC could regulate the broadcast of indecent material primarily to protect child viewers. After *Pacifica*, broadcasters' concern with FCC indecency regulation continued, resulting in the formation of a coalition to challenge such regulation. We designated Action for Children's Television as the lead party to help emphasize that many who favored broadcast regulation to protect the interests of children were opposed to indecency regulation ostensibly designed to protect children.

The objective of our coalition was to get federal indecency regulation relaxed rather than eliminated. Elimination seemed a bridge too far. There were cases in which I represented the coalition, both at Wilmer Cutler and at Jones Day. We had only modest success, but we did establish two propositions. The first of these was that FCC indecency regulation could not be justified as designed to protect adults. Second, there needed to be a safe harbor, after children had presumably gone to bed, when indecent material could be broadcast and made available to adults. Ultimately, the D.C. Circuit, in an opinion written by later justice Ruth Bader Ginsburg, determined that a safe harbor was required after 10:00 p.m. in the evening (*Action for Children's Television v. FCC*, 852 F.2d 1332 (D.C. Cir. 1988)). Congress then enacted a statute imposing a 24-hour ban on broadcast indecency (Pub. L. No. 100–459, §608, 102 Stat. 2228 (1988)). In 1991, we convinced the D.C. Circuit to hold the statute unconstitutional (*Action for Children's Television v. FCC*, 932 F.2d 1504 (D.C. Cir. 1991)). Congress enacted another statute limiting broadcast indecency to the hours of midnight to 6:00 a.m. Representing the same group, we again challenged that statute in the D.C. Circuit, which held the statute unconstitutional for the period from 10:00 p.m. to midnight when children were likely asleep (*Action for Children's Television v. FCC*, 58 F.3d 654 (D.C. Cir. 1995)) (en banc), *cert. denied*, 116 S.Ct. 701 (1996)).

None of these cases went to the Supreme Court, but I recall that my efforts led Howard Stern to characterize me as a "great American hero." Since that time, the Supreme Court has revisited the issue in *FCC v. Fox Television Stations, Inc. v. FCC*, 567 U.S. 239 (2012). The broad challenge to FCC indecency regulation, which continues to this day, has been largely unsuccessful, though the *Fox* case found vagueness problems in the particular case. New media (cable, satellite, streaming) remain unconstrained. The Supreme Court has even invalidated a statute regulating indecent trademarks as I discuss later (*Iancu v. Brunetti*, 588 U.S. ——, 139 S. Ct. 2294 (2019)). Broadcasting alone continues to be subject to the indecency regime.

## Building an Appellate Practice

When I joined Jones Day, one of the things that was apparent to me was that an appellate practice needed to have Supreme Court work. It was a very competitive field because there were many firms with former members of the Office of the Solicitor General and other leading appellate advocates competing for that work. As a result, Supreme Court work was not generally profitable. The work was necessary, however, for visibility. Though I had argued many appeals, I was conscious of the fact that I had only argued one Supreme Court case, which had been a decade earlier in the *WNCN Listeners Guild* case (450 U.S. 582 (1981)). Though Don Ayer had solid Supreme Court credentials through his stint in the Solicitor General's Office, and Bob Klonoff and Glen Nager had been assistants in that office, I thought it was important both for me and for other members of the Issues and Appeals practice to have more Supreme Court experience. So, we set out to seek Supreme Court cases, some of which at reduced rates or pro bono. Our theory was the same as former Solicitor General Cox: who needs to be compensated for cases in the Supreme Court of the United States?[32] We were successful in getting some of these cases, and, ultimately, I argued eight additional Supreme Court cases, and my colleagues argued several others. To my great regret, perhaps being overly scrupulous, I turned down Larry Silberman's invitation to join the weekly Chief Justice Rehnquist poker game; it seemed to me that I should not be losing money to the chief justice before whom I was appearing—which was certain to happen since I was a poor player.

## Lubrizol

In addition to Supreme Court work, it was also necessary for Issues and Appeals to become involved in the firm's specialty practices. One of these was patent law. Largely thanks to one of my partners, Herb Hansell, patent law became a significant focus of our group. Herb was a distinguished figure. He had been the legal advisor to the State Department in the Carter Administration. Years later when I was on the bench, he was asked to represent the Palestinian Liberation Organization (PLO) in negotiating a peace agreement with Israel; Ehud Barak was then the prime minister and eager for a resolution of hostilities. Herb declined the representation because the PLO was simply unable to decide what its position should be. A tragic lost opportunity.

When I arrived at Jones Day, Herb had been a longtime advisor to Lubrizol, a manufacturer of motor oils and other products, and had a very close relationship with Roger Hsu, who was the general counsel, and with Joe Bauer, who was then the deputy general counsel. Lubrizol and Exxon had been litigating for many years over various patent issues, each asserting patents against the other, and Jones Day had been Lubrizol's counsel in many of these cases, sometimes partnered with another firm. There were several pending Lubrizol cases. One of them went to the Federal Circuit. This was an Exxon patent being asserted against Lubrizol. Leslie Misrock, who was a well-known patent lawyer in a New York boutique firm, had been primarily responsible for the case, but Herb thought it would be best for the client if I argued the case in the Federal Circuit. The client was appalled, thinking that no lawyer who had not spent his life as a patent lawyer could possibly argue a patent case in the Federal Circuit.

Ultimately, a compromise was reached. I would share the argument with Leslie. At the close of the argument, Judge Nies, a member of the panel, complained about the size of the appendix, which contained record materials cited in the briefs. It was about a dozen volumes, well over two feet high when stacked. Leslie began to argue that the large volume of material was necessary, indeed required by the court's rules. I thought this was not earning us any good will and stood up, put my arm around Leslie and said, "we apologize your honor," so the immediate crisis was averted. Eventually, we were victorious, though Judge Nies dissented (*Exxon Chemical Patents, Inc. v. Lubrizol*

*Corp.*, 64 F. 3d 1553 (1995)). The client was kind enough to give me some credit for that. So, I became Lubrizol's lawyer in other Federal Circuit cases and ultimately was given responsibility at Jones Day for all their litigation, which included district court litigation.

Even though I ultimately replaced Leslie Misrock as the lead lawyer, I became quite friendly with Leslie who continued to play a role in the Lubrizol litigation. Leslie unfortunately died shortly after I was confirmed to the Federal Circuit. The original memorial service in New York, to which I was invited, was scheduled for either September 11, 2001, or shortly thereafter. Obviously, the service was rescheduled for a later time. When I appeared for the rescheduled service, I opened the printed program and noticed that my name was listed as one of the speakers, which no one had bothered to tell me. Between the time that I opened the program and the time that I was to speak, I had 10 minutes to prepare a memorial tribute to Leslie. Suppressing panic, I managed to do it. I do not think anyone noticed that I was unprepared.

Lubrizol was a good client and my relationship with them was a close one for several years. I remember one of the district court cases involving Exxon in particular. The Exxon lawyers on the other side were a tough bunch, but competent. We disagreed about the appropriate number of deposition days. My recollection is that Exxon wanted 300 days (presumably to drive up the cost to Lubrizol which had shallower pockets than Exxon), and my counter proposal was 150 days—still a huge number of days. Unable to agree, we asked the Ohio district judge to resolve the issue. We ended up in a conference in the judge's chambers, each of us presenting his side of the dispute. The judge then said, "Well, that is my ruling." We said, "Excuse us. What is the ruling?" He said, "My ruling is that you have to work this out yourselves." We said, "We cannot. That is why we are here." His response was to ask us if we would like to see the plans for the new courthouse. That had a big impact on me. Now on the occasions that I sit as a district judge, I make myself available to resolve discovery disputes.

As a result of the Lubrizol work, I became involved in other patent cases, and that would have continued to be a major area of practice, save for the fact that on April 1, 1998, I was nominated to the Federal Circuit. By that time, I had argued five cases in the Federal Circuit. I thought it appropriate under those circumstances to withdraw from all patent cases that I was then handling in the Federal Circuit and not to take on others.

In one way, my nomination to the Federal Circuit was beneficial to Lubrizol because it gave me a unique opportunity to settle all of the then pending Lubrizol/Exxon litigation in the district courts. In the course of the negotiations, I got to know Ken Cohen, the in-house Exxon counsel who was responsible for the Lubrizol litigation. He thought that perhaps a round of golf would oil the wheels (so to speak). I am a very inept golfer and lost badly. The Exxon outside counsel was very good (his devotion to golf being confirmed by an office a foot deep in golf balls with a path to his desk). We were able to settle the cases because the opposing lawyers had developed a good and productive working relationship.

## Other Litigation

Another specialty area of Jones Day's practice in which I became involved was state tax litigation, thanks to Jim O'Hara. The litigation involved issues of state law, but it also included interesting issues of federal constitutional law. The bulk of the work was for taxpayers, but occasionally the states themselves would need outside representation. I recall arguing once in the Tennessee Supreme Court, twice in the Ohio Supreme Court, once in the Colorado intermediate appellate court, and once representing the state of Kansas in the Kansas Supreme Court. I also represented the Seneca Indian tribe in the New York Court of Appeals.

There were two problems in these cases. The first was that Washington counsel was not always welcome in state court, where all of these cases were litigated, though on constitutional issues the courts often thought we had something to contribute. The other problem was that the state courts were conscious of the state need for revenue, so representing the taxpayer was an uphill battle. In the Seneca case, the issue was whether a treaty between the Seneca tribe and the United States barred New York from requiring the tribe to collect taxes on reservation cigarette sales. The argument went well, and we thought that victory was likely. The Court of Appeals dodged the issue, finding that the original complaint (not drafted by us) did not sufficiently raise the issue, an argument that had not been raised by the state in opposing the tribe (*Snyder v. Wechsler*, 644 N.E.2d 1369 (N.Y. 1994)).

There were significant and politically charged cases that I became involved in as a result of my move to Jones Day. One of these was the striker replacement case. In 1995, Andy Kramer, one of the partners in the Washington office of Jones Day and a consummate rainmaker, was instrumental in securing the representation of the Chamber of Commerce. The case involved an Executive Order issued by President Clinton that barred federal contractors from hiring permanent striker replacements in the case of labor disputes. The Executive Order relied on the federal contracting power. When I was asked to undertake the representation, it seemed to me likely that I would be forfeiting any chance of being nominated by Clinton to a judgeship, but I was enthusiastic about handling the case and was willing to accept any adverse consequences that flowed from doing so. We lost in the district court on the ground that the controversy was not ripe. Ultimately the case ended up in the D.C. Circuit, and I argued. The Executive Order was held invalid on the ground that the claimed statutory authority did not exist (*Chamber of Commerce v. Reich*, 74 F.3d 1322 (D.C. Cir. 1996)). This was the first time in decades that an Executive Order had been invalidated. I was wondering whether the Justice Department was going to take the case to the Supreme Court. They called and said they would not. They told me that a lot of the Clinton people had not been very favorably disposed to the Executive Order in the first place. It turned out that this was not something that made me a pariah in the eyes of the administration.

Another significant case was the *Trinity Broadcasting* case, which came to me as a result of earlier work that I had done on the *RKO* license renewal cases and ironically partly because of my work in *Mozert*. Trinity Broadcasting was one of the major religious broadcasters in the United States. Its Miami TV license had been challenged, and the FCC had stripped Trinity of the license, which was worth many millions of dollars. The FCC's theory was that Trinity had failed to comply with the FCC's minority ownership rules, which (the FCC claimed) required de facto minority control. It also argued that Trinity and Colby May, one of Trinity's lawyers who was affiliated with the Christian Coalition, had displayed a lack of candor before the FCC. I thought that the facts did not remotely support a finding of lack of candor. I had no doubt that part of the FCC motivation for taking away the license was because Trinity was viewed as a right-wing religious broadcaster, which seemed to me indefensible. I wrote the brief and argued the case in the D.C. Circuit. Trinity prevailed (*Trinity Broadcasting v. FCC*, 211 F.3d 618 (D.C. Cir. 2000)). Both Trinity and Colby were delighted. It was a great experience to work with Colby and the Trinity executives.

One of the most unusual representations, again as a result of Herb Hansell, was of a Kuwaiti citizen named Talal Alzanki. He and his wife were accused by the Justice Department of enslaving their nanny, slavery being a crime under federal law. The nanny was free to come and go from their residence. The theory was that she was enslaved psychologically, as well as by threats of deportation. This seemed to be a reach based on the underlying facts, though it was clear that the nanny was not treated well. We tried to get the Civil Rights Division to drop the charges, but they refused, the case having become a cause célèbre in the women's movement. I did not handle the trial (at which Alzanki was convicted based on evidence of psychological coercion by a rape trauma expert), but I assisted in the sentencing phases. Tears were running down Alzanki's face at the prospect of being separated from his wife and their baby with spina bifida. Mercifully, he was sentenced to a year in Allenwood, one of the "Club Fed" prisons. The conviction was affirmed on appeal ((which I did not argue since the Kuwaiti government had stopped paying), *United States v. Alzanki*, 54 F.3d 994 (1st Cir. 1995)). There are some horrific cases involving noncitizen domestic workers, but I was convinced, on the facts presented, this was not one of them.

The efforts by Herb Hansell and Andy Kramer resulted in my involvement in another significant case. A coalition led by the National Foreign Trade Council challenged a Massachusetts law barring state agencies from contracting with any company that did business with Myanmar (Burma). We argued that the Massachusetts law interfered with the exclusive federal authority over foreign relations and that the state law was preempted by federal law, which had occupied the field. The coalition looking for counsel held a beauty contest where they interviewed a number of different law firms. I was told later that I was hired because I did not come to the beauty contest with a PowerPoint presentation and instead just sat and talked to them about the case. I am not a fan of PowerPoint and have, with the agreement of my colleagues, banned its use by counsel in oral argument on the theory that an oral argument is not a lecture by the counsel to the court. We were successful at the district court and at the First Circuit (*National Foreign Trade Council v. Natsios*, 181 F.3d 38 (1st Cir. 1999)). Sandy Lynch, who later became the chief judge of the First Circuit, was very kind in an article she wrote years later, saying that I had made a good argument and that my approach to the dialogue between counsel and the bench made a difference.[33]

Massachusetts was successful in getting the Supreme Court to agree to review the case. At that point I was hoping to be confirmed as a judge on the Federal Circuit, and I was wondering what would happen if I were confirmed before the argument took place. I discuss this later. We won in the Supreme Court, my last case as an advocate (*Crosby v. National Foreign Trade Council*, 530 U.S. 363 (2000)).

## Amicus Briefs

Amicus briefs are often the result of the desire of a trade association or other entity to enhance its own visibility, as well as to enhance the visibility of the case. In the Supreme Court now, there are often 25 or 50 amicus briefs in a major case. Typically, those briefs do not say anything that is much different from what is in the parties' briefs, and usually they are ineffective in influencing the outcome of the case, particularly in the Supreme Court. There is one exception to the general rule and that is at the cert stage. There, the filing of amicus briefs probably can often have a significant impact, convincing the Supreme Court that the case is important and that review should be granted.

Amicus brief influence at the merits stage is rarer. In the *Quill* case, an amicus brief that we filed did appear to have an impact on the Court. North Dakota urged that prior precedent in the *National Bellas Hess* case (*National Bellas Hess v. Department of Revenue*, 386 U.S. 753 (1967)) be overruled so that states could require the collection of state use taxes from out-of-state companies that were selling by mail, telephone or the nascent Internet. Our amicus brief on behalf of the Direct Marketing Association, arguing against overruling *National Bellas Hess*, listed all the state statutes of limitations and the amount of back taxes that companies would be liable for if the Court were to overrule the earlier case. The Supreme Court crafted a compromise in which it said that the Due Process Clause did not forbid the imposition of these collection obligations, but that the Commerce Clause remained a barrier unless Congress acted to approve the state tax collection (*Quill Corp. v. North Dakota*, 504 U.S. 298 (1992)). The Supreme Court has since largely overruled *Quill* and allowed states to impose collection obligations (*South Dakota v. Wayfair, Inc.*, 585 U.S. ——, 138 S. Ct. 2080 (2018)).

Another influential amicus brief involved the Appointments Clause and Tax Court judges (*Freytag v. Commissioner*, 501 U.S. 868 (1991)). The amicus brief argued that the Tax Court should be considered a "Court of Law," able to appoint inferior officers, a view ultimately shared by the Court, even though both petitioner and the Commissioner disagreed (*Freytag*, 501 U.S. at 870). Erwin Griswold, the author of the amicus brief, had been Dean of Harvard Law School (when I was a student there) and later the solicitor general. When he wrote the amicus brief (before my time at Jones Day), he was a member of the Issues and Appeals practice at Jones Day.

One of the great pleasures of being at Jones Day was to get to know Griswold better. He was a very formidable man who was not given to small talk. We had him over to dinner at our house a couple of times, and he loosened up a good deal, telling stories of the old days at the Solicitor General's Office. Griswold, despite having served as solicitor general in both Republican and Democratic administrations, was not very good at developing business. He was not interested in trawling for clients. Also contrary to my own views as to the responsibility of a lawyer, he was not interested in taking on cases where he did not agree with the ultimate objective of the client. The result was that Griswold did not have much work to do. What he did do was write a memoir called *Ould Fields, New Corne.*[34] I thought it was riveting, revealing how vulnerable a person Griswold was despite all his bluster. Griswold only knew one publisher, the West Publishing Company (the leading publisher of legal and other regulatory materials), so he asked West to publish his memoir, which it did. The result was that the memoir was not available in regular bookstores, and it probably had few sales. I recommend it.

Overall, my experience at Jones Day was a happy one, and I was able to help build an important firm practice and start a firm-wide pro bono program.

As at Wilmer Cutler, it was a pleasure working with able colleagues in a collective effort to provide the best possible service to our clients. I still miss private practice.

* * *

My time in private practice spanned almost one thousand volumes in the *Federal Reporter*. I was fortunate to participate in many high-profile cases. I learned that a lawyer's ability to influence the outcome of litigation is inversely proportional to the level of the court. The higher the court, the less the influence. I think that I did many things right, thought a lot about each case and tried to be creative, sometimes coming up with new theories on appeal (reinventing the case) that prevailed. In every case in which my name was on the brief, I was intimately involved in developing the theory of the case and in writing and rewriting the brief. At oral argument in later years, I was able to argue without notes, and to conduct a conversation with the court—all the things that judges preach to advocates. I also made mistakes, such as the failure to restart the ship arbitration discussed earlier. I will spare the reader and myself a description of other mistakes I made in practice.

One of the difficult things about private practice is that doing a good or even outstanding job does not always correlate with success. Sometimes that results from the failure of judges or justices to see the light. Sometimes that is the result of the inherent weakness of the legal or factual arguments. Carl Sandburg famously wrote:

> "If the law is against you, talk about the evidence," said a battered barrister. "If the evidence is against you, talk about the law, and, since you ask me, if the law and the evidence are both against you, then pound on the table and yell like hell."[35]

I tried to avoid the latter alternative.

## Notes

1   Lewis J. Paper, *Empire: William S. Paley and the Making of CBS* (New York: St Martin's Press, 1987), 256–58.
2   Jonathan Kandell, "Laurence A. Tisch, Investor Known for Saving CBS Inc. from Takeover, Dies at 80," *The New York Times*, November 16, 2003, https://www.nytimes.com/2003/11/16/business/laurence-a-tisch-investor-known-for-saving-cbs-inc-from-takeover-dies-at-80.html.
3   Peter J. Boyer, *Who Killed CBS? The Undoing of America's Number One News Network* (New York: Random House, 1988), 292–95.
4   Boyer, *Who Killed CBS?*, 298–312.

5    Michael T. Kaufman, "Lloyd N. Cutler, Counselor to Presidents, Is Dead at 87," *The New York Times*, May 9, 2005, https://www.nytimes.com/2005/05/09/politics/lloyd-n-cutler-counselor-to-presidents-is-dead-at-87.html.

6    Anne Kornhauser and Eleanor Kerlow, "Litigator Dyk to Exit Wilmer for Jones, Day," *Legal Times*, February 19, 1990, 7.

7    From a PR Newswire at the time: "Mr. Ayer, 41, expressed excitement about rejoining a growing group of appellate specialists at Jones Day and cited as a special attraction the arrival of Timothy Dyk earlier this year. "The practice seems to be taking off, and I look forward to rejoining my friends and being part of that." See "Deputy Attorney General of the United States to Rejoin Jones, Day, Reavis & Pogue," *PR Newswire*, May 11, 1990.

8    "Jones Day recalls with gratitude Pat McCartan's leadership," Announcement, Jones Day, December 1, 2020, https://www.jonesday.com/en/news/2020/12/jones-day-recalls-with-gratitude-pat-mccartans-leadership.

9    Andrew M. Kramer, "Leading Labor Lawyer, Dies at 67," *The New York Times*, November 29, 2011, https://www.nytimes.com/2011/11/30/business/andrew-kramer-leading-labor-lawyer-dies-at-67.html.

10   Herb Hansell Obituary, *The New York Times*, May 26, 2015, https://www.legacy.com/us/obituaries/nytimes/name/herbert-hansell-obituary?pid=174936613.

11   Jones, Day, Reavis & Pogue, Encyclopedia.com, https://www.encyclopedia.com/books/politics-and-business-magazines/jones-day-reavis-pogue.

12   The same thing happened at Wilmer Cutler with regard to former Supreme Court clerks, but to a lesser extent. David Westin became an executive at ABC (and ultimately head of the news division); Ray Clevenger became a Federal Circuit judge; Boyden Gray became White House counsel.

13   "History of Cameras in Courts," About Federal Courts, United States Courts, last accessed June 4, 2021, https://www.uscourts.gov/about-federal-courts/judicial-administration/cameras-courts/history-cameras-courts.

14   Ibid.

15   Ibid.

16   Douglas O. Linder, "Hauptmann (Lindbergh) Trial (1935)," Famous Trials, last accessed June 4, 2021, https://famous-trials.com/hauptmann.

17   Ruth Ann Strickland, "Cameras in the Courtroom," The First Amendment Encyclopedia, last accessed June 6, 2021, https://www.mtsu.edu/first-amendment/article/989/cameras-in-the-courtroom.

18   "The Lindbergh Case: The Trial of the Century," thelindberghcase.com, archived at Internet Archive: Wayback Machine, last accessed June 6, 2021, https://web.archive.org/web/19990224112920/http://lindberghtrial.com/html/trial.htm.

19   Strickland, "Cameras in the Courtroom."

20   "History of Cameras in Courts."

21   Ibid.

22   Gabe Roth, "Why Doesn't the Supreme Court Have Cameras?," MSNBC, July 24, 2015, https://www.msnbc.com/msnbc/why-doesnt-the-supreme-court-have-cameras-msna647191.

23   Jess Bravin, "Justice Kennedy: Cameras at Court Would Be 'Insidious,'" *The Wall Street Journal*, March 14, 2013, https://www.wsj.com/articles/BL-LB-44568.

24   "On Cameras in Supreme Court, Souter Says 'Over My Dead Body,'" *The New York Times*, March 30, 1996, https://www.nytimes.com/1996/03/30/us/on-cameras-in-supreme-court-souter-says-over-my-dead-body.html.

25   "The Nation," *The Los Angeles Times*, November 22, 1988, https://www.latimes.com/archives/la-xpm-1988-11-22-mn-309-story.html.

26   Tony Mauro, "Is the Court Finally Camera-Ready," *Legal Times*, May 14, 1990, 10.

27   "History of Cameras in Courts."

28   Jack Karp, "Fed. Courts' Audio Pilot Starts Slow but Finds Some Success," *Law360 Pulse*, April 30, 2021.

29   Madison Adler, "Judiciary Opposes Cameras in Courts Bill Ahead of Markup (1)," Bloomberg Law, June 23, 2021, https://news.bloomberglaw.com/us-law-week/judiciary-opposes-cameras-in-courts-legislation-ahead-of-markup.

30   Ibid. The Second (1996), the Third (2017), and the Ninth Circuit (1996) Courts of Appeals adopted rules and guidelines to allow camera coverage. Recording of live streams is however prohibited by the Audio Streaming Pilot Guidelines at https://www.uscourts.gov/about-federal-courts/judicial-administration/audio-streaming-pilot.

31   The words are still dirty today apparently. See Timothy Bella, "The 7 Dirty Words Turn 40 but They're Still Dirty," *The Atlantic*, May 2012, https://www.theatlantic.com/entertainment/archive/2012/05/the-7-dirty-words-turn-40-but-theyre-still-dirty/257374/.

32   Ken Gormley, *Archibald Cox: Conscience of a Nation* (Reading, MA: Addison-Wesley, 1997), 200.

33   :

> The very best oral arguments are conversations with the court. And very frequently in the courtroom you can get a chemistry going where both sides are thinking through the issues well beyond what was said in the briefs. And the good advocates understand their case well enough […] they go in there, they have this certain confidence level, and then they can take it up to the next level. To pay tribute to one of my colleagues on the Federal Circuit – Timothy Dyk, when he was in private practice, argued an extremely important case in front of me that went to the Supreme Court. But he was superb, and he was superb in part because he had thought through all of the problems that the panel had thought through, and he had answers for all of them. And that's unusual, and it was such a pleasure to have him. It's such a pleasure to have good lawyers appear in front of us.

Chief Judge Sandra L. Lynch, *Scribes Journal of Legal Writing* 15 (2013): 70.

34   Erwin N. Griswold, *Ould Fields, New Corne: The Personal Memoirs of a Twentieth Century Lawyer* (St. Paul, MN: West Publishing, 1992).

35   Carl Sandburg, *The People, Yes* (New Yprk: Harcourt, Brace, 1936).

# Chapter 8

# REFLECTIONS ON CHANGES IN THE LEGAL PROFESSION

The history of the Cravath firm covers the period from the inception of the predecessor firms in the nineteenth century to the period after World War II.[1] Most of the book is a boring listing of railroad reorganizations and other firm representations, but there are other parts that describe the way the practice used to be, and they are fascinating. That led me to attempt to describe the changes that occurred from the time that I started in practice to the time I went on the bench and to some extent thereafter.

Many of the changes in the legal profession in the past 50–60 years are readily apparent and were summarized in Chapter 1. My goal here is to describe some aspects of those changes and other changes not so well known. The focus is on changes in what is fondly known as "Big Law" in Washington, the venue of my 35 years in private practice. The major changes can be easily summarized: Over the past 60 years, what used to be a profession has morphed into big business with all the attendant problems.

## Size of the Legal Profession

There are now many, many more law schools[2] and many, many more law school graduates[3] than there were when I entered the profession. This has produced a great surplus of lawyers (though not a surplus of lawyers representing individuals, particularly the disadvantaged). Only a small percentage of recent graduates is hired by one of the leading firms. Many law school graduates do not end up practicing law at all.[4] Interestingly, the same problem—a surplus of lawyers—has existed in vastly different contexts in nineteenth-century Europe and in China today.[5] As a result of the lawyer surplus, there is a tremendous amount of anxiety at many US law schools about getting a job after graduation.[6] That was not a problem when I was in law school. Even if you were toward the bottom of the class in a good law school, it was pretty much certain that you would have a job when you graduated, if you wanted one.

## Composition of the Legal Profession

When I went to law school in 1958, there were very few women in the class. Harvard had only opened its law school to women in 1950. Generally speaking, only 3 percent of the law school class were women through the 1960s and remained less than 5 percent in all ABA-approved law schools through the 1970s.[7] There were also very few minorities—virtually no Asian Americans or Hispanics and very few African Americans. That has changed dramatically. The year 2016 was the first that female enrollment overtook male,[8] and by 2020, 55 percent of first-year students were female.[9] There are also a great deal more African Americans, Hispanics and Asians who graduate from law school and enter the profession. In the 1964–65 academic year, an estimated seven hundred African Americans were attending law school.[10] Data on other minority groups was not even collected until 1969.[11] In contrast, today around a third of the 2019 J.D. enrollments are minorities, of which 7.9 percent are African American (approx. 8,500 students).[12] About one quarter of my law clerks have been minorities.

When I started in private practice in 1964, the legal profession was very much an old boys' club, and Lloyd Cutler was the essence of someone who was a member of that club. Cutler had been born Jewish, but had converted and became an Episcopalian, which in those days was helpful, a necessity even, for entry into the old boys' club. When you were working with Cutler on a project, he would frequently ask you to come to his office. The work would often be interrupted by calls that he would receive from, or make to, other leading lights—journalists like Scotty Reston, administration officials, law professors or corporate CEOs. These leading lights belonged to the same clubs. They socialized together. They knew each other, and that was an important way of getting business and influencing government.

There were few women partners or associates in the major firms. My wife Sally was the first female associate and the first female partner at Wilmer Cutler. Some sense of the problems faced by women in those times can be gleaned by Sally's experience in applying for a Supreme Court clerkship. When Sally was at Michigan Law School, she was the first female editor-in-chief of the *Michigan Law Review*, and one of the first to head the Law Review at any leading law school. The law school held an annual moot court competition, where a Supreme Court justice was always invited to judge the finals. Sally got a call from the dean's office saying that Justice Potter Stewart was coming for the event; that Mrs. Stewart was with him; and asking Sally to entertain Mrs. Stewart. Over lunch, they connected in part because Mrs. Stewart's daughter was either applying to or was at

Smith College, where Sally had gone. Sally's one-hour lunch turned into a three-hour lunch. Sally had been invited to the dinner that evening celebrating the winners of the moot court competition. When Sally arrived, Mrs. Stewart, who was sitting next to her husband on the dais, went over to Sally and invited her to meet the justice. They had a good conversation. He knew that Sally was going to be clerking on the D.C. Circuit for Judge Wright (earlier one of the courageous district judges enforcing desegregation in the South) when she graduated. He indicated that if she had any thoughts about a further clerkship, he would be happy to have her apply to be one of his clerks.

With a strong recommendation from Judge Wright in hand, Sally applied to, and got an interview with, Justice Stewart. The interview went well. Then she met with his clerks and that went well too. About two weeks later, she got a handwritten note from the justice stating that he was very sorry he was unable to offer her the clerkship, and he wished her success in her career. She was baffled by the rejection.

Many years later, we were at Cape Cod and met Dick Stewart, a professor at Harvard Law School. Sally said something like, "Oh, I've always wanted to meet you. I've heard so much about you." He said, "We did meet many years ago. I was clerking for Justice Stewart at the time. And I remember you came out of his study, and you looked like you were on top of the world. You talked with us for a while, and you were very confident, very cheerful, and then you left. Justice Stewart came out of his study and said, "She's a definite. I will make her an offer. She's great." Then Justice Stewart's secretary said, "I'm not having a girl in chambers. You hire her, I will quit." Sally always said that Justice Stewart was wise enough to know that a clerk was there for one year, but a secretary was there for decades, and he was sensibly not going to risk losing a very good secretary for a one-year clerk.

This was not unusual. Some women felt resentful as younger women began to get positions that the long-time secretaries had been unable to get when they had started out. Carmel "Kim" Prashker Ebb graduated first in her class at Columbia Law School and was the first female clerk for a federal judge in the 1940s.[13] She had clerked for Judge Jerome Frank on the Second Circuit. She then tried to get a Supreme Court clerkship. She was turned down because the justice to whom she applied said his wife would never let him work in such close proximity to a woman.[14]

Minorities suffered even more significant discrimination and continue to do so today: There remain real barriers for Black law graduates entering the profession.[15] My Tennessee experience with John Payton was only the tip of the iceberg. There has been progress, but there is a long way to go.

## Firm Size and Management

In the 1960s, a large law firm would have been around 150 to 200 lawyers, and none of them was in Washington. Covington had 100 lawyers in 1960.[16] At the end of 1963, Arnold & Porter had 31 lawyers and 18 partners, Wilmer Cutler 22 and 15.[17] Many Washington firms dealt with real estate or local businesses. Only a few of the bigger firms dealt with federal issues and federal agency practice. By 1973, the numbers of lawyers at most of the bigger firms had doubled and, in some cases, quadrupled by 1977.[18] The growth continued thereafter, with new firms entering the market and firms all across the country opening D.C. offices and, sometimes, as with Jones Day (originally headquartered in Cleveland), making Washington their home office. Today most major law firms, with some exceptions, have offices in multiple cities, including Washington, and in many countries. The growth in the size of firms, much of it through mergers and acquisitions, has been exponential. There are quite a few firms now that have over one thousand lawyers.

The overall numbers for Washington are phenomenal. There are now 80,000 lawyers in the D.C. area, nine times as many per capita as in New York.[19] To be sure, many of these are government lawyers, but the number in private practice is dramatically larger than it was. The reasons for the increase in Washington practice are not hard to find. There is a lot more government activity, including legislation and federal regulation, and the proximity to the center of power and the talent pool in Washington leads to the retention of Washington firms to do the work. Washington practice is not limited to federal legislative and regulatory matters. It extends to litigation nationwide because of the talented lawyers in the Washington firms. Many federal regulators choose to stay in Washington when they leave government. Other talented lawyers come to Washington to join firms straight out of law school or after clerking. Washington is a good place to live and raise a family. So, lawyers are attracted to living here. In addition, National Airport, in my view, is the best airport in the country, putting the city within easy reach of many other cities.

The increase in size and the opening of branch offices by major firms and the increasing number of lateral entrants have had a dramatic effect on the relationships within the firms. As noted earlier, lawyers these days in the mega firms are unlikely to know all the other lawyers in the firm. Lawyers within one branch office may not even be well acquainted with those in the same branch office. Laterals did not have past work relationships within the firms. The collegiality that existed in the early days has been to a significant degree lost.

As the size of the firms has increased, the management structure of the firms has necessarily changed. When I started at Wilmer Cutler, John Pickering was the de facto chairman of the firm, and later there was a younger managing or administrative partner who served on a one-year basis. Decisions of any consequence were made by the partners as a whole. There were firm meetings in which all the partners would sit around the table and make decisions. One of the most important decisions was admitting new partners, and those decisions were always made by the partners as a group. Eventually, Wilmer Cutler created a committee to make recommendations for partnership, and it created a management committee to run the firm. That transition had a rocky start. The firm asked the partners to rate and comment on the first management committee's performance, leading to some critical and bitter comments. The problem for any firm management is that partners are as hard to manage as a herd of cats, and partners do not always like or respect their colleagues. I recall a Wilmer Cutler partners' meeting where a partner remarked that he liked or respected half of the people sitting around the table, leaving his partners to wonder whether they were liked or respected or neither.

When I was at Jones Day, there were no partner votes on firm matters, nor even votes by the partners on who would make partner or who would run the firm. The firm was run by the managing partner who named his own successor and selected the other members of the firm management. Under the system prevalent now, if you are at a firm with a good managing partner or management committee, it works well. It does not work well if the managing partner or committee is poor. A lot hinges on the quality of those running the firm, and few lawyers are trained in management. The increasing trend to hiring nonlawyer managers creates further distance between management and firm lawyers doing the day-to-day work.

## Firms and Partners

Firms themselves have markedly changed and not just in terms of size, composition and branching. One significant change has been in the relationship between the firm and its partners. In 1964, if you became a partner in a law firm, it was generally assumed that you would stay at the firm for your professional life, though stints in government were common in Washington firms. While firms sometimes merged or split apart (as with the inception of Wilmer, Cutler & Pickering), it was very unusual for an individual partner in a major law firm to leave that firm or to join another firm unless there was some scandal that caused the partner to leave.

In the 1960s, firms had remarkable tolerance for partners who were incompetent or unable to perform. There was one partner who was finally let go from Cravath because he attended movies every afternoon instead of doing his work, but there had to be something really extreme before a partner was shown the exit. The firms' tolerance in particular for alcohol and for alcoholics was remarkable. As in many other firms, there was more than one partner at Wilmer Cutler who was an alcoholic. One Wilmer Cutler partner was responsible for an important client. He did do the work, but he was so impaired that he was not able to send out the bills! For years, there would be no bill, and the client would be demanding, "Where's the bill for services?" But the bills were never sent. The company eventually went bankrupt, and the firm never got fully paid.

Since the 1990s, it has become much more common for partners to move between firms. Some leave because they are offered better opportunities. Partners can be offered tens of millions to move firms.[20] Judgeships, corporate and political/government positions draw partners away as well. But other partners leave because they are asked to leave. When I was at Jones Day, partners were pushed out because their practice did not align with the firm's objectives, or they were not sufficiently productive. The decline in productivity was not always their fault. Clients often prefer working with younger lawyers who are seen as more responsive, particularly when the in-house lawyer is younger than some of the firm's older partners. This has created a lot of partner anxiety, particularly as partners get older. That has become another significant feature of the legal profession. Older partners, unless they are rainmakers or otherwise indispensable, are often gently pushed aside within the firms. Some of the firms that are UK-based even have the expectation that you will retire at the age of 55 and have another career. Life as an older partner at some of these firms is not as pleasant as it used to be. Perhaps the UK model should be adopted by US firms.

## Firms and Associates

There is also a different relationship between the firm and its associates. In the beginning at Wilmer Cutler, the assumption was that associates were going to become partners unless—in the language of the time—they tripped over their own shoelaces. In the early years, few did. To be sure, that was not the model in New York, at Cravath or other large New York firms, where a relatively small number of the associates ended up making partner. But the large New York firms took care of the associates who did not make partner. For example, at Cravath, it was very common to place associates who did not make partner with the in-house law departments of clients or with various satellite firms. Cravath was very generous in supporting the satellite firms by referring them business that was too small for Cravath or where there was a conflict. Today most young lawyers do not expect to become partners and do not expect the firm to find positions for them when they leave. Though the standard for making partner has changed, one thing has not changed: bitter intra-firm fights about who makes partner.

The feeding frenzy to hire former Supreme Court law clerks is also new. As discussed earlier, when I left the Supreme Court as a law clerk, there were no clerkship bonuses or rush to hire Supreme Court clerks. Hiring bonuses now are as high as $400,000 for a Supreme Court clerk.[21] When I was at Jones Day it was less, but still a significant amount. Singling out Supreme Court law clerks as super lawyers is not justified. Yes, the justices have the pick of the litter and try to choose the best and the brightest, but the selection process is imperfect, and many outstanding law school graduates are not selected. There is nothing that Supreme Court law clerks learn that is particularly valuable to them in later positions. The characteristics that make good clerks (a bookish mindset and the ability to excel in a subordinate position) are not the things that matter most in private practice where entrepreneurship is valued above all else. The attention paid to hiring Supreme Court clerks is not a good thing for either the clerks or the firms. It is difficult to learn or to be successful in practice if you view yourself as already having been anointed as a remarkable talent. And the benefit to the firms is problematic. The firms can trot out the Supreme Court clerks in making pitches to prospective clients. But the Supreme Court clerks often stay only a few years and then move on to something less mundane than practicing law. For others who stay more than a few years, the lure of judgeships, government, the academy or in-house counsel positions often is too great to resist.

## Lawyer Compensation

Another change is in the approach to partner compensation. Most senior partners in big firms now earn more than $1 million a year. My recollection is that in the early 1960s, $25,000 a year would have been considered to be very good compensation for a young partner and compensation for a senior partner was only two or three times higher. When I started, at many large firms, there were variations among partners because of seniority, but less variation, or none at all, between partners at the same seniority level. At Wilmer Cutler, there were only a few partners who were not in the lock-step model, and those were Cutler, Pickering and Wollenberg. Manny Cohen, when he joined the firm, was not in the lock-step model. But by and large, almost everybody with the same seniority was paid the same in the early years, and that did not produce much grumbling. At most firms now, the differences in partner compensation are phenomenal. The ABA reports that the spread between lowest- and highest-paid partners at Kirkland & Ellis is 43:1 and even in less extreme cases, the pay spread is still considerable.[22] Rainmakers are very much in demand, and there is a lot of jumping ship from one firm to another. To keep rainmakers, firms pay them disproportionately.

Not only has partner compensation dramatically increased, but its importance in firm life has also increased. Many partners in law firms measure
their worth by how much they make, not so much by their accomplishments
in the cases or other matters that they handle. The law has become what
Lewis Coster has described as a "greedy profession."[23] Part of that has to do
with the enormous increase in the cost of college for children and housing
and the need to save for retirement. Most firms no longer have pensions for
partners, so saving for retirement is each partner's responsibility. Even with
people making over a million dollars a year, there is a great deal of anxiety
about compensation.

In the early 1960s, associate compensation, like partner compensation, was
much less than it is today. The starting associate compensation at the D.C. firms
was on the order of $6,500 a year, which would be approximately $60,000 in
today's money. Starting associate compensation now is at or above $200,000
a year. The enormous increase in associate compensation has become necessary in part because of college/law school loan burdens, but also because the
firms no longer take care of departing associates. In this new world, attracting
good associates requires higher compensation. But this golden handshake has
not increased association satisfaction. When I entered the profession, lawyers
were either associates or equity partners (with the occasional counsels). Firms
now have a variety of different levels between associate and equity partner,
including non-equity partner, of counsel and counsel, in part to enable firms
to retain talented lawyers not chosen as equity partners.

## Hours and Hourly Rate

The dramatic increase in compensation of both associates and partners has
been made possible by two developments: an increase in the hours lawyers are
expected to work (the source of much lawyer unhappiness) and an increase in
the hourly rates charged by firms.

When I was a young lawyer, lawyers worked very hard. I think the number
of chargeable hours that I put in at the firm as a young associate was often
on the order of 2,300–2,400 hours in some years, which would be a respect-
able number even today at the big firms. But there are differences in today's
world. First, there is an expectation that lawyers will put in a large number of
chargeable hours each and every year. Second, there are specific yearly hours
requirements, and lawyers are required to keep time on a computer timeclock
in six- or ten-minutes intervals, which is itself a distraction from substantive
work. Third, in an earlier time, vacations and weekends were accommodated.
You were not expected to work on the weekend on a regular basis and were
not expected to routinely respond to communications from partners outside

of office hours, though court and other deadlines could lead to late nights and weekend work.

The history of the Cravath firm shows that early in the twentieth century, long vacations existed and the firms closed down in the summer.[24] Part of this was the result of the lack of air conditioning, but routine lengthy summer vacations still existed when I was a young lawyer even with air conditioning. Lawyers, both partners and associates, took such vacations. I remember when I was a young lawyer at Wilmer Cutler, it was expected that you would take a month's vacation, and people actually went away to Cape Cod or to Europe or wherever. The firm even instituted a sabbatical program where partners could take time off from the firm with pay, either for a single six-month period or for two separate three-month periods every six or seven years. When you were on vacation, you might occasionally receive a draft brief to review or return to the office for an important matter, but it did not happen very often. Now, vacations are usually short, and they are never real vacations because you are expected to have your smartphone and laptop with you. Lawyers are expected to respond at any hour of the day or night.

Associates (and partners too) now risk what the Japanese call *Karoshi*—death by overwork. The speed with which matters are addressed leaves less time for reflection and sound judgment. The consequence of all this is that many young graduates typically do not look forward to joining firms and those who do rarely enjoy firm life. The goal for many is to land elsewhere.

The hourly rates charged by firms have also increased dramatically. When I started practice, hourly billing was the norm. This apparently was something of a new phenomenon. The influential "The 1958 Lawyer and His 1938 Dollar" (the title is telling itself), published by the Special Committee on Economics of Law Practice, recommended a move to hourly billing and contemplated a billing rate of $20 an hour ($190 an hour in today's dollars).[25] My recollection is that in the early 1960s, associates would be billed at less than $50 an hour and senior partners at only a couple hundred dollars an hour. Today, top hourly billing rates are over $1,200 an hour and associate rates are several hundred dollars.[26] This has affected how the law firms provide services for clients.

## Client Charges and Relationships

When I started out, the size of firm billings was not a major source of conflict between firms and clients. I do not recall in the first few years of practice that there were many complaints by clients about the size of the bills. The descriptions of services performed tended to be much shorter and with less detail than they are now, and the clients generally were not concerned that they were being overcharged. I am not suggesting that there were no concerns about legal fees. I remember that Bob Evans, who was CBS' general counsel, decided that he would have a special conference room for meetings with outside lawyers, and he would crank down the temperature in the room to around 62/63 degrees. His theory was that he would shorten the length of the meetings and the legal fees. Now, in many cases, the hourly rates and the size of legal fees are of paramount concern to clients. One consequence is that clients negotiate fees in advance and insist on discounts from the "regular" rate or a set fee for a particular project.

When I started in practice, the size of the team was generally determined by the law firm, and the law firms did not bloat the teams in order to increase the size of the bills. They couldn't; the lawyers were needed for other projects. Because there was trust and the expectation of a long-term relationship between the firms and the clients, and the fees were not so high, the firms could involve young lawyers on the teams, even though the value to the client was modest. Young lawyers, even those fresh out of law school, gained experience by working on firm matters large and small and by watching the more senior lawyers conduct discovery, try cases or argue appeals. If you took an out-of-town deposition in those days, it was assumed that a junior associate would go with you to the deposition. The junior associate would handle the documents, and the senior associate or partner would concentrate on asking the questions. So too, close partner involvement in brief drafting was expected. Today, clients have little tolerance for paying lawyers to learn their craft. My understanding is that when people take out-of-town depositions, it is much more typical that only a single lawyer is present. Briefs are typically written by associates, often with little partner review. At the same time, unnecessary work is done. As a result of billing concerns, there is also a much more adversarial relationship between firms and clients than used to exist. In some few cases, the clients do not worry about fees—in the bet-the-company cases, where there is an agreement that the lawyers should spare no expense. These bet-the-company cases are very popular with firms.

The changes in the relationship between firms and their clients go beyond fees. Fifty years ago, many of the relationships were both long-term and exclusive, at least in particular practice areas, and the result was that there was a comfort level between the firm and the clients that was very beneficial. This is much less true today. There is also a lot less substantive contact between outside counsel and corporate general counsels and executives. This is the result of the growth of the in-house law departments. When I started, the in-house law departments were much smaller than they are today in most cases. The role of the corporate law department was not to do the work, but to supervise the work that was being undertaken by the outside law firms. Today, in-house law departments often will do what is called commodity work themselves instead of referring it to outside firms, and often junior in-house lawyers supervise outside counsel.

I think the quality of legal work has also suffered as a result of the increasing size of legal fees. In the early days of Wilmer Cutler, if there were a significant brief in a court of appeals or the Supreme Court, several partners and associates would sit together and discuss and revise the draft page by page. There was a two-partner rule, requiring that at least two partners review each brief and opinion letter. The challenges by other lawyers would sharpen arguments and lead to abandoning arguments that did not work or to developing new arguments that might be better. That was a process that often also included the in-house counsel.

Today, except in bet-the-company cases, the firms are under a great deal of pressure from the clients to spend fewer hours on briefs or memoranda with the result that work product has sometimes suffered, though many lawyers are willing to forgo fully recording their time or write-off time spent to ensure a quality product. Partners can be frustrated when associates have not learned to write well in college or law school and their work requires extensive revision (and non-chargeable hours). At the other extreme, briefs are sometimes produced by associates and only lightly reviewed by the partner, who does not begin to really think about the case until oral argument. The result is that often firms are not testing their own arguments. Now, after oral argument, my fellow judges and I sometimes comment on the poor quality of briefing and oral argument. There are, to be sure, many firms devoted to quality, and many fine briefs and arguments, but not as many as one might hope or expect.

The process by which clients choose firms has also changed markedly. The competition among firms for client work is intense. As noted, many fewer clients have long-term relationships with particular firms. Those long-term relationships were often founded on personal friendship. One of my former partners at Wilmer Cutler once said, clients do not hire lawyers because they are going to be able to do good work; they hire lawyers because they like them. That was an overstatement, but I think there was more truth to it than one might like to think. Now, personal relationships play less of a role and competitive bidding and beauty contests are the order of the day. The role of safe choices plays another part—that is, a tendency on the part of in-house counsel to make the safe choice by hiring well-known lawyers rather than hiring lawyers who are less known but perhaps more able, so they can avoid second-guessing by superiors or the board of directors if things turn out badly. One wonders why clients are not more diligent in seeking out those lawyers who have proven they can do an excellent job, of which there are many.

The intense competition for client work has led to an increased willingness of some firms to take unsavory clients (though in some cases objections from younger lawyers have caused firms to withdraw). The tradition in private practice was then, and is now, to undertake representations where you might not feel entirely comfortable with the client and its position. It always seemed to me that, in general, a lawyer was obligated to put aside personal predilections though there was some selectivity in client choice. But most big firms in earlier days drew a line against taking unsavory clients.

When I started practice, firms felt comfortable refusing to make arguments that they thought were frivolous or not supported and refusing to write briefs that sounded like a client press release. I always took the position with clients that I would not make arguments that I thought were frivolous, and I did not do so. I think that approach had value for the client, because in court cases nothing is more damaging for the client's position than making frivolous arguments, which inevitably dilute the impact of the meritorious arguments. Equally, in developing a case, if you are willing to reject frivolous arguments, you necessarily have to think harder and more creatively to come up with meritorious arguments that will support the client's ultimate objective. My perception is that the ability of lawyers to reject frivolous or extraneous arguments favored by the client is less today than it used to be.

## The Liberal/Conservative Divide

During the New Deal period, Republicans and Democrats were often bitterly divided over the desirability and constitutionality of various New Deal measures. By the early 1950s, with the election of President Eisenhower, mainstream Republicans were less opposed to federal regulation, and when he was elected, Nixon even championed the creation of the Environmental Protection Agency.[27] There was still a liberal/conservative divide, but in the larger firms any disagreements were not the source of day-to-day friction. When I started out, firms were mixtures of Republicans and Democrats. The politics did not much matter. Now there is once again a significant left-right divide as to the proper role of the federal government. This is very much a feature of the country at large, but it has become much more pronounced in the profession. I first encountered it in 1985 when I was teaching at the University of Virginia, and some of the students on the left and the right would almost come to blows in the classroom over legal theory. This eventually found its way into law firms.

I remember one particularly unpleasant incident when I was at Jones Day working on a challenge to President Clinton's Executive Order on striker replacements, a case I discussed earlier. An associate who was working on the case wanted me to refer to President Clinton in the briefs as "King William," not something that I thought would be particularly helpful in producing the desired result. The associate went behind my back suggesting that I was trying to throw the case because my wife was an official in the Clinton administration. Without King William, we won the case, and the associate went on to bigger and better things.

The unpleasantness in firms results partly from philosophical divisions but also because opposing counsel have become much less pleasant and accommodating to each other, which, some have remarked, seems common in patent cases. The Inns of Court were formed to address the problem but have had only limited success.

## Firms and Publicity

With the increased competition among firms for business, firms have sought ways to distinguish themselves. One way is through lawyer advertising. In the 1960s and early 70s, lawyer promotion was restrained. There were, to be sure, efforts by firms and individual lawyers to secure favorable mentions in the general press. But the self-promotion was subtle. Then came the Supreme Court's decision in *Bates v. State Bar*, 433 U.S. 350 (1977), which afforded some First Amendment protection to lawyer advertising. Now, self-promotion by firms and individual partners is the order of the day. There is nothing subtle about it. All big firms have marketing departments and even regular newsletters. Correspondingly, there is a legal press that covers the firms and how much they are making and profits per partner and who has just won big cases or is the "best" lawyer in America. It is not clear that these enhanced promotional efforts have made for better lawyering or a more informed selection of lawyers by clients.

## Public Service Organizations and Pro Bono Work

Another significant change in the legal profession is the decline in the participation of government-funded public service organizations in litigation. In 1974, the federal government created the Legal Services Corporation with a significant allotment of funds.[28] Legal Services organizations funded by the federal government ultimately became controversial, and the funding was decreased, particularly for cases with broad impact in the development of law.

Firm pro bono work continues at a high level and makes a significant contribution. It seems to be driven in large part by the desire to give associates (and younger partners) the opportunity to argue in court. When I was a young lawyer, leading figures such as Cutler, Pickering and Fortas did a good deal of pro bono work. What is significant is that they did not only high-profile cases like *Gideon* (Fortas) and *NAACP v. Claiborne Hardware Co.*, 458 U.S. 886

(1982) (Cutler), but also a significant amount of other pro bono work that did not reach the headlines.[29] The example of Brandeis and his extensive public interest work was a beacon.[30] The involvement of senior active partners appears to have declined with the exception of a few cases involving, for example, same-sex marriage or other high-profile issues. Often the pro bono work of younger lawyers is supervised by a pro bono partner.

## Legal Research

Another important change is in the area of legal research. The cost of the books used by lawyers to do legal research was part of firm overhead; each firm maintained its own library. In one of its old offices, Wilmer Cutler maintained a two-story library, where lawyers actually went, read hard copies of books, and worked alone or with other lawyers on the team. Most firms today have only skeletal libraries.

When I started in 1964, much legal research was focused on the West keyword system that still exists but is not much used today. You would find the right key numbers (representing legal principles) and look for the cases under that key number. The output was only as good as the input, and the input was not particularly good. There was also a US Code Annotated Westlaw publication that annotated various statutes of the US Code and collected the cases that cited the relevant provisions of the statute. This was a research source for statutory interpretation, and it is still in use. There was also the Shepard's Citations, which would list all the cases which cited another case or a statute or regulation. Shepard's would have signals indicating whether the earlier case had been cited, overruled or distinguished.

Another important source of research was treatises, and in those days, they were considered an important contribution that law professors made to the profession. Moore's *Federal Practice* and Wright and Miller's *Federal Practice and Procedure* are examples. There were treatises in many, many areas, some better than others. Today law schools unfortunately often discourage professors from treatise work, viewing it as insufficiently theoretical. Nonetheless, the number of treatises has proliferated.

Then, too, law review articles and notes were a major source of research. Generally, the articles were prepared by the faculty, and the notes were prepared by students. They would review areas of the law, analyze the cases, review legislative history of statutes and engage in legal analysis that was relevant to what the bench and bar were actually doing. Most law review articles now are either theoretical or empirical and not much use to judges. They seem to be written for other law professors. What is written today about pending litigation, and the issues that come up in pending litigation, tends to be written in specialty journals, blogs or the legal press, and it does not address the subject in depth. Often, the professors and practitioners who write these articles have an axe to grind, for many professors are themselves representing clients. It is an enormous loss in terms of having an independent source of scholarly analysis published in the law reviews focusing on the problems that we are dealing with on a day-to-day basis. This is a perception that is not only mine, but I think is widely shared in the judiciary. We note with amazement that law school professors keep track of the number of mentions they get in the press or in judicial opinions as it is somehow relevant to their compensation or stature in the academy. Given this focus, it is a little bit surprising that they are not more interested in writing articles that would be useful to judges and would get mentioned in opinions. The writing of amicus briefs by law professors is an inadequate substitute.

Currently, the bulk of legal research is done using full-text computer searches of prior court and agency decisions, statutes and regulations. It is a marvelous technology that makes it possible to do things that one could not even dream of doing 60 years ago. The problem is that young lawyers often do not do anything except full-text searches. The result is that they miss things that a full-text search does not turn up, such as analogous court rulings or analogous statutes. It produces the green elevator case (as the saying goes), but not an elevator of another color. The cost of research materials has often been shifted to the clients in the form of Lexis and Westlaw and other charges. Significantly, research can be done from home electronically, and lawyers do not need to come to the physical office to access the library.

Finally, artificial Intelligence (AI) is replacing routine work done by lawyers, such as aspects of document review and the preparation of routine documents. We can look forward in the future to increased use of AI to produce legal documents, but I am skeptical that AI will have the significance that some predict. The law is simply too complex in many instances for a computer to do the work.

## E-mail, Smart Phones and Laptops

Another profound change in the legal profession has resulted from the introduction of new methods of communication, particularly e-mail and cell phones. Cell phones have created the ability to contact lawyers day and night, regardless of their location. E-mail has made it possible to communicate instantaneously in writing and to transmit lengthy documents across the world in seconds. Laptops have made it possible to work remotely. The result has been a 24/7 work cycle, remote working and a notable decline in in-person meetings, which has had serious adverse effects on the profession—making it both less (rather than more) efficient and less collegial.[31]

## Production of Legal Documents

During my time in practice, there was an enormous change in the technology used in the legal profession to produce documents. Very few lawyers in those days knew how to type or, if they did, they were mostly not interested in doing it. Typically, one would begin a brief or memorandum by dictating to a secretary. Each lawyer had his or her own secretary, and all secretaries in those days knew how to take dictation. Some of them were astonishingly good at it, rivalling the speed of a good court reporter (Bridget McCoy, Lynne Leonard and Candy Clayton being examples of those who worked with me). Briefs and memoranda were then typed on an electric typewriter. After the initial draft was created, it would be revised multiple times with handwritten revisions. Deciphering my handwriting presented a substantial problem for my secretaries. There are now few secretaries (called assistants) and even fewer secretaries or assistants who can take dictation. The production of first drafts on word processors and the input of changes, formerly done by secretaries, now falls on junior associates, who are spending considerable time on what used to be secretarial work. At the same time, some of the cite checking and document work formerly done by associates is now done by paralegals, a position virtually unknown in the early 1960s.

Once the draft was finished, there were basically three mechanisms for reproducing briefs or other documents. One mechanism was xeroxing the material, another was mimeographing (retyping the text on mimeograph stencils), and the third was printing it—that is, sending the text to a professional printer and having it set in lead type and printed. Changes were not easily accomplished.

If the document were to be xeroxed, minor changes in the draft could be made by whiting out part of the typing and then typing over it. But that could not be done for extensive revisions. For those, to create a clean copy, the whole page would have to be retyped. To avoid retyping entire pages, we would cut and paste parts of pages together and then copy it. In one case, I recall District Judge Pratt's objection that we were not respectful when submitting a cut-and-paste job, and he insisted that we retype the whole brief. In some instances, in the trial courts and in federal agencies, instead of xeroxing, the filing would be done by mimeographing the document. But at the Supreme Court and the courts of appeals, briefs were typically printed by a professional printer.

When I was young lawyer at Wilmer Cutler, Cutler had a great fondness for a printing firm in New York known as Ad Press. I think that Cutler liked Ad Press because, when he was a young lawyer at Cravath before World War II, the owner of Ad Press had invited Cutler out to his Long Island estate on the weekends to listen to opera records. That established a long-term relationship. Ad Press did a lot of the financial printing for Wall Street, but also printed briefs.

Our briefs would be sent to Ad Press in New York in typescript and then set in lead type. We would fly to New York, go to the printer and stay there well into the night, reviewing page proofs and making corrections. We would then take the final product back to Washington for filing the next day. Making changes in page proof was very expensive. I recall one filing for the FCC on which Cutler and I worked together, and the printing bill was $30,000, which would have been equivalent in today's money to almost $275,000. In fact, I think that the printing bill for that particular document was larger than the legal fees that were charged for producing the document. In that case, Cutler had decided to set the initial draft in type. He thought he was like Justice Brandeis. Brandeis would send first drafts to the printer, rewrite the opinions in page proof and send them back for multiple revisions. That is what Cutler did with this document, which explains why the printing was so expensive. However, sitting and watching Cutler work helped me learn to write.

Ad Press made so much money from the printing of these documents that it was lavish in its treatment of the lawyers. Ad Press had a bowling alley so that you could bowl while you were waiting for type to be set. It had a relationship with an astoundingly good restaurant in Little Italy that was frequented by the mafia. Ad Press would send you there in a limousine. The limo would wait for you while you had dinner and then bring you back to do further work on the page proofs. In a pinch, Ad Press even had its own plane to fly you from New York back to Washington, if your work on the proofs extended beyond the last shuttle flight.

One of my favorite pieces of correspondence generated while I was a young lawyer was a letter from the owner of Ad Press to Cutler. Regrettably, I did not save a copy. At the time I was going to Ad Press regularly to work on briefs. Then, as now, my tendency was to rewrite even at the last minute, which caused a good deal of expense in resetting the type. It also kept the linotype operators at Ad Press beyond their normal working hours. So, the owner of Ad Press wrote a letter to Cutler telling him that I was banned from the premises forever.

I do not remember whether that was the reason, but at some point, Wilmer Cutler switched from Ad Press to a printer in Washington called Wilson-Epes, which was a lot easier, cheaper, and just as good as Ad Press. No one prepares briefs by setting them in lead type anymore. Instead briefs are produced on word processors and duplicated to look like printing.

Also, in the days before the amendments to the Federal Rules of Appellate Procedure imposing word limits, the then-existing rules had page limits.

Creativity was required to bring a long brief into compliance. Now word limits have put a stop to this.

## Travel

At the time I went to Wilmer Cutler, I had probably flown in airplanes a dozen times and had never flown first class. When I first started flying, I enjoyed it very much and never gave a thought to airline safety. However, when I was clerking, my father was diagnosed with cancer of the small intestine, and he was being treated at Sloan Kettering in New York. On several occasions I received calls in the middle of the night that he was in dire straits and I should fly immediately to New York to see him, which I did. My concern about flying dated from that period.

When I was clerking and even when I was working in the Justice Department, this was not much of a problem because plane trips were rare except for out-of-town arguments. But in private practice it was necessary to fly several times a month, sometimes several times a week, because both Wilmer Cutler and Jones Day had clients and consultants all over the country, and in the case of Jones Day, multiple US offices. CBS was located in New York. Lubrizol was in Cleveland, and one of its cases was being litigated in Canada. There were also consultants used for various projects, such as Arthur D. Little in Boston for CBS and the Stanford Research Institute in California for General Motors. Frequent flying was unavoidable. In the early years, one was reminded of the dangers of flying by the regular newspaper accounts about plane crashes and by one's own experience and the experience of friends. I had a friend who worked at a Philadelphia firm, who had been in a plane crash at LaGuardia Airport and survived. A woman I had gone out with several times was killed in a private plane crash in the Caribbean. I had an acquaintance who was the managing editor of Playboy; he and his wife were killed in the American Airlines DC-10 crash in Chicago in 1979.

I also had my own experiences with airline safety. On at least one occasion, maybe more, an engine of a Lockheed Constellation in which I was flying caught fire on the trip between New York and Washington and the props had to be feathered. A bit later, flying to New York or Boston, you would typically take a Lockheed Electra, a model that had crashed several times. In the original design, the stresses on the wings were not properly accounted for, and the wings would fall off. You would be sitting in a plane and see where they had cut out the wing to reinforce it so that the wing would stay on, which was not terribly reassuring. I remember one trip to Boston in a snowstorm where the Electra was bouncing up and down and drinks were flying all over the place. I wondered whether the wings would hold up. They did.

On another occasion, Sally and I and our good friend, Conrad Cafritz, and his then wife had rented a small plane to fly from Washington to the Greenbrier resort in West Virginia. At takeoff there were thunderstorms around National Airport. The pilot either misunderstood or received wrong instructions from the tower and turned directly into the storm. Quite a ride. Conrad yelled to me that if we survived this, he would kill me. We survived, and he did not make good on the threat.

Remarkably, in the 1960s, you could fly to Boston and there would be a helicopter waiting on the tarmac, which would fly you to Arthur D. Little. No need to worry about the Boston traffic. I recall the time the helicopter pilot said that the week before his tail rotor had stopped working so that the helicopter spun around, and one of the passengers had been so frightened by this that he jumped to his death.

There was an ever present sense in the early days that what you were doing was not the world's safest activity. I was very interested in the equipment on the flights that I was taking, particularly after the long New Yorker stories about the dangers of the DC-10. I would always avoid taking a DC-10 if I could, and I preferred flying commercial to smaller company planes. The safety concerns are now much less, though the Boeing Max 8 brought safety concerns back into the headlines for a time.

There were compensations for the occasional dangers of flying. In those days, lawyers were not expected by clients to fly coach. Lawyers flew first class. Cutler flew all the time and his method of getting to New York was on American Airlines that, unlike the Eastern Shuttle, had first class and breakfast. Amtrak then was not a desirable option, being slow and ill-kept. On the transatlantic or transcontinental flights, first class was particularly special. In those days, you would not eat dinner at your seat. On the 747, the upper deck of the plane was reserved for the first-class passengers to have dinner. My recollection is that there was separate seating for dinner on the L1011 as well. There was also a separate bar, and it was all very nice.

When I began at Wilmer Cutler, there was no airport security. You did not have to go through metal detectors to get on the plane. You did not even need to buy a ticket in advance on the Eastern Shuttle or give your name before boarding the plane. The fare was collected on board via a cart that went up and down the aisle. The result of this was that you could arrive for a flight at the very last minute. Cutler did this regularly, and I emulated him. He arrived just a few minutes before the plane left, and there were times when he had to pressure the gate attendant to reopen the plane door so that he could get on the plane. One time I decided to have my shoes shined before getting on the plane. This was in old Terminal A of National Airport. The shine was unusual in that it involved setting the shoes on fire to get a glossier shine. All of a sudden, I heard last call for my flight, and ran to the gate with smoking shoes. One can imagine how that would be received today by the gate attendant, but I was allowed on the plane. The cockpit security in those days also was lax. I remember flying on the Concorde with the cabin door open to the cockpit. You could walk up and talk to the captain.

There were amusing episodes about flying. One involved Lloyd Cutler and his casual attitude about getting on planes. In this instance, he got on the plane, talking to his distinguished companion, and then did not realize that he was on the wrong plane flying to the wrong destination until the plane was in the air. Cutler being Cutler, he spoke to the pilot, insisting that the plane turn around and come back to National Airport where they could let him off. Of course, the pilot refused. This would have all remained unknown except for the fact that the pilot happened to be the brother-in-law of one of my partners at Wilmer Cutler (Bob McCaw). The pilot told his brother-in-law about this nut, who insisted on turning the plane around and flying back to National Airport. Cutler took a good deal of ribbing about that, at least outside his presence.

Another one of my partners, Joel Rosenbloom, had been on a fishing trip and was flying back to the District of Columbia. Joel at the best of times was not a sharp dresser, and he was dressed in his fishing gear. He called the flight attendant over to tell her a story. He asked whether she had ever heard about the man who carried a bomb on the plane because he had heard that the chances of there being a bomb on a plane was one in a million, but the chances of there being two bombs on a plane was one in a billion. The attendant did not find this story amusing, and she had the marshals or the police take Joel off the plane and hold him for questioning. Only through Cutler's intervention with his friends in the government was Joel released and allowed to come back home.

\* \* \*

What goes before has fleshed out themes that I described in the introduction: a focus on compensation as the primary objective, startling changes in the number of lawyers and firms and in the client relationships, a lessening of collegiality, and increasing distance between liberals and conservatives. This has definitely made the practice of law less enjoyable than it used to be.

## COVID

What I have said so far about changes in the legal profession now describes changes from the early 1960s to the year 2020. Beginning in March 2020, COVID upended the legal profession like most others. For more than a year, few lawyers have gone to physical offices, face-to-face meetings with clients have been nonexistent, and trials, oral arguments and almost everything else have typically been held remotely. It is much too soon to assess what changes in the profession will result as vaccines bring us back to a semblance of normality. It seems clear that business travel (with its attendant costs) is likely to be curtailed and that remote working is likely to increase: many lawyers enjoy working at home and avoiding the daily commute.

## Notes

1   R. T. Swaine, *The Cravath Firm and Its Predecessors, 1819–1948* (Clark, NJ: Lawbook Exchange, 2007).

2   There were 136 accredited US law schools at the start of the 1960s. The number today is over 200. "Enrollment and Degrees Awarded: 1963–2010," Legal Education Statistics, American Bar Association, last accessed 6 June 2021, https://www.amer icanbar.org/content/dam/aba/administrative/legal_education_and_admissions_ to_the_bar/stats_1.authcheckdam.pdf.

3   1L enrollments in 1963 totaled 20,776 with 9,638 JDs or LLBs awarded. By 2010, first year enrollment had more than doubled to 52,404, and 44,004 JD/LLBs were awarded. Since then, there has been a decline in 1L enrollment to 38,284 in 2019. See Ibid.; and "Law School Enrollment," Law School Transparency Data Dashboard, last accessed June 6, 2021, https://data.lawschooltransparency.com/enrollment/all/ ?scope=national.

4   Debra Cassens Weiss, "'After the JD' Study Shows Many Leave Law Practice," *American Bar Association Journal*, April 1, 2014, https://www.abajournal.com/magaz ine/article/after_the_jd_study_shows_many_leave_law_practice.

5   On England, see Lenore O'Boyle, "The Problem of an Excess of Educated Men in Western Europe, 1800–1850," *Journal of Modern History* 42, no. 4 (1970): 471–95. On China, see C. Minzner, "The Rise and Fall of Chinese Legal Education," *Fordham International Law Journal* 36, no. 2 (2013): 334–95.

6   "Looking Back at ITLSS," *Inside the Law School Scam*, August 7, 2014, http://insidet helawschoolscam.blogspot.com/2014/.

7   S. E. Martin and N. C. Jurik, *Doing Justice, Doing Gender: Women in Legal and Criminal Justice Occupations* (Thousand Oaks, CA: Sage, 2007), 110.

8   Stephanie Francis Ward, "Women Outnumber Men in Law Schools for the First Time, Newly Updated Data Show," *ABA Journal*, December 19, 2016, https://www. abajournal.com/news/article/women_outnumber_men_in_law_schools_for_first_t ime_newly_updated_data_show.

9   "Various Statistics on ABA Approved Law Schools," *American Bar Association*, https:// www.americanbar.org/groups/legal_education/resources/statistics/statistics- archives/.

10  William C. Kidder, "The Struggle for Access from *Sweatt* to *Grutter*: A History of African American, Latino, and American Indian Law School Admissions, 1950– 2000," *Harvard BlackLetter Law Journal* 19 (2003): 7.

11  Ibid.

12  "Law School Enrollment by Race and Ethnicity (2019)," Enjuris, last accessed June 8, 2021, https://www.enjuris.com/students/law-school-race-2019.html.

13   Debra Cassens Weis, "First Female Clerk to a Federal Appeals Judge Dies at 94," *American Bar Association Journal*, February 12, 2019, http://www.abajournal.com/news/article/first-female-clerk-to-a-federal-appeals-judge-dies-at-the-age-of-94.

14   Ibid.

15   Debra Cassens Weiss, "Black Law Grads Trail in Employment Overall and in Bar-Passage-Required Jobs, New NALP Report Finds," *American Bar Association Journal*, October 21, 2020, https://www.abajournal.com/news/article/black-law-grads-trail-in-employment-overall-and-in-bar-passage-required-jobs-nalp-reports.

16   "Firm History," About, Covington & Burling LLP, last accessed June 8, 2021, https://www.cov.com/en/about/firm-history.

17   Daniel J. Cantor, "Law Firms Are Getting Bigger … and More Complex," *American Bar Association Journal* 64, no. 2 (1978): 218.

18   Ibid.

19   "Washington, DC Legal Market," Georgetown Law, last accessed June 8, 2021, https://www.law.georgetown.edu/your-life-career/career-exploration-professional-development/for-jd-students/explore-legal-careers/legal-markets/washington-d-c-legal-market/.

20   Debra Cassens Weiss, "As Law Firm Culture Changes, Old Partnership Model 'Is All but Dead,'" *American Bar Association Journal*, August 12, 2019, https://www.abajournal.com/news/article/changed-law-firm-culture-exemplified-by-kirkland-which-pays-up-to-10m-to-lure-top-lawyers.

21   Adam Liptak, "Law Firms Pay Supreme Court Clerks $400,000 Bonuses. What Are They Buying?" *The New York Times*, September 21, 2020, https://www.nytimes.com/2020/09/21/us/politics/supreme-court-clerk-bonuses.html.

22   Weiss, "As Law Firm Culture Changes, Old Partnership Model 'Is All but Dead,'" *American Bar Association Journal*, August 12, 2019, https://www.abajournal.com/news/article/changed-law-firm-culture-exemplified-by-kirkland-which-pays-up-to-10m-to-lure-top-lawyers.

23   Lewis A. Coser, *Greedy Institutions. Patterns of Undivided Commitment* (New York,: Free Press, 1974).

24   Swaine, *The Cravath Firm and Its Predecessors, 1819–1948*.

25   American Bar Association, *1958 Lawyer and His 1938 Dollar* (St. Paul, MN: West Publishing, 1958).

26   Debra Cassens Weiss, "More Top Lawyers Break Through $1,000 Hourly Billing Barrier," *American Bar Association Journal*, February 23, 2011, https://www.abajournal.com/news/article/more_top_lawyers_break_through_1000_hourly_billing_barrier/.

27   "The Origins of the EPA," Environmental Protection Agency, last accessed October 18, 2021, https://www.epa.gov/history/origins-epa.

28   "Our History", Legal Services Corporation, last accessed June 8, 2021, https://www.lsc.gov/about-lsc/who-we-are/our-history.

29   Siobhan Roth, "The Public Lawyer: John Pickering Looks Back," *Legal Times*, August 2, 1999, 16.

30   Among the many biographies of Justice Brandeis, see Alpheus Thomas Mason, *Brandeis: A Free Man's Life* (New York: Viking Press, 1946).

31   William R. Coulson, "A Generational Perspective: Retro Is Trending", *The Bencher. The Magazine of the American Inns of Court*, May/June 2021, 23–24.

# Chapter 9

# BECOMING A FEDERAL JUDGE, 1993–2000

## Leaving Private Practice

Despite the satisfactions I found in private practice, I had always wanted to be a federal judge. This opportunity only existed for me during a Democratic administration since I was a Democrat, and Republican presidents rarely nominated Democrats. I never pursued a judgeship under President Jimmy Carter, in part because I had no significant connection to the administration (even when Cutler was White House Counsel) and in part because Carter very appropriately recognized that it was important to increase the number of women and minorities on the bench.[1] Carter's Executive Orders required that selection panels "make special efforts to seek out and identify well qualified women and members of minority groups as potential nominees."[2] The assumption was that there were going to be fewer white men appointed. In the District of Columbia, in particular, Carter appointed only one white male to the D.C. Circuit (Abner Mikva who had been a congressman). The Federal Circuit did not yet exist. Although Carter made five appointments to the Federal District Court for the District of Columbia, only two were white males: Louis Oberdorfer and Harold Greene, both of whom had long records of public service. I was much too junior to compete with them for the bench.

In 1992, when Bill Clinton was elected president, it was clear to me that, if I wanted to pursue a judicial appointment, this was the time. I was getting along in years, being 55 when Clinton was elected, so I would likely be aged out if I waited much longer. In addition, continued private practice as a long-term alternative seemed problematic. Though I loved private practice, and I had every reason to think that I would be welcome at Jones Day for some years to come, the firm then had a mandatory retirement age of 66, which in some instances was extended to age 70. I knew law firms and could not conceive that I was going to be able to practice law at Jones Day after age 70. The judiciary offered the added benefit of allowing me to remain active in the law beyond normal retirement age.

But, there were obstacles. Getting nominated and confirmed even in the best of times can be a long and difficult process. Even legendary Judge Edward Weinfeld took over four years to get nominated and confirmed for the federal district court in Manhattan and was never nominated for the Second Circuit despite his sterling reputation.[3] The early 1990s were not the best of times. Some history is useful to understanding the problem.

During the constitutional convention in 1787, there were various proposals for the selection of Article III judges (those with life tenure). After the convention settled on presidential nomination and Senate confirmation, Alexander Hamilton in the *Federalist* wrote that "it is [...] not very probable that [the President's] nomination would often be overruled."[4] Right from the start, this proved unduly optimistic. The controversy over judicial nominations goes back as far as *Marbury v. Madison*, and Jefferson's opposition to the last-minute (midnight) Federalist judges.[5] During the nineteenth century, almost a quarter of the nominees for the Supreme Court failed to secure Senate confirmation,[6] though most lower court nominees encountered no problems "owing both to the large number of appointments and to the tradition known as senatorial courtesy, in which presidents consulted with senators who represented the state of a potential nominee."[7]

Despite the early controversy over Supreme Court nominations, in later years, nominations or potential nominations to the Supreme Court were only occasionally controversial—Brandeis being one example. Another example was Martin Thomas Manton, a judge on the Second Circuit in the 1920s and 30s, who was thought (correctly) by his opponents to be on the take in patent cases. He was only narrowly denied a Supreme Court nomination that went to Justice Pierce Butler.[8] Eventually Manton was tried and criminally convicted of accepting bribes in patent cases, and his conviction was affirmed by a specially constituted Second Circuit panel, with Justice Harlan Stone, retired Justice George Sutherland and new appointee to the Second Circuit, Judge Charles Clark, sitting in place of the recused Second Circuit judges.[9] From 1894 through 1968, only one Supreme Court nomination failed in the Senate (Judge John J. Parker in 1930).[10] During the Eisenhower years, Chief Justice Warren and others even received recess appointments on the assumption that confirmation was a foregone conclusion.[11]

The bitter modern partisanship over judicial nominations began in 1968, with the then associate justice Fortas's nomination to be chief justice.[12] This was defeated by a filibuster and a failed cloture vote in the Senate. Ostensibly the Republicans objected to Justice Fortas's opinions about obscenity and other liberal decisions of the Warren Court, although the real reason appeared to be to deny the appointment to President Johnson and preserve it for the next president, hoped to be a Republican (Nixon). (Fortas later resigned as associate justice due to his unsavory connection to Wall Street raider, Louis Wolfson.) Then in retaliation for Fortas, Haynesworth and Carswell, who were nominated by Nixon, were not confirmed by the Democratic Senate. Next was Judge Robert Bork, nominated by Reagan, and not confirmed by a Democratic Senate in one of the most lopsided defeats in US history.[13] Justice Thomas was barely confirmed after a bruising confirmation hearing, and more recently, Harriet Miers (White House Counsel), nominated by George W. Bush, withdrew because Senate confirmation seemed unlikely. Most recently, then chief judge Merrick Garland failed even to get a hearing before a Republican Senate after being nominated by Obama.

As time passed, senators began to focus on court of appeals nominees. During the Clinton Administration, circuit confirmations became considerably more difficult. According to data available at the Federal Judicial Center, Clinton had more unsuccessful judicial nominations (all positions in total) than his predecessors. Clinton had 126 (20 withdrawn by president, 105 no Senate vote, 1 rejected by the Senate (Ronnie White, Eastern District of Missouri)) compared to Reagan's 64 (8 withdrawn, 55 no Senate vote, 1 rejected (Bork)) and George H. W. Bush's 58 (1 withdrawn, 57 no Senate vote). After Clinton, there were even more unsuccessful nominations: Presidents George W. Bush had 194 (13 withdrawn, 181 no Senate vote) and Obama had 222 (7 withdrawn, 215 no Senate vote). President Trump had 151 unsuccessful nominations (8 withdrawn, 143 no Senate vote) even though Republicans controlled the Senate during his presidency.[14] When I was considered in the 1990s, everyone was acutely conscious of the ideological battle over circuit judicial nominations.

The Republicans cared more about judges than the Democrats, at least until recently. This has been a continuing feature of the confirmation process in large part as a result of *Roe v. Wade* (410 U.S. 113 (1973)) and the dramatic effect that the decision had on the Republican base. Judicial nominations became an election issue for the Republicans both in the primaries and in the general elections. That has been much less true with respect to the Democrats. That may be changing now, but even during the Clinton and Obama administrations, where in each case the president was a lawyer, it appeared that ideological considerations played a relatively minor role in nominations to the appellate courts. I am not saying that either Clinton or Obama would have nominated someone, for example, who thought that *Roe v. Wade* should be overruled, but ideological considerations like those that energized the Republicans did not play so much on the Democratic side. As long as the nominee was a Democrat or the equivalent, competent and a good character, there was little concern about judicial philosophy assuming there were no speeches or publications taking problematic positions. President Biden seems more interested in diversity than ideology.

My ability to get confirmed was a major issue, not for a district court position, but for a circuit judgeship. The Democrats held the Senate in the first two years of the Clinton presidency in 1993 and 1994. But then, beginning in 1995, the Senate went Republican and stayed Republican through the remainder of the Clinton presidency. Even in 1993 and 1994, because of the then filibuster rule, Republicans could block a nomination. Concerns about confirmation could make it difficult to get nominated in the first place.

There were reasons for Senate Republicans to oppose me for a circuit position. One was that I had worked on cases as a lawyer in private practice which were viewed by some Republican Senators and their allies outside of the Senate, such as Gary Bauer and Paul Weyrich, as evidence that I was unsuitable for a judicial position. For example, as discussed earlier, I had worked on behalf of a coalition trying to limit FCC indecency regulation. I had represented the school board in the *Mozert* case, and I had helped represent a Palestinian in challenging an exclusion order based on secret evidence. In addition, I had served on the board of People for the American Way, an organization opposing conservative groups on various issues. There was also the fact that I was married to Sally, and various Republican Senators, particularly Senator George Voinovich, were not happy with some of the work that she had done in the Clinton administration. She held various positions, including heading the Office of Information and Regulatory Affairs and ultimately the Deputy Director for Management at the Office of Management and Budget (OMB) (after my confirmation). Just how much of a role this opposition to my wife played was not entirely clear, but I was told at times that it played a significant role.

## US District Court for the District of Columbia

Because of my concerns about confirmation for a circuit judgeship, I initially sought to become a judge on the US District Court for the District of Columbia. The Republican Senators at that time cared less about the district courts: the focus of controversy was on the Supreme Court and the courts of appeals. With some exceptions, if you were nominated for the district court, you were likely to be confirmed rather easily by the Senate. However, I was not well positioned for a district court nomination. President Clinton had given Eleanor Holmes Norton, the District of Columbia's Representative in Congress, the senatorial prerogative to determine who would be nominated to district court positions in the District of Columbia. The White House was hands off in that process, and I had no particular connection to Ms. Norton. Indeed, at times in the past, we had been on opposite sides of some issues, such as in the *Red Lion* case.

Norton had established a nominations committee to recommend candidates. The committee was composed of prominent lawyers and nonlawyers. The process involved submitting an application and then being interviewed by the nominations committee. The committee would recommend three people for each slot. Norton would interview the three and make her choice.

I first applied for a district court position on May 12, 1993, and was recommended as one of the three finalists. I was scheduled for a meeting with Norton. In the interview, she asked what to her was a critical question: "Why do you want to be a judge?" I did not give the right answer to that question. The answer that she undoubtedly was looking for was that I viewed being a federal judge as an opportunity to redress wrongs done to the less fortunate or disadvantaged in society. My background would have made such an answer credible. I had been a clerk to Chief Justice Warren, had been on the board of various migrant organizations, had represented migrant workers, had some extensive other pro-bono work, and had represented a number of indigent criminal defendants over the years. I did not give this answer. I mumbled something about how I had always wanted to be a judge, and it would be a high honor to help make the system better. The position ultimately went to my former Wilmer Cutler partner, James Robertson, who was sworn in in October 1994. It is not surprising that Robertson received the nod from Ms. Norton because he had been active in the South in civil rights cases and that very much appealed to her.

The same problem existed in 1995 when I was again considered for a district court position. Again, I was recommended by the committee. I decided to be better prepared for my second interview. Through a friend and client, I arranged lunch with one of Ms. Norton's confidants at Georgia Brown's Restaurant. Just as the lunch started, in walked Marion Barry with his security detail. He was then councilman for D.C.'s Ward 8 in between stints as the city's mayor. He said hello to my companion and, uninvited, joined us at the table, ordering an ample lunch. The table conversation never turned to my efforts to get nominated. Barry left. I was stuck with the check, and I was no better prepared for my interview with Ms. Norton. Again, I gave the wrong answer to the question "Why do you want to be a judge?"; again, I mumbled the same unsatisfactory answer, and again I was not selected. In April 1997, I once again applied for the district court. And this time I had run out the string and was not selected by the committee to be one of the three finalists. My only remaining opportunity was at the circuit level.

After the first district court position went to Robertson, I began in late 1994 and early 1995 to talk to the White House Counsel's Office about a possible circuit nomination, with a focus on the Federal Circuit and the D.C. Circuit. For the regional circuits outside of D.C., the candidate would be nominated for a slot allocated to a particular state. If there were one or two Democratic Senators from that state, those Democratic Senators had quite a bit of influence over the nomination. With respect to the D.C. Circuit and the Federal Circuit, however, there was no home state Senator, so the president had more latitude. In the Senate, the primary players were the chairman and ranking member of the Judiciary Committee, the members of the Judiciary Committee, and the majority and minority leaders of the Senate.

As noted, in the early 1990s, because of the filibuster, the White House was very concerned about whether the president's nominees would be confirmed. Indeed, Republican Senator Orrin Hatch, ranking member and then chair of the Judiciary Committee, had written a letter to the White House demanding preclearance. The White House was therefore interested in whether a nominee would face strong opposition from the Republican Senators and also whether the nominee had support in Republican quarters, for example, as Justice Breyer did when he was nominated to the Supreme Court. The White House was very deferential to the Senate Republicans, taking the position that it would not nominate somebody for a circuit position until the Republicans approved that nomination.

In late 1994, I made an effort to secure a favorable signal from Republican Senators that I would be acceptable. They were unwilling to send such a signal. Nor did I receive help from Lloyd Cutler, my former partner, who was White House Counsel in 1994.[15] Interestingly, there is a view, and I think it was correct, that the filibuster threat tended to moderate circuit and Supreme Court appointments both for Republicans and Democrats because of the need to get support from members of the other party for the nominations to be approved. The Senate filibuster has since been eliminated for judicial nominees, first as to lower court nominees (2013)[16] and, more recently, to Supreme Court nominees (2017).[17]

## Federal Circuit Nomination

Eventually, after Clinton was reelected in 1996, the White House attitude toward the confirmation process changed even though the Republicans continued to control the Senate and could block nominees with both party-line votes and filibusters. Potential difficulties in the confirmation process did not now deter the White House from nominating people who might face some opposition. The White House was willing to nominate without preclearance, even though there could be quite a bit of work to do to convince the Senate to take up the nomination and vote favorably. That was not only true of me, but of others, like Richard Paez and Marsha Berzon for the Ninth Circuit.

Starting in 1997, I focused my attention exclusively on a circuit nomination. There were vacancies on both the D.C. Circuit and the Federal Circuit.

There were several significant players in the nomination process—the president, the chief of staff, the White House Counsel's Office, the Justice Department's Office of Policy Development (now Office of Legal Policy), the FBI (which vetted the nominees) and the American Bar Association, from which the Democrats solicited ratings before the nomination occurred. There were also various interest groups that played a role, like the Alliance for Justice, or various bar associations, but they had lesser influence. Erskine Bowles and then John Podesta was chief of staff. Jack Quinn and then Chuck Ruff and then Beth Nolan was the White House Counsel. Mark Childress was senior counsel to the president for nominations, and Sarah Wilson was associate counsel and senior counsel to the president in the Office of the White House Counsel. Eldie Acheson was head of the Office of Policy Development at Justice. Those who worked most directly on my nominations—Podesta, Childress, Wilson and Acheson—were excellent and fully supportive.

Despite the change in White House attitude, I was not seriously considered for the D.C. Circuit. The White House was convinced that I would never be confirmed if I were nominated. Indeed, no one was confirmed to fill the D.C. Circuit seats during the Clinton presidency after Merrick Garland was confirmed in 1997. The nominees that Clinton did name thereafter for the D.C. Circuit, Elena Kagan and Allen Snyder, never secured a vote on their nominations.

With the D.C. Circuit out, the administration turned to the possibility of nominating me for the Federal Circuit to fill the seat vacated by Glen Archer when he took senior status. That court was much less of a lightning rod because of the specialized nature of its jurisdiction, which focused on patent cases, government personnel cases, veterans' cases, foreign trade cases and non-tort monetary claims against the government. Abortion issues and high-profile constitutional cases were largely foreign to that court.

Ultimately, I was chosen for the Federal Circuit vacancy. Various considerations played a role in my nomination. Surely my wife's support was a factor. Perhaps I benefited also from the fact that John Podesta and I had been co-coaches of a little league baseball team and I had a close relationship with Tony Podesta, John's brother, developed when I litigated the *Mozert* case. It is always said that in order to get nominated, you need a rabbi—that is, someone who will care about your nomination and shepherd it through. My good friend, Tom Udall, was still years from being in the Senate. I had no single individual who was my rabbi during the nomination process.

I was nominated for the Federal Circuit on April 1, 1998. The method of notifying me was evidence of the different party attitudes to judicial nominations. My recollection is that when President Reagan and the two President Bushes nominated individuals to the circuit courts, they would call the nominees, tell them of the nomination and offer congratulations. Biden appears to be doing the same. Calling the circuit nominees was not something that Clinton did. I was notified of my nomination to the Federal Circuit by a White House paralegal on April Fool's Day. I was nonetheless happy to get the call. The happiness at the nomination was offset by the dreadful news that same day that Sally had been diagnosed with stage IIIB breast cancer. Her aggressive and ultimately successful treatment continued throughout the confirmation process, though she hardly missed a day of work.

The confirmation process began with the Judiciary Committee, where Senator Orrin Hatch was chairman and Senator Pat Leahy the ranking member. At that stage, the process was more or less transparent. When you got to the floor, the confirmation process was very much a black box, with only the majority leader knowing the full extent of what is going on. At that time, the majority leader was Senator Trent Lott (R-MS), because the Republicans controlled the Senate. The minority leader was Senator Tom Daschle (D-SD).

Even though I faced opposition from conservatives, I also had some support on the Republican side of the aisle as a result of work that I had done in private practice. This included the challenge on behalf of the Chamber of Commerce and others to President Clinton's striker replacement Executive Order. That work led the Chamber and the National Association of Manufacturers to support my nomination. As discussed earlier, I also represented Trinity Broadcasting in an FCC license challenge. That led Trinity Broadcasting, as well as Colby May, associated with the Christian Coalition, to support my nomination. I also represented a business coalition headed by the National Foreign Trade Council in the Massachusetts Burma case (mentioned earlier), and they were supportive. So, there were various things that I had done as a lawyer that earned me some credit on the Republican side. A significant part of the Federal Circuit jurisdiction was patent cases, but I did not receive support from the patent community or the Federal Circuit Bar Association. I was not a member of their fraternity and was unknown to them. The White House told me to be careful and not allow myself to be interviewed by the various patent bar associations, because I was not seen as one of their own and they were not likely to be friendly. Bringing them into the picture risked giving additional weight to the opposition.

There is no doubt in my mind that one of the reasons that the confirmation process was so difficult and took so long for me was that I did not have a Senate supporter who really cared about my being confirmed. This was brought into sharp relief by the experience of my now colleague, Dick Linn. Dick did not have the baggage that I had, having been almost exclusively a patent lawyer, and he was a friend and neighbor of Pat Leahy, the ranking member on judiciary. Because Leahy wanted him, his nomination was taken up before mine even though my nomination had been earlier. Dick was confirmed rather easily. Both the White House and other Republican senators would do their best to accommodate Senator Leahy. I did not have a Senate supporter like that.

After my nomination, during the time that I waited for my hearing, Sally and I were invited (for the first and only time) to attend a movie screening in the White House theatre. The president and other White House staffers attended. The Monica Lewinsky scandal had broken in January of that year, and Clinton's relationship with her was front page news. In that light, the choice of movie was an odd one. The title was *Dangerous Beauty*, and it was about a sixteenth-century courtesan who excelled at oral sex, and her relationship with the doge. The audience was unusually quiet.

## Notes

1   Exec. Order No. 11,972, 42 Fed. Reg. 9,155 (February 15, 1977); and Exec. Order No. 12,059, 43 Fed. Reg. 20,949 (May 16, 1978).

2   Cited in Sheldon Goldman, *Picking Federal Judges: Lower Court Selection from Roosevelt through Reagan* (Yale University Press, 1997), 238–39.

3   William E. Nelson, *In Pursuit of Right and Justice: Edward Weinfeld as Lawyer and Judge* (New York: New York University Press, 2004), 113–14.

4   The Federalist No. 76 (Alexander Hamilton).

5   Winston Bowman, "The Midnight Judges," Federal Judicial Center, https://www.fjc. gov/history/spotlight-judicial-history/midnight-judges.

6   Paul A. Freund, "Appointment of Justices: Some Historical Perspectives," *Harvard Law Review* 101, no. 6 (1988): 1147.

7   "About Judicial Nominations: Historical Overview," Art & History: Powers & Procedures, United States Senate, last accessed June 8, 2021, https://www.senate. gov/about/powers-procedures/nominations/judicial-nominations-overview.htm.

8   David J. Danelski, *A Supreme Court Justice Is Appointed* (New York: Random House, 1964).

9   *United States v. Manton*, 107 F.2d 834 (2d Cir. 1939).

10  Paul A. Freund, "Appointment of Justices: Some Historical Perspectives," *Harvard Law Review* 101, no. 6 (1988): 1154; and Josh Chafetz, "Unprecedented? Judicial Confirmation Battles and the Search for a Usable Past," *Harvard Law Review* 131, no. 1 (2017): 96–132.

11  Norman Dorsen, "The Selection of U.S. Supreme Court Justices," *International Journal of Constitutional Law* 4, no. 4 (October 2006): 652–63.

12  On partisanship in Supreme Court confirmations, see John A. Tures, "Partisan Supreme Court Battles Are as Old as the United States Itself," *The Conversation*, September 29, 2020, https://theconversation.com/partisan-supreme-court-battles-are-as-old-as-the-united-states-itself-146657.

13  "Senate's Roll-Call on the Bork Vote," *The New York Times*, October 24, 1987, https://www.nytimes.com/1987/10/24/us/senate-s-roll-call-on-the-bork-vote.html.

14 "Unsuccessful Nominations and Recess Appointments," History of the Federal Judiciary, Federal Judicial Center, last accessed June 8, 2021, https://www.fjc.gov/hist ory/judges/unsuccessful-nominations-and-recess-appointments.

15 Gwen Ifill, "President Chooses Another Counsel; Openness Is Vowed," *The New York Times*, March 9, 1994, https://www.nytimes.com/1994/03/09/us/president-choo ses-another-counsel-openness-is-vowed.html.

16 Jeremy W. Peters, "In Landmark Vote, Senate Limits Use of the Filibuster," *The New York Times*, November 21, 2013, https://www.nytimes.com/2013/11/22/us/ politics/reid-sets-in-motion-steps-to-limit-use-of-filibuster.html.

17 Matt Flegenheimer, "Senate Republicans Deploy 'Nuclear Option' to Clear Path for Gorsuch," *The New York Times*, April 6, 2017, https://www.nytimes.com/2017/04/ 06/us/politics/neil-gorsuch-supreme-court-senate.html.

# Chapter 10

# THE CONFIRMATION PROCESS, 1998–2000: SELECTED DIARY ENTRIES

During the confirmation process, I kept a daily diary. Here are some entries following my April 1, 1998, nomination. These entries, which appear here substantially as written at the time (with some supplementation), are only a small portion of the whole. For almost two years I made calls and met with people, seeking support for my confirmation on a daily basis, weekends included. I replicate the diary entries to give a sense of the uncertainty and chaos of the rollercoaster ride as it unfolded. As far as I know, there is no similar published record of such an experience. There are 785 days between my nomination and my confirmation on May 24, 2000. The median waiting time for circuit court confirmation during the Clinton presidency was about 140 days.[1]

April 8, 1998: The White House tells me that Hatch (the chairman of the Senate Judiciary Committee) and John Podesta (then deputy chief of staff) do not get along.

April 12, 1998: Hatch and Lott (the majority leader) also have tensions between them. Republican Senators Ashcroft and Sessions are Lott's eyes and ears on the Judiciary Committee. Lott does not want to move too fast with nominations.

April 16, 1998: Colby May, associated with the Christian Coalition and the lawyer for Trinity Broadcasting, agrees to help with my confirmation. For the first time, I hear that my wife Sally is a problem because of Republicans' concerns about regulatory reform.

May 5, 1998: The ABA letter concerning my nomination is released. It rates me "qualified" rather than "well qualified." The primary reason, as later explained to me privately by an ABA committee member, is that a district court judge that I appeared before said that I screamed at him in court. That is not my style, and it never happened. I assume that this was a Cleveland district judge who sat on one of the firm's cases and was unhappy with my predecessor's attitude toward him before I took over the case. In fact, I had never met the judge nor been in the judge's courtroom. (This weaponization of the ABA process by sitting judges I later learned happened to at least one other Clinton

nominee.) This emphasizes the difference between FBI investigations, where
people are concerned about lying to the FBI, and ABA investigations, where
there are no consequences. Ironically, this problem would not have existed if
I had not suggested that opposing counsel in that case, who was a member of
the ABA committee and with whom I had a good relationship, recuse himself.
He did not participate in reviewing my nomination. The White House says a
qualified rating makes no difference, and that no one cares whether you are
rated well-qualified or qualified by the ABA.[2] Judge Posner also received a
qualified rating.[3]

July 16, 1998: The hearing on my nomination takes place. I am introduced
by Senator Kerry of Massachusetts (logical because I was born in Boston). The
hearing has a bit of theater. I am asked about the role of legislative history,
cameras in the courts and a variety of other topics. Then comes once again
the question: Why do you want to be a judge? Senator Michael DeWine, "Can
you tell me why you want that job [at the Federal Circuit]? For some of us,
looking at the jurisdiction, we might think it might not be the most interesting
job [...] [W]hy do you want it?"[4] This time I manage a satisfactory answer.

I bring my then 97-year-old mother, my wife, my two daughters, my son,
and my granddaughter to the hearing. My 2-year old granddaughter speaks
up from the audience at one point: "Talk louder Grandpa! I cannot hear
you." She starts to cry. As my daughter starts to leave with my granddaughter,
Senator DeWine, who is presiding at the hearing along with Senator Richard
Durbin, says that my daughter need not take the crying child out of the
hearing as he had many children, and it was perfectly okay. I also mention that
I had coached my son's little league baseball team. So, I am able to establish
myself as a good family man. (I did not go as far as a Trump nominee, who
had his child take the stand to tell the committee that "the law keeps us safe"
and "vote for my daddy").[5]

After the hearing, Mike O'Neill with the Republican committee staff tells
me that things went well; that there should be no problem; and it is likely I will
soon be confirmed.

July 17, 1998: I receive the first set of written questions from the committee.
I respond to them over the course of the next several days.

July 20, 1998: The Judiciary Committee Republican Staff Director is
named Manus Cooney. He telephones me and asks if I want to be confirmed,
and I say, "Yes, I do want to get confirmed," and he says, "Well, you are going
to have to do something that you are not going to like doing." I say, "What
is that?" He said, "You are going to have to humiliate yourself." By that he
meant that I would have to call people and get them to support me and play
the politics of the situation, which he knew would be uncomfortable for me.
I take his advice, which was very good advice, and I am very grateful for it.

In the coming months, I make one call after another after another asking for help.

August 5, 1998: Colby May says that Grassley, Ashcroft and Sessions think that I was the architect of the Bork opposition and are holding me up as payback for Bork's defeat. In fact, I had nothing to do with the Bork confirmation battle.

August 7, 1998: Conservatives also appear to be concerned about comments that I made on a Federalist Society panel about the virtue of looking to committee reports (legislative history) in connection with statutory interpretation.

August 11, 1998: Colby May tells me that he has received pressure to stop supporting me and that he has declined to stop.

September 9, 1998: Thurman does not like my positions, but will vote for me.

September 10, 1998: The committee votes on my nomination. I am approved with apparently four negative votes (Grassley, Sessions, Kyl and Ashcroft).

September 15, 1998: The Judiciary Committee reports on my nomination "with the recommendation that he be confirmed."

October 7, 1998: Senator James Inhofe on the Senate floor recites my work on indecency regulation and the Tennessee textbook case and my board membership at People for the American Way: "I believe that Mr. Dyk is [...] an extremist and should not be confirmed."[6]

October 20, 1998: John Podesta is chosen to succeed Erskine Bowles as White House chief of staff.

October 21, 1998: The White House and Lott relationship is deteriorating. I am not included in a unanimous consent resolution. The congressional session will soon expire, and my nomination with it. The view is that I should go through next year. Apparently, Ashcroft held me up.

January 7, 1999: There is a lot going on—the impeachment trial for President Clinton begins. The White House has more significant things to worry about than my nomination. On January 23, Sally and I take our son to watch the impeachment trial from the first row of the balcony.

January 26, 1999: I am re-nominated for the Federal Circuit. The question is whether I will have to have a new hearing.

January 29, 1999: There is a new concern that I might sit by designation on other circuits if I were confirmed for the Federal Circuit. The thought is, if I were to sit on other circuits, I might do more damage than would be possible at the Federal Circuit. The White House tells me not to promise to forgo such sittings. I make no promises (a good thing since I have been able to sit on the First Circuit by designation).

February 12, 1999: The Senate votes in the Clinton impeachment trial. He is not convicted.

February 22, 1999: There have been in the past, and will be in the future, repeated suggestions that I meet with various Republican senators who oppose my nomination. Such meetings never take place, but, on February 22, I have my first meeting with a senator. A meeting with Senator Daniel Moynihan (Democrat, New York) is scheduled for the morning. He is an hour late, and obviously the worse for wear in terms of alcohol consumption. He has little interest in my nomination, though he promises to help. I spend about an hour talking with him about the Clintons. He is not a fan of the President, but very much a fan of the First Lady.

February 23, 1999: Mike O'Neill confirms that Ashcroft and Grassley held me up last year.

March 12, 1999: A new hearing may be necessary. A new member of the Judiciary Committee, Bob Smith, a nonlawyer and Republican from New Hampshire, announced his candidacy for president in February and seems to be a problem. Morality is his issue. He fastens on the *Rafeedie* case, where I had served as supervising partner. (As mentioned earlier, the case involved the exclusion of a US resident with Palestinian background from reentry into the United States after a trip abroad, based on secret evidence). Wilmer Cutler took the case on pro bono, and we eventually succeeded in setting aside the exclusion order because of the inappropriate use of secret evidence (*Rafeedie v. INS*, 880 F.2d 506 (D.C. Cir. 1989)). Some conservatives, such as Bruce Fein, supported that outcome.[7] The White House tells me that this makes it necessary for me to secure support from Jewish groups. Eventually, I am able to secure letters from the American Jewish Congress and the Anti-Defamation League supporting my nomination. At least one other Jewish group refuses on the ground that Rafeedie is a bad actor.

March 24, 1999: I meet with Republican Senator Arlen Spector. He will support me.

May 10, 1999: *The Legal Times* publishes an article on the Federal Circuit and the conservative opposition to my nomination. The article states:

Federal Circuit nominations have rarely inspired the bare-knuckle political fighting common to other appointments. One exception was Tim Dyk [...] He found himself under attack from two conservative D.C. lobbying groups, the Family Research Council and the Free Congress Foundation. Gary Bauer, a leading social conservative and presidential hopeful, was then head of the former group. Thomas Jipping, an oft-quoted conservative critic of liberal judicial appointees, guides the latter's Judicial Selection Monitoring Project.

Both wrote to the Senate Judiciary Committee to denounce Dyk's nomination.

Their letters dwelt on Dyk's representation of broadcasters [...] on indecent programming. Dyk's arguments in those cases "mirror those of pornographers," Bauer claimed. Jipping assailed Dyk as a nominee who "uses his legal talents to undermine protecting children and parental rights." More generally, both groups warned, Dyk bore the hallmarks of an "activist" who, as a judge, would twist the law to serve his sociopolitical agenda. The concern about Dyk's alleged anti-family leanings seemed a bit misplaced, given the narrow jurisdiction of the court to which he had been nominated.
Still the campaign effectively stalled Dyk's nomination.[8]
For the first time, there are concerns mentioned about the Federal Circuit's jurisdiction over takings cases. That is a matter of some interest to conservatives.

May 21, 1999: There are reports that the iconic judge Giles Rich of the Federal Circuit is quite ill.

May 24, 1999: Meet with Senator Chuck Hagel, Republican from Nebraska. He will support me.

June 5, 1999: According to the *Washington Post*, Hatch is holding up all judicial nominations because he wants Ted Stewart, who held various positions in the Utah state government, to be nominated to be a federal district court judge.

June 9, 1999: Judge Giles Rich of the Federal Circuit dies at age 95, creating another vacancy on the court. Part of the opposition to my nomination has been based on the idea that the Federal Circuit only needs 11, rather than 12 judges, echoing a debate that happened earlier with respect to the D.C. Circuit. I communicate the existence of this additional vacancy to the White House and others, but nobody seems to care.

June 23, 1999: Hatch announces that he is running for president. How is this going to affect the confirmation process?

June 29, 1999: I hear that Senator Jeff Sessions opposed my nomination because he thought I was being nominated for the D.C. Circuit.

July 1, 1999: Clinton nominates Sally as deputy director for management at the Office of Management and Budget (OMB).

July 2, 1999: Clinton agrees to nominate Ted Stewart to the district court, eliminating that log jam.

July 8, 1999: The White House reports that Grassley (previously mildly opposed) is now strongly opposed to my nomination.

July 16, 1999: The Federal Circuit Bar Association proposes to meet with me to consider supporting my nomination. The White House says do not do it because any bar opposition would just give additional fodder for the Republicans. The patent bar wants one of their own, but they did not have a great deal of influence with the White House or in the Senate. I decline the interview.

July 22, 1999: Rumor that a Democratic senator (Schumer?) opposes me because of *Rafeedie*. This proves to be untrue.

July 26, 1999: Judge Randall Rader of the Federal Circuit opposes filling the 12th seat. Grassley and Sessions are using this.

August 9, 1999: The president complains in an ABA speech about the pace of confirmations.

August 13, 1999: Dick Linn, a friend and neighbor of Leahy, is to be nominated to fill the Rich seat. Leahy is ranking on Judiciary.

August 18, 1999: Sessions, Smith and Grassley, though opposed, do not plan to place holds on my nomination.

August 21, 1999: I attend the wedding of my cousin in Utah. She is marrying a law partner of Hatch's son, Brett Hatch. I am seated with Hatch but say nothing about my nomination. Eventually I leave to go to the rest room. My cousin Bob (uncle of the bride and a well-known broadcaster) tells Hatch that I am nominated to the Federal Circuit. I come back, and Hatch says: "Now I know why I am at this table," but he offers to help.

September 15, 1999: Sally has a hearing on her nomination to be deputy director of OMB. Voinovich is strongly opposed. Our son and I attend. Voinovich states his opposition: "I am being very candid with you. I am not for your nomination. From all the experience that I have had with you and your people, and my people have had, I don't believe—and I say it in all due respect—not in terms of integrity, and I hate to say this in front of your husband and your son. But I just disagree with your approach as I have seen it in many, many instances."[9] I tell my son: "This is not going well." The next day, the *Washington Post* describes the "earful" Sally received.[10]

September 21, 1999: The Republicans seek cloture on the Stewart district court nomination, but the cloture motion is defeated. My nomination is also discussed on the floor of the Senate, along with the nominations of Paez and Berzon for the Ninth Circuit. Leahy voices strong support for Paez and Berzon but does not mention me. Senator Herb Kohl chimes in to support me, no doubt courtesy of his staffer Jon Liebowitz, a longtime friend.[11]

September 27, 1999: Linn is to be nominated tomorrow. The White House opposed this because of concerns that Leahy will bring up the Linn nomination before mine, thereby jumping the line and making my confirmation even more difficult since the court will have 11 judges if Linn is confirmed.

September 30, 1999: Grassley is concerned that I undertook business representations only after my nomination to secure support. Grassley wants a list of representations with dates.

October 1, 1999: There is agreement between Republicans and Democrats about the Stewart district court nomination. He is eventually confirmed. Only Smith wants a new hearing on my nomination.

October 6, 1999: I am told that business groups have objected to Linn's jumping the line and have told Hatch. I tell the White House: "I didn't ask for this," that is, this is not my fault. Leahy and Hatch are angry at the Chamber for fomenting opposition to Linn. The Chamber will not oppose Linn—but won't support him.

October 13, 1999: One of my Republican supporters runs into Manus Cooney at a fundraiser for Republican Senator Abraham and asks how things are going. Cooney: "I hope we can do it. But tell him to ask his friends in the White House why the Senate should move any white males." This is a reference to the rejection of Ronnie White, a Black nominee to be a Missouri district judge, purportedly on the ground that he is weak on capital punishment. Clinton said, "The vote adds credibility to the perception that [...] minority and women nominees [are treated] unfairly and unequally."[12] The Republicans are offended or pretend to be.

October 20, 1999: Allen Synder, nominated for the D.C. Circuit on September 22, calls for advice. "When should I start cutting back on my practice?" I do not tell him that he is never going to be confirmed.

October 21, 1999: Without a second hearing, my nomination is voted out of committee along with Linn's. I have six negative votes. This includes the four who voted against me the first time (Grassley, Sessions, Kyl and Ashcroft). The fifth is Smith. Senator Thurmond, who voted for me last year, also votes against me. The story of Thurman's vote is amusing. Various supporters of mine had talked to Thurman's aide, Duke Short, affectionately known as "Senator Short," who had assured them that Thurman would vote for me as he did last year. Immediately before the vote, one of the Republican committee members leaned over to Thurman and yelled in his ear, Thurman being somewhat deaf, "Senator, he's a liberal." That being the last word that Thurman heard about me before the vote, he voted no. Linn also has 4–5 negative votes, but the opposition to him is perfunctory.

October 25, 1999: Bruce Cohen, the committee chief of staff on the Democratic side, telephones to tell me that Leahy is working equally for the Linn nomination and for mine. He does not sound convincing. Cohen is critical of the Chamber for not lining up more votes for me. Leahy offers to cosponsor a bill with Grassley to prospectively reduce the size of the Federal Circuit to 11 judges in exchange for my confirmation. There are no takers.

November 7, 1999: My mother, having been active in the women's suffrage movement many years ago, appears in the introduction and closing to the Ken Burn's documentary on women's suffrage, *Not for Ourselves Alone: The Story of*

*Elizabeth Cady Stanton and Susan B. Anthony.*[13] In the closing, Ken Burns asked her how she felt the first time she voted. She said that she was "terribly fright-ened." Frightened about what? "Frightened about pushing the wrong lever." She then added, with a mischievous smile, "I still go into that booth with the same feeling—what if I vote Republican!" Fortunately, Republican Senators do not watch PBS. Sarah Wilson sees the program and calls me the next day to ask if that was my mother. I tell her yes.

November 10, 1999: Lott and Daschle have an exchange on the Senate floor. Lott agrees to move the Berzon and Paez nominations for the Ninth Circuit by March 15, 2000, but waffles on other nominations (mine included), saying that "my hope" is to move the other nominations by then. This leads to a period of some White House pessimism about the prospects for my confirmation. Again, the issue of Sally surfaces, and concern that she would receive a recess appointment for the position of deputy director of the Office of Management and Budget, which the Republicans strongly oppose. Cohen: "You will not get a vote until next year."

November 18, 1999: White House reports that someone has a hold on me. Speculation that this could be Voinovich because of Sally. "This has a bad feel to it. Never been in a situation like this. Can't find out anything."

November 19, 1999: The Linn nomination is hotlined by the Democrats—that is, given priority.

Senator Inhofe threatens to put a hold on all judicial nominations if Sally and others receive recess appointments.[14]

November 22, 1999: Linn is confirmed. The White House reports that Leahy says that Hatch says that he cannot move me "because of the wiretap thing." What is this about? A Republican friend: "You can't imagine how much the Republicans hate Clinton."

December 5, 1999: Meet with John Podesta for an hour. He will ask the President to ask Lott why I am a problem. Does not think Sally is the problem, but she should not take recess appointment because this would be a problem. The Republicans are unhappy that the Chamber is pushing me.

December 16, 1999: Bruce Cohen says that Leahy has no idea what is going on, and that he never knows what is going on with respect to bringing nominations up on the floor. This seems hard to believe. Nonetheless, Cohen is "sort of" confident about my prospects.

January 11, 2000: Childress says Smith, who had apparently placed a hold on my nomination, has agreed to lift the hold. I am the last one in the "hope" category in the Lott-Daschle floor exchange. Difficult environment, even now.

February 9, 2000: It now appears that the nomination of a Republican choice, Brad Smith, for the Federal Election Commission is an issue, which is holding up judicial nominations.

February 17, 2000: Mark Childress is leaving the White House Counsel's Office to become Daschle's chief of staff, though this is not going to happen immediately. What effect will this have on my confirmation?

February 23, 2000: Childress confirms that the Lott statements in the Lott-Daschle exchange on the floor did not represent a solid commitment to bring up my nomination before March 15. Lott wrote in the waffle ("hope") himself. Childress calls later in the day to say that my nomination is likely to come up tomorrow on the floor. I have a sleepless night.

February 24, 2000: Tomorrow comes, and my nomination does not come to the floor as a result of a presumed hold. Smith? Grassley?

February 29, 2000: The *Trinity* oral argument (the FCC case about Trinity's Miami TV License) takes place. I receive a lot of compliments.

March 2, 2000: The oral argument in the Supreme Court in the *National Foreign Trade Council* case (Massachusetts sanctions on companies doing business with Burma), mentioned earlier, is scheduled for March 22. I am concerned that I might be confirmed before the argument takes place. The White House tells me no problem, we will simply not sign your commission until the argument takes place. So, I face the prospect of arguing before the Supreme Court as a confirmed federal court of appeals judge. Fortunately, I am not confirmed before the argument takes place, saving me that awkward situation.

March 5, 2000. Childress: "I woke up at 4 a.m. worrying. It's time to leave this job." Please don't leave just yet. I tell Childress that the Chamber's theory is that the Republicans see me as valuable and want something in exchange. Childress: "That is really funny. The Republicans never asked for anything concerning you but were not shy about asking for something in exchange for Berzon and Paez." The White House is irritated that the Chamber opposed Paez.

March 6, 2000: My nomination is supposed to come up tomorrow. Wilson calls later in the day. "You are off."

March 7, 2000: Paul Crouch, the CEO of Trinity Broadcasting, calls Lott, with whom he is friendly. Crouch relays the call to me:

CROUCH:   You certainly have your hands full with these nominees.
LOTT:     Yes, we do not want to fill vacancies.
CROUCH:   Well, I certainly hope that there is no problem with respect to our good friend Tim Dyk.

Stunned silence from Lott. He eventually says we should be able to work that one out. I tell Sarah Wilson about this. She says, "I don't know where you come up with these people."

Senator Ted Kennedy supports my nomination of the floor. He says I am supported by "corporations" and business organizations like the Chamber of Commerce and the National Association of Manufacturers.[15]

March 8, 2000: The issue of *Rafeedie* surfaces again. The FBI apparently has been talking to senators about the issue, and this appears to dampen the concern. But an investigation may be necessary. Paez and Berzon are confirmed for the Ninth Circuit.

March 9, 2000: One of the business groups tells me that the Republican senators are concerned that Linn was confirmed ahead of the pro-business candidate for the Federal Circuit. That is me.

March 16, 2000: Hatch sends a letter to FBI director Louis Freeh asking him to look into the *Rafeedie* matter.

March 22, 2000: I argue the *National Foreign Trade Council* case in the Supreme Court. It goes well.

March 25, 2000: Our son Abe and I go to Rochester for my mother's 99th birthday party.

March 27, 2000: The White House tells me that the FBI is looking again into the *Rafeedie* issue.

March 29, 2000: An FBI agent comes to my office for an interview about *Rafeedie*. She is clearly embarrassed by the whole thing and says that the questions that she was about to ask me are not her questions. I answer the questions.

April 8, 2000: The FBI report on *Rafeedie* becomes available. It says that there is no problem.

April 12, 2000: The FBI director is supposed to meet with Lott, Hatch and Smith about the *Rafeedie* problem to tell them there is no problem. The meeting never takes place.

April 20, 2000: The White House offers to trade funding for a beach for my confirmation. The offer is rejected.

April 27, 2000: Chief Justice Rehnquist calls Sessions and complains about the pace of confirmation of judges. This was organized by the White House.

May 3, 2000: Daschle threatens to close down the Judiciary Committee if there are no actions on the pending judicial nominations.

May 5, 2000: The *Trinity* case is decided in favor of Trinity (*Trinity Broadcasting v. FCC*, 211 F.3d 618 (D.C. Cir. 2000)). The client is very happy.

May 18, 2000: Paul Crouch, the CEO of Trinity, writes a letter of support to the Committee.

May 19, 2000: My nomination is supposed to be brought up on Monday. There is a lot of activity preparing talking points. However, Senator Feingold is lining up Democratic votes to oppose the confirmation of Smith for the Federal Election Commission. This could anger the Republicans and derail the agreement to bring me up.

May 23, 2000: Lott is going to vote against my nomination. The Chamber is concerned, as this might sway other Republican senators. There is floor debate on my nomination. Smith opposes my nomination to be a "District Judge" even though I "might turn out to be one of the greatest judges in the history of the world." I am a judicial activist who has represented People for the American Way in suing the "Texas" Board of Education for teaching that evolution be taught "as only one of several explanations of the origins of mankind." Also, because "Terrorists were represented pro bono by Mr. Dyk." Accuracy is not Smith's strong suit. The only other opposition is voiced by Sessions who argues at length that there is no need for a twelfth judge on the Federal Circuit. He does not oppose me because I am not a "good lawyer" but because I will "burden the taxpayers with $1 million a year for the rest of his life." I think it is worth it. Many Republicans do not.[16]

May 24, 2000: Around four o'clock, I sit in the fourth-floor conference room at Jones Day to watch C-SPAN. Sally, our son and others join me. Finally, my nomination is brought up. The vote is 74 to 25 in favor of my confirmation. We drink champagne, and I receive congratulations. I feel more relief than exhilaration.

That evening, Sally and I have dinner with friends. They apparently think that I was confirmed for the D.C. Circuit.

May 25, 2000: The president signs my commission. I visit my new colleagues. I do not know most of them. Bob Mayer, chief judge, to the *Legal Times*: "if it were me, I'd be relieved."[17] Justice Ginsburg tells me how my confirmation makes her very happy. Sally will not get a recess appointment yet since the administration still has more judges that it wants to get through. Her recess appointment does not happen until August 3.

June 9, 2000: I am sworn in at the Federal Circuit by Chief Judge Mayer. I vividly recall that, after the swearing-in, I passed through the courthouse lobby and saw workmen chiseling my name into the marble wall. More than anything else this made me feel that I was now really a federal judge. I purchase a robe at the Washington Uniform Shop, where they do not have any particular interest in selling robes to judges because this is not a frequent item. Nurses and postal workers are better customers. They have a rack of robes in the back of the store. I pick a standard Murphy robe. I hire a judicial assistant and law clerks.

August 8, 2000: I have my first sitting on the Federal Circuit. My first opinion is a dissent from denial of rehearing en banc (*Little Six, Inc. v. U.S.*, 229 F.3d 1383, October 12, 2000). The case, involving federal taxation on Indian gaming revenue, goes to the Supreme Court, which, in a related case, agrees with my dissent (*Chickasaw Nation v. United States*, 534 U.S. 84 (2001)).

September 26, 2000: I have a formal investiture ceremony at the Federal Circuit. Chief Justice Rehnquist and Justices O'Connor, Scalia, Kennedy, Souter and Ginsburg attend, and Justice Scalia administers the oath. I have various connections with him. He and I were on the *Harvard Law Review* together; Sally testified for him at his confirmation hearing, and his father and mine taught at Brooklyn College at the same time. We see each other socially occasionally. One of these times was shortly after his appointment to the Supreme Court. Scalia said the best thing about it was that, with the title justice rather than judge, he will no longer be taken for an administrative law judge. In taking the oath I am nervous and misspeak. After the oath, Scalia complains that, since I am a liberal, it is not surprising that I stumbled over the obligation to follow the Constitution. My grandson Christopher, sitting behind Justice Souter, manages to annoy him by kicking his chair. The investiture is an occasion for various people who have known me throughout my life to say nice things about me. It is an opportunity for me to thank those who helped with the nomination. Anybody who is interested will find the investiture ceremony at the first pages of the 304 Federal Third Reporter.

October 2000: I attend my 40th reunion at Harvard Law School. Larry Silberman has researched our class and found that we have the most federal appellate judges (six) in any class in the history of the school. He suggests a panel at the reunion of the six of us, but Larry later concludes that he is irked at Harvard Law School for some reason and does not attend. The moderator of the panel keeps referring to me as being appointed to the D.C. Circuit, despite efforts by me and others to correct him. In a meeting with Dean Clark, one of my classmates asks why Harvard Law School does not have a patent professor. Clark is dismissive. "Patent law, animal rights law. We can't satisfy everyone." As of this writing, Harvard Law School still does not have a full-time traditional patent professor on the permanent faculty.

Now 20 years later, 20 of the 25 Republicans who voted against me are gone from the Senate. Jeff Sessions gave up his Senate seat in 2017 to serve as President Trump's attorney general until 2018. His confirmation, while appreciably shorter than mine, was more newsworthy.[18] Dick Linn and I became good friends on the court. He took senior status in October 2012 and has moved to Florida. I am active in the Federal Circuit Bar Association. Kagan, whose nomination to the D.C. Circuit failed, became solicitor general and then Supreme Court justice. Of the active judges when I joined the court, all but two have either taken senior status or left the bench.

More than twenty years after the fact, I remain puzzled as to why so much energy on both sides went into the question of whether or not I should be confirmed. Contrast the way judges are appointed in other countries: In Canada when judges are appointed, they cease to practice and take the bench immediately after the selection. Opposing Canadian counsel in one of the cases I participated in did exactly that, and I was envious. After all, my 20 years' experience shows that any individual judge has only a limited effect on the development of the law. My work is not as important as the controversy over my confirmation would suggest. I also continue to be struck by the amount of confusion that surrounds the nomination process, and the amount of horse trading that is involved in getting judges brought up for a vote.

The most encouraging thing about the whole process is that there were a lot of people who care about doing the right thing, and who were not prevented from doing so by political considerations, including a number of people on the staffs of Republican senators, such as Manus Cooney, Mike O'Neill, Lee Liberman Otis, and there are many people outside of the Senate (and elsewhere) who spent a great deal of time and energy supporting my nomination for no particular personal gain to themselves. I remain grateful to all of them, and without their help, my nomination would never have gotten through.

I never took the criticism that I received during the process personally, nor did I think it was meant personally. That was reflected in the fact that none of the opposing Senators seemed to want to get to know me: none met with me. It was just that I was caught up in a war between the Democrats and the Republicans. Nominees for judgeships were collateral damage.

While it certainly was always a possibility that I would not be confirmed, I thought that if that occurred, I would not be devastated. If it happened, I was prepared to continue with my career in private practice, which I enjoyed. If you are nominated at a time when the president and the Senate are not of the same party, you have to accept the fact that confirmation might not happen. Allen Snyder, whose nomination for the D.C. Circuit failed, had a different experience. Allen was apparently devastated by not being confirmed, though he had been told by many people, exceptionally qualified as he was, that it was never going to happen. He had a notable career thereafter in public service. Perhaps, if I had not been confirmed, I too would have been devastated despite my outward calm during the process.

In the course of the process, I received a lot of compliments from people, some a little over the top, comparing me to Job in terms of my endurance. I think that my ability to be restrained and contained about what was going on was enormously helpful to me ultimately in achieving a favorable result.

It is interesting to speculate what impact the trials and tribulations of the confirmation process might have on judicial performance. I think that in the case of a couple of Supreme Court nominees who were ultimately confirmed, the experience was a bruising one. It may have affected their jurisprudence. In my own case, I do not think that the confirmation process and the difficulty of getting confirmed has had any influence on my decision-making as a federal judge.

# Notes

1    "Judicial Nomination Statistics and Analysis: U.S. Circuit and District Courts 1977–2020," *Congressional Research Service*, 2021, 15, https://crsreports.congress.gov/product/pdf/R/R45622.

2    The White House ended cooperation with the ABA during the nomination process under Presidents George W. Bush and Donald Trump. While President Obama restored the relationship, President Biden announced in early 2021 that it would not restore the ABA's role in the vetting process before nominations. Charlie Savage, "Biden Won't Restore Bar Associations' Role in Vetting Judges," *The New York Times*, February 5, 2021, https://www.nytimes.com/2021/02/05/us/politics/biden-american-bar-association-judges.html.

3    Richard A. Posner, *Reflections on Judging* (Cambridge, MA: Harvard University Press, 2013), 27.

4    Hearings on Confirmation of Appointees to the Federal Judiciary Before the Senate Committee on the Judiciary, 105th Cong. 563–64 (1998).

5    Mary Kay Linge, "Senate GOP Is Pushing Through Trump's Judicial Nominees," *The New York Post*, November 17, 2018, https://nypost.com/2018/11/17/senate-gop-is-pushing-through-trumps-judicial-nominees/.

6    144 Cong. Rec. S23915 (daily ed. October 7, 1998).

7    Bruce Fein, "Giving Secrecy a Bad Name," *Washington Times*, 1992, F1.

8    H. Otis Bilodeau, "The Federal Circuit's Favor," *Legal Times*, May 10, 1999.

9    Hearing on the Nomination of Sally Katzen, to Be Deputy Director for Management, Office of Management and Budget Before the Senate Committee on Governmental Affairs, 106th Cong.14 (1999).

10   Stephen Barr, "OMB Nominee Gets Earful at Confirmation Hearing," *The Washington Post*, September 16, 1999, https://www.washingtonpost.com/archive/politics/1999/09/16/omb-nominee-gets-earful-at-confirmation-hearing/263f4d6a-dcf3-4c03-8927-908f50c552ed/.

11   145 Cong. Rec. S22006 (daily ed. September 21, 1999).

12   Roger Clegg, "Civil Rights Lite," *Legal Times*, November 22, 1999.

13   "Not for Ourselves Alone," Public Broadcasting System, last accessed: October 18, 2021, https://www.pbs.org/kenburns/not-for-ourselves-alone/.

14   145 Cong. Rec. S31050-51 (daily ed. November 19, 1999).

15   146 Cong. Rec. S2147 (daily ed. March 7, 2000).

16   146 Cong. Rec. S8791-94 (daily ed. May 23, 2000).

17   Jonathan Ringel, "Still Standing; He Finally Takes a Seat," *Legal Times*, June 5, 2000.

18   Protestors interrupted the confirmation hearing of Senator Sessions in January 2017. Ailsa Chang, "Protestors Interrupt Confirmation Hearing for Sen. Sessions as Attorney General," *NPR*, January 10, 2017, https://www.npr.org/2017/01/10/509139945/protesters-interrupt-confirmation-hearing-for-sen-sessions-as-attorney-general.

# Chapter 11

# LIFE AS A FEDERAL JUDGE, 2000–THE PRESENT

I left the practice of law in the twentieth century and began as a judge in the twenty-first century. When I was sworn in as a circuit judge on June 9, 2000, I was 63 years old. I was secure financially. My three children had been, or would be, able to go through college without any debt, and the two older ones were employed and self-supporting. Sally, who had had her bout with breast cancer, was then finishing her treatment and on the road to recovery. Because of my age, I had no realistic ambition of doing anything else in government other than sitting on the court. True, I would be eligible for senior status or full retirement in 10 years and could in theory reenter private practice or serve as a mediator or arbitrator. I had seen what that world was like for retired judges in private practice, having spent time working with George Pratt, who retired from the Second Circuit, and Charles Clark, who retired from the Fifth Circuit. That was not for me. I note that four judges on our court left the court for greener pastures that perhaps turned out to be not as green as they thought they would be. Thus, I came to the bench knowing that I would remain for the rest of my professional life—a prospect that I found most congenial.

Like all new judges, I felt a profound sense of privilege—the opportunity to contribute to American jurisprudence and to decide cases fairly and pragmatically within the bounds of precedent. The feeling of responsibility was enhanced by our location overlooking Lafayette Park and the White House.

Any new circuit judge coming from private practice is aware that there are major differences from the world that he or she has just left. There is life tenure (unlike most state appellate courts) and fixed compensation. There is no client to establish the lodestar of a desired outcome. A judge no longer has to be concerned about where the work is coming from and whether there will be work to do.

There is enough time to address the issues properly and, apart from the need to show up on time for oral argument, few deadlines (the lack of deadlines is not as beneficial as one might think; judges sometimes can take years to produce an opinion that should take a couple of months). When you take the bench, in large part you give up your right to free expression on political and other controversial issues, but it is a small price to pay. As an appellate judge, in the words of Judge Coffin, you become a "media cipher,"[1] and you join a world where life is governed by seniority and precedent.

I will discuss other features of judicial life later in the chapter, but by way of background, I begin by addressing what I will call the common approach to the process of judging, that is, how federal appellate judges typically approach the task of deciding cases.

Federal circuit courts function as the intermediate appellate courts between the 94 federal district and territorial courts (and multiple agencies) and the Supreme Court. In all, there are 13 circuits, with the jurisdiction of the 11 numbered circuits and the D.C. Circuit defined geographically and our court uniquely having a nationwide specialized subject-matter jurisdiction. All courts of appeals have multiple members ranging in size from the First Circuit (six active judges) to the Ninth Circuit (29 active judges). Each court has senior judges who sit part-time. There are now around 175 active Federal circuit judges and nearly 120 in senior status. These courts normally sit in panels of three. The composition of the panels and the cases assigned to the panels is randomly determined.

Typically, briefs are distributed to the panels some weeks before argument, although oral argument is not guaranteed. In the cases that are argued, the judges read the briefs one or more times before oral argument. The judges are well prepared for oral argument and ask questions of counsel. The judges are not mailing it in. Every active judge has four law clerks, most of whom are employed for one-year terms. The clerks mostly do not come directly from law school but have one or more years' experience clerking at the district court level or at a firm before they begin. The clerks prepare a bench memo for the judge before oral argument, summarizing the briefs, record and prior precedent. The presiding (senior active) judge on the panel (if in the majority) makes the writing assignments to the other judges. The opinion may be precedential (binding on future panels) or non-precedential (not binding) and describes the basis for the court's disposition. The clerks (for the judge who is assigned to write the case) prepare a draft opinion. The judge revises the opinion and circulates it to the other judges on the panel. The other judges vote to join the opinion or dissent.

As we will see, various circuits and individual judges (including myself) depart from this model and have their own traditions and procedures, but it is I think an accurate summary of what is typical. What is clear is that almost without exception federal judges work very hard, are highly ethical (despite the recent disclose that a significant number of district judges failed to follow recusal obligations resulting from stock ownership)[2] and avoid ex parte contacts with the litigants or their counsel. Despite an apparent public perception that judges, like legislators, engage in horse trading (I will support you on this one, if you support me on the other), I think this never occurs. In my experience, the discussion about each case is separate and uninfluenced by positions on other cases.

This description of the common framework leaves important questions unanswered. How much influence do clerks have in deciding cases and over the content of opinions? To what extent do judges discuss the cases with other judges before oral argument? How much influence do judges have on each other? Are judges collegial or antagonistic? Do they socialize with each other outside of court? To what extent do judges come to cases with a predetermined view of the outcome (e.g., criminal convictions should be affirmed)? What guides the judge in decision-making apart from statutes, regulations and prior precedent? Chief Justice Roberts, during his confirmation hearings, famously said that he viewed himself as an umpire calling balls and strikes.[3] Any baseball fan knows that different umpires have quite different strike zones. Each judge must ask: what is my strike zone?

These questions are difficult to answer. Judges are generally secretive about these issues, and the available evidence is fragmentary and anecdotal. As one distinguished judge noted, "for the most part, judges in recent times have largely left to others the writing about their craft and calling."[4] Legal empiricists have spent a substantial amount of energy and thought trying to model precisely how judges reach their decisions. In my view, their work has little value. Although I do have answers to some of these questions based on more than twenty years on the bench, sitting on both my own court and on the First Circuit, my knowledge is incomplete, and my assumptions may be inaccurate. What I can do is describe how I operate and how what I do diverges from the common model. Judge Coffin, when a judge with the First Circuit, wrote two books (14 years apart) describing his judicial process.[5] His approach has both interesting similarities and some dissimilarities from mine.

## The Federal Circuit's Docket and Jurisdiction

As courts of appeals go, the Federal Circuit is the new kid on the block. Our court was created in 1982, in large part to consolidate all patent cases in a single appellate court and thus to create greater uniformity in decision-making. Unlike other courts of appeals whose jurisdiction is geographic, our court has nationwide jurisdiction of specified types of civil cases. We have no criminal cases.[6] On paper our docket is diverse, and it was certainly designed that way by Congress, which did not want a specialist court.[7] In addition to patent cases, we have cases involving monetary claims against the government other than tort claims (that is, contract claims, bid protests, takings cases), international trade (dumping), customs classification, veterans benefits, government personnel cases and vaccine cases (compensating people who are injured by common vaccines). Despite the congressional design, in recent years, our docket has been dominated by patent cases. When I joined the court in 2000, about 30 percent of our docket was patent cases. It is now over twice that, and

I have estimated that the time devoted to patent cases is probably on the order of 80 percent.[8] The nature of our docket makes us somewhat isolated from the other courts of appeals and from the Supreme Court. Our docket is nonetheless just as interesting, perhaps more interesting, than most circuit dockets. We are blessed by having an excellent court staff, headed now by Pete Marksteiner and earlier by Jan Horbaly.

Despite the patent-heavy nature of our docket, the prior experience of our judges is diverse. By my count, 10 of our 19 judges (active and senior) came to the bench with significant patent experience. Two had been corporate patent counsel (Newman and Lourie); one had been a professor specializing in patent law (Moore); one had been a district judge, handling significant patent cases (O'Malley); one had been the solicitor of the Patent and Trademark Office (PTO) (Chen); three had primarily practiced patent law (Linn, Stoll and Cunningham); and two others had some patent litigation experience (Taranto and myself). Of the nine with little or no experience, one had been a claims court judge (Mayer). Another had been the deputy director of the Commercial Litigation Branch of the Justice Department Civil Division (Hughes). Two had significant experience in international trade law (Reyna and Wallach). The other five had important experience on the Senate Judiciary Committee and at the National Labor Relations Board (NLRB) (Prost), at Justice (Shall and Bryson), law teaching (Plager) or private practice (Clevenger). All are both very intellectually capable and diligent.

Patent law is unusual because so many of the issues are framed as legal issues, encouraging routine appeals since appellate courts give de novo review to legal issues. There are primarily two issues in a patent case: (1) does the accused product or method *infringe* the patent claims (requiring an interpretation of claim scope), and (2) are the patent claims *invalid* for various reasons, the most common being that some earlier inventor got there first (anticipation) or some earlier inventor would easily have gotten there first (obviousness) or the subject matter is not patentable in the first place because it is an abstract idea or natural phenomenon (known as a Section 101 issue). Patent protection has been, and continues to be, an important driver of innovation, but issuing and litigating unwarranted patents can stifle legitimate competition.

Severe problems exist because the PTO issues hundreds of thousands of patents each year, often with inadequate review, leaving to courts and other post-issuance proceedings by the PTO to sort out patent eligibility and patent validity. These cases come to us from a wide variety of sources—primarily from the district courts and the PTO in post-issuance review proceedings (where the PTO has been asked to revisit questions of patent validity). Patent cases in many instances are one-off cases. In those cases, our job is to figure out the scope of the patent claims and to address infringement and invalidity.

While important to the particular litigants, we render many decisions that have little consequence for future cases. Others have considerable consequence. We decide many cases that establish the rules for patent infringement and invalidity. We have also had a number of cases in the last few years involving constitutional and statutory interpretation issues related to the America Invents Act (AIA) (Pub. L. No. 112-29, 125 Stat. 284 (2011)). The AIA was passed in 2011 and altered the patent system from a "first to invent" to a "first inventor to file" system, eliminated priority contests and allowed post-issuance patent challenges at the PTO.[9] A number of the cases challenging the post-issuance PTO review process have gone to the Supreme Court which, so far, with the exception of a case involving the appointment process for administrative patent judges (*United States v. Arthrex, Inc.*, 594 U.S. ——, 1415 S.Ct. 1970 (2021)), has generally rejected the challenges.

I have written a couple of law review articles suggesting that Congress should give us a more diverse jurisdiction, in accordance with the original design.[10] Most of my colleagues would agree that we would be better off if we had a more diverse docket, including criminal jurisdiction. In the early years of the court, Congress did give us additional civil jurisdiction, such as jurisdiction over veterans' cases. In recent years, there have been no non-patent additions to our jurisdiction. The most prominent proposal had been to give us jurisdiction over all immigration cases. This was quite impractical. Even though the proposal would have given us three additional judges (15 active judges instead of the existing 12), the legislation itself recognized the impossibility of processing all those immigration cases with three-judge panels, providing that many of the appeals would be heard by a single judge. There were objections from the bar and from our court, and, eventually, the proposal died.[11]

One of the reasons, I think, that there has not been a push to give us additional jurisdiction is that many other courts of appeals do not have enough cases. That is certainly true of the D.C. Circuit and various other circuits as well. There would probably be some reluctance by those courts to surrender jurisdiction. At the time that our court was created in 1982, one of the proposals was to give us exclusive copyright jurisdiction, but that fell through when other courts of appeals objected because they liked the copyright cases. While occasionally we now get copyright cases (such as the recent case, *Oracle America, Inc. v. Google Inc.*, 750 F.3d 1339 (Fed. Cir. 2014), which went to the Supreme Court (*Google LLC v. Oracle America, Inc.*, 593 U.S. ——, 141 S. Ct. 1183 (2021)), it is always because the copyright case is paired with a patent claim in the first instance. Under our authorizing statute, we have exclusive jurisdiction over any case that includes a patent claim (28 U.S.C. § 1295(a)(1)). We do have very interesting non-patent cases, some resulting from our exclusive jurisdiction over takings cases and other monetary claims against the government. I enjoy the diversity and wish there were more.

## The Work of the Court

Each year, I, like my colleagues, meet with all the law clerks to discuss our history and experiences on the court. In one recent meeting, I mentioned that, unlike private law practice, there are few good stories about the work of the court. I then corrected myself to say that there are quite a few stories about the work of the court that would be worth retelling, but I will not repeat them. I remember my experience with my colleague, Dan Friedman, who had a long and distinguished career at the Office of the Solicitor General. He had been on our predecessor court, the Court of Claims, and continued his remarkable career on the Federal Circuit. At lunch Dan would tell us stories of his time in the Office of the Solicitor General and his time on the court during its earlier days. When the Federal Circuit Historical Society decided to do an oral history of Dan, I asked if I could participate in the interview so that I would be able to ask him questions to bring out the many stories that he told his colleagues. I joined the interview and asked these questions, but Dan never answered them. The stories were forever lost.

I think there is an important lesson from that experience—that is, that the confidentiality of the court experience to a great extent takes precedence over the demands of history, at least in the years you are a sitting judge. The stories of internal court conflicts are best not recorded. So, I have followed Dan Friedman's example, leaving some of the best stories unrecorded.

There nonetheless were events appropriate to record. The most significant event during my time on the court was the 9/11 attacks. That morning I was driving to work with my colleague Ray Clevenger. We heard (on the radio) that a plane had flown into a World Trade Center building. Assuming that this had been an accident similar to the incident many years earlier with the Empire State building, we continued on to work. After we arrived, it became apparent that this was a terrorist attack, and we could see the Pentagon burning across the river. A secret service agent, golf bag in tow (containing surface-to-air missiles) charged up to our roof. It seemed like a good time to go home. The drive home was surreal. It was as though nothing had happened. Minutes later Washington became a giant traffic jam, and it took many people hours to get home. We went to work the next day, though I recall that some clerks took a couple of days before they felt comfortable returning. The COVID experience I treat at the end of the chapter.

## Law Clerks and Judicial Assistants

As noted, one of my first steps after I was confirmed was to hire chambers staff. At that time, each judge was entitled to three law clerks (in later years, four) and a judicial assistant. My first clerks were Nathan Judish, John Cuddihy and Troy Grabow. Nathan had previously clerked for Judge Selya on the First Circuit, so at least one of us had some experience in a court of appeals chambers. My first judicial assistant was Vivian McCallum, who stayed with me for a few years. She was excellent at her work; however, she made my life difficult because she loved to bake and brought cake, brownies and cookies to the office on a regular basis. She never ate her own baking, but the rest of us did, with the attendant weight gain. She and the man she later married, Ray Dearie, a distinguished judge on the Eastern District of New York, have remained good friends. Henrietta Jessie has most ably served with dedication as my assistant for over a decade now, and I dread her impending retirement.

The selection of law clerks is one of the most difficult and important aspect of any judge's job. I have had really outstanding clerks. As Justice Scalia was quoted as saying in regard to hiring clerks, "you can't make a mistake. I mean, one dud will ruin your year."[12] I have been lucky; I have not had dud clerks. The great majority of my clerks have been exceptional. But the "one and done" approach is beneficial, I find, because the clerk's enthusiasm often begins to fade after a year, and in those rare cases where the clerk is not exceptional, it is best that the clerk leaves after a year. My clerks have gone on to clerk in other circuits and district courts and one (Ruthanne Deutsch) on the Supreme Court. Many teach at leading law schools (including Stanford and Columbia). Others have gone into government or public interest firms or have become partners in leading private law firms. Most notably, one of my former clerks, Tiffany Cunningham, has been appointed to serve on the Federal Circuit, an exceptionally good choice. We are all thrilled to have her as a colleague. She is working hard to call me by my first name rather than referring to me as "judge." A list of my clerks with their current employment appears as an appendix.

The process of selecting clerks has changed somewhat over the years. The Judicial Conference at times has tried to encourage judges to agree on the process for selecting clerks. During my early time on the court, there were voluntary guidelines. Judges were not supposed to interview law clerks until after their second year in law school. Judges were to begin the process of contacting the clerks for interviews on a specified day, start their interviews on a specified day and so on and so forth. This led to unpleasant chaos during the hiring season, including manipulation of the process by both judges and prospective clerks. After a number of years, so many judges were departing from the guidelines that the guidelines became meaningless and were abandoned. More recently, the Judicial Conference has tried once again, with a less detailed process. Basically, judges are still asked to agree not to interview prospective law clerks until after the second year in law school and give offerees time to consider the offer (no "exploding offers"), but there is no effort to micromanage the rest of the process. This seems to have worked reasonably well.

There has been quite a change over the past 20 years in the kinds of applicants selected for law clerk positions on our court and other courts as well. When I first joined the court, most law clerks came to the court immediately after law school or after a district court clerkship or a clerkship on another circuit. There were occasions when law clerks had a year or two of law firm experience, but that was unusual. The law firms did not like lawyers to join the firm and then leave to clerk. That has changed. On our court, many of the law clerks now have several years of post-law school experience before coming to the court, often having been in private practice for two, three, four or five years. This can be quite useful to the judge because the clerk will have been trained in private practice to be a better lawyer, a better writer and researcher and hence a more useful clerk. I have, by and large, avoided hiring clerks with more than a year or two of practice experience. My goal has been to hire clerks immediately out of law school or, more recently, after a year or two of firm work or a clerkship elsewhere. I am now hiring for two years in the future. The less experienced the clerk, the less likely the clerk will be afflicted with what I call "the junior judge syndrome"—that is, forgetting the clerk's appropriate role. More importantly, I enjoy the teaching function and helping them learn to be better writers, better researchers and better lawyers. My relationships with my clerks past and present has been one of the great rewards of being a judge. Having 80 some clerks is like having 80 or so additional adult children.

The process of hiring clerks involves using a system called OSCAR, which is an online system where law students can submit applications and easily distribute them to a large number of judges. In my early days on the court, many of the applications came in hard copy by mail or FedEx, but now almost all of the clerkship applications come through OSCAR. Because it is so easy to apply, there are many applications. I leave to my current law clerks the task of sorting the applicants, showing me only highly promising candidates. A decade or so ago, I would interview more people than I had slots available. Now I have fewer interviews and almost never interview candidates without making an offer. The process is painstaking. I read the applications, call law school professor and law firm references, and the applicant is interviewed by my current clerks and by my former clerk, Ruthanne Deutsch. The purpose of the interviews is to identify a problem in attitude or work ethic, which is infrequent. I have hired many clerks from Harvard and Yale but also multiple clerks from Stanford, Michigan, Georgetown, George Washington, Chicago, Northwestern, Texas, Duke, NYU and Columbia, and individual clerks from schools as disparate as Brigham Young, Minnesota and Vanderbilt. My clerks have been diverse in other ways as well. About one quarter have been minorities, and they have come from poor as well as rich families, small towns as well as big cities.

I have always looked for students who were at the top of their class, but I have not been as insistent as many of my colleagues in hiring clerks with a science background, though I have had quite a few science PhDs. In the beginning, I did not even require that the applicants have a particular interest in or knowledge of patent law. Now that patent cases have become a much larger proportion of our docket, I do generally insist that the candidates have taken patent law in law school whether or not they plan a patent law career. Patent law is sufficiently complicated that it is hard to learn on the job. With rare exceptions, I do not hire interns. Competition among judges to hire particularly exceptionally well-qualified clerks can sometimes be unpleasant.

In my early years on the court, most of the work was done in chambers. Working on Saturday was common. I come in on Saturdays only rarely now given my ability to work at home and the ability of the clerks to work at home as a result of new technology. I probably work five or six hours on cases routinely every weekend. When I was a law clerk on the Supreme Court, Saturday work in chambers was routine, and the justices would take the clerks to lunch, almost every week. As pay back for the generosity of Warren, Reed and Burton when I clerked, and for the very hard work by my current clerks, I take my clerks to lunch after the conclusion of each argument week and when they started and finished their clerkships. We have a law clerks outing each year at our house, and also invite the clerks to our year-end holiday party. However, COVID has changed much of this for the time being.

## The Judicial Process

Having assembled my chambers staff, the next question was: how to process the cases? Typically, our court sits in the first full week of every month, and the obligation of each judge is to volunteer for 40 sittings a year. In general, that means that I sign up for four sittings a week for 10 months of the year with four argued cases a day—160 cases a year in theory, but judges do not always get four days each month and cases sometimes drop off the calendar. With nonargued cases added to the total, an active judge usually participates in about 150 cases a year. I write about fifty opinions, almost one per week. I always have elected, with few exceptions, not to sit in July and August, and I have always been able to take vacation while I am a judge, something which is increasingly difficult in law firm life. Unfortunately, even for a judge, as a result of smartphones and e-mail, it is impossible to get away entirely. When

I am on vacation, I still have to check my phone several times a day and respond to messages, except on weekends and holidays.

The briefs become available to the judges six weeks before argument. Before the briefs are distributed, each judge has advised the clerk's office of any conflicts, resulting from stock ownership or relationships with one of the parties or the lawyers. The cases are assigned randomly to the panels, and the judges are assigned randomly to the panels. In the past, it was not always the case that the random approach was honored, as I discuss later. As far as I know, in the time that I have been on the court, there has been nothing but random assignment with few exceptions, such as assigning a judge to a new case when the judge heard an earlier version of the same case, which I think is important to continuity in decision-making.

I early on concluded that I would not make the work assignments for the clerks, but instead I allow the clerks to decide who would work on each case. After the arguments are completed for the previous month, the clerks sit down and divide the cases among themselves. The process of preparing the upcoming cases for argument varies from chambers to chambers. In general, I do not look at the briefs until the arguments from the previous month are completed. In most chambers, the clerks read the briefs before the upcoming oral argument and prepare a bench memo. In the Ninth Circuit and perhaps in a couple of others, the cases are divided up in advance of argument, and the assigned judge prepares a bench memo for the other judges on the panel, with the memo-writing judge the presumptive author of the opinion—in my view a bad approach that discourages independent decision-making by each panel member.

I had my clerks prepare bench memos for me my first month or so that I was on the court, but soon decided that bench memos summarizing the parties' arguments were not useful to me. Because I was going to read the briefs anyway, I did not need summaries of the arguments, and did not need recommendations from the clerks as to how I should decide the case. Instead, I decided to prepare a bench memo for my clerks based on my first quick read of the briefs. This memo is usually one or two pages, single-spaced, summarizing the case and the issues, telling the clerks my tentative decision on each issue, and asking them to do legal or record research on selected questions. This work by the clerks is essential in complex cases where understanding the technology can be a major challenge and the parties usually take directly opposite positions as to what the record shows as to the facts and what the statutes, regulations and cases show as to the law. The clerks have to become conversant in the technology and sort out the conflicting positions. Based on my bench memo and preliminary discussion of the case, typically they have a substantial task ahead of them to provide me the information I request. I also ask either my judicial assistant or the clerks to supply me with copies of the relevant cases so that I can read them before the argument.

After the clerks finish their memoranda, and I have read them, I begin my second read of the briefs. The result is that I read over thirty thousand pages of briefs each year. With the benefit of those memoranda, I always find additional things that I had previously missed. When I finish my second read, I again discuss the case with the assigned clerk and my discussions with that clerk continue up to the moment that I would go down to be robed for the oral argument.

Except in rare cases, I do not involve other clerks in the preparation process. In some chambers, all the clerks sit down together with the judge and discuss all the cases. I cannot understand how this is productive because a clerk cannot meaningfully contribute to the discussion of a case without reading the briefs. It always seemed to me impossible to have all the clerks read all the briefs of all the cases in addition to their other work.

Some judges want to discuss the upcoming cases with their colleagues before the oral argument, which is usually done on a one-on-one basis. Other judges never want to do that. I have found those discussions to be quite useful, and I often learn about issues in the case that I had not seen before. Sometimes I have learned about authority that other chambers have uncovered, of which I was not aware.

An unusual feature of our court, which as far as I know does not occur in other circuits, is the meeting of panel members' law clerks before the oral argument. These law clerk meetings usually do not happen with respect to submitted cases—that is, cases submitted on the briefs without oral argument, and they almost never happen with respect to en banc cases—that is, cases heard by the full court rather than a panel. In argued panel cases, the meetings among law clerks are fairly common, occurring in the majority of difficult cases. I am not a fan of those meetings, because I think it tends to suggest that the law clerks are junior judges who have a collective role in deciding the cases. Admittedly, there are benefits. Because so much of our docket consists of patent cases, often with difficult technology, it is a challenge for the judges to understand the technology, and that is necessary before they can address the legal issues in the case. Many judges have law clerks who are experts in different technology areas, and they can help explain the technology to the other clerks, enabling them to help educate their judges.

Another useful aspect of the clerks' meetings is that the judges get a window into the other panel judges' thinking about the case before oral argument. Often the clerks will say that they do not know the views of their judges, but I think it is generally understood that the clerks' comments do reflect what their judges are focusing on and concerned about at that stage. I certainly never send my clerks to one of those clerks' meeting without making sure that the views they are going to express are compatible with my own views.

Oral argument is the favorite part of the job for most judges. Unlike most other circuits, we hold oral argument in virtually every counseled case. We are what is known as a "hot bench." We are well prepared and ask a lot of questions of counsel and, indirectly, of each other.

As far as I know, after argument in all circuits, the three judges take off their robes and sit down at a table in a conference room adjoining the courtroom (unless one or more of the judges is participating remotely—a very rare event in our court). They then discuss and decide the case. The process varies from circuit to circuit. Our court has always had a very formal process for discussion and voting. The judges sit in assigned seats according to seniority, and the case discussion and voting begin with the judge with the least seniority speaking first, the next judge in order of seniority speaking second and finally the presiding judge speaking last. The position of the junior judge can be a position of considerable influence in some cases, because, in general, judges do not like to have disagreements. In our court, the presiding judge, if in the majority, decides who gets the writing assignment for an opinion. For the first few years, I did not preside on any cases, and I was almost always the junior judge on the case. Now in most instances, I do preside. In our court there has always been plenty of work to go around, and the presiding judges are often generous with the junior judges, assigning them interesting cases to write. In the First Circuit, the process is quite different. There is not assigned seating or ordered discussion. The judges just sit around a table and discuss the cases. The discussion is called a "semble" rather than a conference, and the assignment process is less structured. The presiding judges have always been generous to me as a visitor.

At the conference in our court, the judges must decide whether the opinion of the court should be precedential (i.e., binding on later panels) or non-precedential (not binding). Another alternative exists in our court that is called Rule 36, referring to Rule 36 of our circuit rules. A Rule 36 disposition results in an order that says affirmed without opinion. That is a different approach than is taken in most of the other courts of appeals where they typically write an opinion in all cases. Our court has been criticized by the bar for using Rule 36, but our court really does not have the time to write opinions in every case and does not want to delegate the task to staff. As noted earlier, unlike most other courts of appeals, where only a minority of cases is orally argued, we grant oral argument in all cases where parties are represented by counsel, so that the lawyers have the opportunity to actually appear before us and address our questions and concerns. Having had that opportunity to argue, it is less important to give them a written opinion.

The general rule has been that Rule 36 affirmances are reserved for cases that have little merit and where a written opinion would serve little purpose. But I think there is a concern in the bar that sometimes our court's Rule 36 disposition is used to paper over differences among judges on significant issues. There are other disadvantages to the Rule 36 dispositions. For example, a Rule 36 disposition can make it difficult to determine the basis for the decision where there are multiple possible grounds for affirmance. In these circumstances, it is impossible to apply issue preclusion to later cases.

After the conference, the judge with the writing assignment prepares a draft opinion. There is no deadline for preparing an opinion, though if a judge gets too far behind on assigned cases, the judge may be precluded from sitting until the backlog is resolved. There is a great deal of variability on how quickly judges circulate a draft for vote. I have always tried to get my draft opinions out within 90 days, but I have not always been successful.

When I have an opinion to write, I prepare an outline for my clerks describing how the panel decided to resolve the case, and my own views as to how the opinion should be organized and how specific issues should be addressed. The law clerk then prepares a draft opinion. The law clerk assigned to help with the opinion is almost always the same law clerk who helped me prepare for argument. The only time that a different law clerk works on the opinion is when the initially assigned law clerk is too busy to produce a draft in a reasonable amount of time.

Working with law clerks on opinions can be tricky. On the one hand, the clerks are indispensable. They are valuable in helping me to understand the technology. Also, I cannot do all the original legal and record research myself. On the other hand, I want the opinion to be mine and not my clerk's. Judge Posner has written frequently on the subject of the clerks' role in opinion writing, and has urged that judges should write the first drafts.[13] I do not agree, and can point to many examples of judge-written opinions that are simply confusing because the judge wrote the first draft. To be sure, the judge has to make the opinion his or her own, but this does not mean doing the first draft. I have two reasons for having my clerk do an initial draft of the opinion. First, I avoid falling in love with my own first draft. If you do the initial draft, it is harder to revise it, and to rethink the case in the process of revision. Second, I can do some research and I can provide leads for my clerks, but I cannot do all the research myself. There is inevitably a good deal of both legal and factual research to be done beyond that done for argument. I find that the most effective way of having the law clerk present that research material to me is in the form of a draft opinion. That focuses both the clerk and me. I always tell my clerks that the most important task that they have is doing legal and factual research and helping to ensure accuracy. The best lesson for incoming clerks is to recount the story about Dean Acheson's work as a clerk for Justice Brandeis. Acheson made a mistake. Brandeis chided him: "Please remember that your function is to correct my errors, not to introduce errors of your own."[14]

There is a tendency on the part of all law clerks to sit in front of their computers and do full text searches, which are quite valuable, but can be confining if you are not entirely sure as to the nature or dimensions of the problem. I am a great lover of books, and books line the walls of my chambers, the hall leading to my chambers, and even my study. I always encourage my clerks to use these books, or better yet, go to the library and get a hard copy of treatises, statutes and regulations and work with those, so they can flip around and look at different parts that may not initially seem relevant, but often provide important context or clues.

It takes my clerk anywhere from one week to three weeks to produce an initial draft. When the clerk finishes the draft of an opinion, I then review it promptly. One of my former clerks told me that I was the only boss he ever had that promptly responded to the work that he produced for review. I read the draft and communicate further ideas about organization or additional research that needs to be done. I then ask for a second draft and sometimes a third draft from the clerk. When the opinion is complete in terms of research and organization, I begin rewriting the draft. The objective is to make the opinion mine rather than my law clerk's. Much to the distress of several generations of clerks, I do this largely in handwriting. If I have long inserts for the opinion, I will type them on the word processor, but, by and large, I take a triple-spaced version of the draft opinion and add text, revise text or move things around by handwriting. Eventually, most of the clerks learn to read my handwriting sufficiently so that they are able to transcribe it (or if not ask me to decipher it), though, as I said earlier, there have been instances in which handwriting transcription mistakes have found their way into the official reporter.

I usually go through many drafts. At a minimum, in a precedential opinion, there are half a dozen, and sometimes as many as 20 drafts, until I am satisfied with the work product. As Paul Freund said of Justice Brandeis, "his opinions went through dozens, even scores of painstaking revisions."[15] If you took the final product and ran a redline against the clerk's first draft, you would in almost all cases see a sea of red. At that point, I do what I consider to be the worst part of my job, which is to read the briefs in the case for a third time. While that is very unpleasant, it is absolutely necessary. In virtually every case, I find issues or authorities on that third reading that have not been addressed in the opinion and that require further revisions. With all these revisions, my desk is constantly cluttered. I remind myself that a Nobel Prize resulted from a cluttered desk.[16]

When I have finished preparing the draft opinion, I then get together with all four of my clerks to discuss it. This discussion with the full complement of clerks is quite useful in clearing up language in the draft, which might not be understandable to someone who has not been working through the case. Most important, it gives the other clerks an opportunity to challenge my reasoning and the way I have resolved the case. I wish they would do more of that. The changes that come out of the clerks' meeting are integrated in the opinion, and then the opinion is cite checked by one of the clerks who did not work on the opinion in the first instance. I ask this clerk to do what I call an adversarial cite check. In other words, the clerk is supposed to try to find fault with the opinion—to try to turn up problems that might not have surfaced. Sometimes they seem reluctant to find fault with the research of the clerk who helped to prepare the draft.

After the cite check has been completed, and the changes based on that process have been integrated into the opinion, I circulate the opinion to my other two colleagues on the panel for vote. And again, this voting is a very formal process in our court. When opinions come in for vote from other chambers, the judge's job is to review those opinions and decide how to vote, and also to make comments to improve the opinion. My view is that comments should be limited to substance and not style, though requests for clarifying language are important and appropriate. Specific proposed language changes are more welcome than fuzzy conceptual objections. The clerk who worked on the case earlier helps me develop comments on the drafts. In joining another judge's opinion, if the opinion is significant, I will usually write something complimentary, a practice prevailing in the First Circuit.

In the majority of cases, the other judges on the case simply vote to join with no or only minor changes, or, if they disagree, vote to dissent. In other cases, the other panel members suggest more significant changes in the opinion which, in general, the authoring judge has to accommodate to get the second vote or should accommodate to make the opinion unanimous. Sometimes the authoring judge can convince a dissenting judge to join the majority opinion by making changes to the opinion, for example, by avoiding certain issues. In recent years, our court has become much better at accommodating dissenting judges so that the dissent is eliminated. When the panel has finished with the opinion and any dissenting or concurring opinions have been prepared by the other judges on the panel, the opinion, if it is to be precedential, is circulated to the full court for comment.

The period of full-court review has varied. It is currently what is called 10-day review, which means 10 working days for other judges to comment on the opinion. Such circulations are common in many other circuits. But unlike many other courts of appeals, the comments on 10-day review in our court are frequent. Most comments are minor—a suggestion to delete a sentence or rewrite a sentence in the opinion or to correct errors. Comments can often be quite helpful. But in some cases, comments reflect a substantial difference in approach. These comments can be significant and extensive, even leading to a threat that if the case is not resolved differently, or the opinion is not written differently, the objecting judge will request an en banc poll. When I first joined the court and for some years thereafter, our technical staff would review and comment on panel opinions on 10-day circulation with a view to pointing out potential conflicts with past precedent, a process with which I was uncomfortable because it seemed to delegate authority from the judges. That practice fortunately no longer prevails.

Once an opinion is issued, there is very often a petition for rehearing. Any judge can request a response to the petition or request an en banc poll. In our court en banc polls, both before opinions are issued and on petitions for rehearing, are much more common than they are in most other circuits. Under our rules, if there is an en banc poll request, before there is a majority vote for en banc, the panel can take the opinion back and revise it to try to respond to the objections of the judge or judges who asked for the en banc poll. That happens not infrequently. If the proposed revision does not satisfy the objecting judges, there can again be a poll asking the court to rehear the case en banc. The number of en banc opinions in our court has averaged several per year since 2001.[17]

In addition to the argued cases, there are what are called submitted cases (cases decided without oral argument), the vast majority of which are pro se cases—that is, cases involving individuals who are not represented by counsel. In general, we do not allow argument by pro se parties, though occasionally we have done that. I remember one case in which the pro se party was allowed to argue and was quite effective. I understand that pro se arguments are common in the Second Circuit. The process for the preparation of opinions in submitted cases is somewhat different from that described above. With rare exceptions, we do not summarily affirm those cases (a Rule 36 disposition). Instead, we write a short opinion that is usually non-precedential and is typically *per curiam* (i.e., the authoring judge is not named). We also have a court staff headed by the able Jeff Goldberg, who assists in the preparation of orders and opinions on motions that come to the court before a panel is assigned.

Most of the panel cases that we hear fall into one of two categories: (1) the outcomes are foreordained by prior precedent, and the case would be decided the same way regardless of the panel, or (2) reasonable judges could differ on the outcome and sometimes do, and a dissenting judge either reluctantly joins the majority or files a routine dissent. But some cases arouse passions among the judges, and some of these end up en banc. The judge or judges on the losing end can be quite unhappy.

En banc opinions are designed to resolve conflicting circuit precedent or otherwise important issues. The en banc court consists of all of the active judges on the court. If a senior judge was a member of a panel whose decision the active judges have voted to rehear en banc, the senior judge is permitted (but not obligated) to be part of the en banc court in deciding the case on rehearing. So, in some circumstances, you could have 13 judges on the en banc court.

All courts of appeals, I suspect, dislike en banc proceedings. En banc arguments are rarely satisfactory, there being so many judges that extended follow-up on a single topic is often impossible. In our court at least, the conferences after the en banc arguments are often perfunctory, without much exchange of information or extended discussion. That is because there is a lot of discussion among the judges individually before the en banc argument takes place. In almost all of those cases, the judges have decided how they will vote before they begin the en banc argument. In other words, the votes are much more preordained than they are in the panels. The writing assignment is again made by the senior active judge in the majority, typically the chief judge. En banc opinions in circulation typically draw extensive comment, and despite the earlier votes, sometimes these comments can lead to a change in result and reassignment of authorship.

A good feature of our court is that, unlike many other courts, such as the Supreme Court and the D.C. Circuit, it is almost never divided internally along liberal and conservative lines. If we have a divided en banc or panel, the division almost never correlates to judges appointed by Republican presidents and judges appointed by Democratic presidents. In other circuits, there are ideological differences among the judges that can reflect the views of appointing presidents along a liberal/conservative spectrum. [18] Even in those circuits, the judges do not vote as Republicans or Democrats, as the recent votes on the Trump election challenges reveal.

A significant feature of our court is the number of our cases that are reviewed by the Supreme Court. From 2000 to 2010, the Court heard more than fifteen of our cases. From 2010 to 2020, the Court heard over thirty, reversing slightly more than 70 percent. Over the past 20 years, the Court has heard almost four of our cases per year, and in more than twenty of those I either wrote the majority opinion (or a dissent) in the case being reviewed or the majority opinion (or a dissent) in an earlier precedential case that had established Federal Circuit law. The judges have a good deal of interest in what happens to their cases in the Supreme Court. We do not attend the oral argument at the Supreme Court. Occasionally, our law clerks will go to the argument, and we do read the transcripts of the arguments and follow all the decisions closely. If the Court disagrees with us or agrees with us, it does not evoke an emotional response, at least in me.

Congress pays less attention to our decisions than does the Supreme Court, though on three occasions Congress has changed the law in response to one of my decisions. The first of these was in the *Forshey* case where Congress expanded our review of Veterans Court decisions, a change that we had suggested in our en banc decision (*Forshey v. Principi*, 284 F.3d 1335 (Fed. Cir. 2002) (en banc), *superseded by statute*, Veterans Benefits Act of 2002, Pub. L. No. 107-330, 116 Stat. 2820, 2832). A second involved rejecting a standard for whistleblowing protection in our decision in *Huffman* (*Huffman v. OPM*, 263 F.3d 1341 (2001), *superseded by statute*, Whistleblower Protection Enhancement Act of 2012, Pub. L. No. 112–199, 126 Stat. 1465, 1465–66). The third was our *GPX* decision holding that the statute providing for the imposition of countervailing duties on imports subsidized by the government of the country from which they came did not apply to imports from nonmarket economies (i.e., China) (*GPX International Tire Corp. v. United States*, 666 F.3d 732 (Fed. Cir. 2011) ("*GPX I*"), *superseded by statute*, Application of Countervailing Duty Provisions to Nonmarket Economy Countries, Pub. L. No. 112–99, 126 Stat. 265, 265 (2012)). In the latter case, Congress overruled our decision a mere 85 days after the decision. We were asked to review this new legislation and found it constitutional (*GPX International Tire Corp. v. United States*, 678 F.3d 1308 (Fed. Cir. 2012) ("*GPX II*")).

An unusual feature of our court is that we sit in a city other than our home city each year, and we hold court at various law schools during that visit. This gives the law students an opportunity to see what a real court is like. It is quite different from the law school moot court experience, which is not really representative of what an actual case argument is like. The judges' mindset in a moot court is to provide a teaching experience for the students. In a real case, even one that happens at the law school, the judges' primary objective is to get the information necessary to decide the case. It is very beneficial for the law students to see the real thing. They seem reluctant to go to the federal courthouse to hear cases in cities where their law schools are located, but they will attend if the cases are brought to them.

In addition to doing the work of the court, most of my colleagues do other things as well, such as attending conferences, teaching or sitting on other courts. Part of the reason may be that our docket is less diverse than the dockets of other courts of appeals, and our judges are searching for a more diverse experience. As I mentioned, in many years, I have sat as a visiting judge on the First Circuit. I have sat on the First Circuit more than thirty argument days to date and have written over sixty precedential opinions. The docket is different, the procedures differ in material ways, and the judges come from different backgrounds but, as with our own court, they are very able and experienced. Mike Boudin on that court was a friend long before I became a judge. I have also sat as a visiting judge on district courts in the District of Delaware, the Eastern District of Texas and in the District of Massachusetts. In the district courts, I have presided over multiple trials and other proceedings. Familiarity with trial court proceedings is essential to an appellate judge, and there is no better way to learn about it than by doing it. One of the things I have learned is that lay jurors take their jobs seriously and can deal with highly complex cases. I found my experiences on the First Circuit and the various district courts to be very beneficial and to have made me a better judge.

There are also many opportunities to speak and to participate on panels or conferences. I do few of those. I find that the task of preparing a speech can be very time-consuming and difficult because I want each one to be original and substantive. Our court has close relationships with the Federal Circuit Bar Association and a number of other associations devoted to patent law. This has good and bad aspects. The good being the opportunity for judges and bar members to learn from each other; the bad being the risk of what is often called industry capture. These associations have a definite view of what the patent world should look like, and they pride themselves on spreading what has been called the "patent gospel." While diverse groups within the industry are represented, public interest groups that might present a different view typically do not have a seat at the table at the various conferences sponsored by the patent bar.

There have also been numerous opportunities to meet with foreign judges, some here and some abroad. The most interesting of these was a trip to China in 2012.[19] This was arranged by the Federal Circuit Bar Association together with the Commerce Department. Shortly before the trip, the Chinese canceled all the scheduled private meetings with the Chinese judges. This was not at all surprising. The Chinese government has a policy against private meetings between its government officials and foreign government officials, the only exception being a private meeting that involves family members. Sally and I had known one of the Chinese central bankers here in Washington, and he invited us to lunch while we were in Beijing. This was possible only because he brought his family along. During one of the public events with the Chinese judges, I had an interesting conversation with one of the Supreme People's Court judges and asked him whether he would like to have a drink with me at an outdoor pavilion after the dinner. He said that he would, but as we were walking down the steps from the dinner venue, he suddenly turned around, said, "Uh oh! I'd better not do this" and retreated back into the building. Yet, at least one judge risked disapproval by joining us at a private dinner with some colleagues in the bar. At the public meetings, the Chinese judges were less than forthcoming. For example, they were asked why their decisions were not all published, to which the only (inaccurate) response was that they are all published. Interestingly, the same reluctance of foreign judges to meet privately occurred when Sally and I visited Cuba. The mother of our tour guide was a judge and declined to meet with us because of the trouble that it might cause. Government-mandated isolation is designed to protect judges from the virus of judicial independence.

## A Few Cases

Some judicial biographies describe the judge's jurisprudence and decided cases to the point that the reader's eyes glaze over. I will not make that mistake, but a few cases merit brief discussion so that the reader will get some sense that our docket, in addition to the patent cases, is both significant and interesting.

One of the cases involved judicial compensation. Justices and judges look sometimes at the lofty compensation of private practitioners with some jealousy. I recall years ago when I was in practice having dinner with Chief Justice Rehnquist and Justice Kennedy at some event. I said that I envied my classmate (Kennedy) because he was on the Supreme Court while I remained in practice. The chief justice consoled me by remarking, "But you make so much more money."

This issue of federal judicial compensation came up in the 2012 *Beer* case. For years, federal judges had not had a pay raise, and their salaries were eroded by inflation. In the past, one common measure of judicial compensation was the salary of law school deans; the compensation of judges was thought to be appropriately the same as that of deans. Dean compensation had grown to the point that it far exceeded that of judges. Judges felt underpaid. Congress had provided for Cost of Living Adjustments (COLA) for executive branch employees and, under the statute, these were scheduled to go to the judiciary as well. For many years, before the COLAs went into effect, Congress eliminated them as to judges. The question was whether this was a violation of the compensation clause of the Constitution protecting judges' salaries from being reduced.

The government's theory was that there was no reduction in compensation because the judges never became entitled to the COLAs. The theory of the plaintiff judges was that the COLAs had been scheduled and the judges were entitled to them, so eliminating them improperly reduced the judges' compensation. This was a matter of considerable interest and concern to federal judges generally. This case presented an awkward situation because obviously the judges were self-interested. The result of the case would potentially determine their entitlement to additional compensation. Because of what is known as the "rule of necessity," the judges nonetheless had to sit on these cases and decide them.

Initially, a few federal judges brought suit in the Court of Federal Claims to secure the withheld compensation. This was the *Williams* case. Earlier, in December 1980, the Supreme Court, in *United States v. Will*, 449 U.S. 200 (1980), had decided a similar issue against the judges. With the background of *Will*, in 2001 a panel of the Federal Circuit in *Williams*, over one dissent, held that the denial of COLAs was not a violation of the compensation cause (*Williams v. United States*, 240 F.3d 1019 (Fed. Cir. 2001)).

Undeterred, another group of federal judges, led by my classmate Larry Silberman, continued to pursue the issue, filing a new lawsuit that became the *Beer* case. The *Beer* case presented two issues: first, whether the *Beer* plaintiffs were barred as a matter of collateral estoppel (preclusion) from pursuing the issue, the original *Williams* case having been a class action of all federal judges. The second issue was the merits of the compensation clause argument and whether that claim was foreclosed by the Supreme Court's *Will* decision. The *Beer* case first came before a panel of our court. In an opinion that I wrote, without addressing the preclusion issue, the panel affirmed the Court of Federal Claims decision on the merits, denying relief, based on the earlier decision in *Williams* (*Beer v. United States*, 361 F. App'x 150 (Fed. Cir. 2010)).

The *Beer* plaintiffs sought certiorari in the Supreme Court, and the Supreme Court remanded the case "for consideration of the question of preclusion" (*Beer v. United States*, 564 U. S. 1050 (2011)). This then led to a panel decision (again authored by me) finding no preclusion but again affirming the denial of compensation (*Beer v. United States*, 671 F.3d 1299 (Fed. Cir. 2012)). The en banc Federal Circuit granted a petition for a rehearing and decided that the congressional action had violated the compensation clause, and the federal judges were entitled to the COLAs (*Beer v. United States*, 696 F.3d 1174 (Fed. Cir. 2012) (en banc)). When the case was heard en banc, I dissented, joined only by Judge Bryson. We noted that the decision seemed more explicable in terms of a desire by the court to do justice rather than following existing precedent, writing:

> The majority opinion brings to mind an exchange between Learned Hand and Justice Holmes. Judge Hand enjoined Justice Holmes to "[d]o justice" on the bench, but the Justice demurred: "That is not my job. My job is to play the game according to the rules." Learned Hand, A Personal Confession, in *The Spirit of Liberty*, 302, 306–07 (Irving Dilliard ed., 3d ed. 1960). If the Supreme Court must play by the rules,

that duty must be doubly binding on subordinate federal courts. Fidelity to this principle mandates adherence to the Supreme Court's opinion in *United States v. Will*, 449 U.S. 200 (1980).

While the majority's approach has much to recommend it as a matter of justice to the nation's underpaid Article III judges, it has nothing to recommend it in terms of the rules governing adjudication. "The criterion of constitutionality is not whether we believe the law to be for the public good," *Adkins v. Children's Hosp.*, 261 U.S. 525, 570 (1923) (Holmes, J., dissenting), but whether the law comports with the Supreme Court's authoritative construction of the Constitution.[20]

The Supreme Court, to the surprise of many, denied certiorari, perhaps because the judgment was not final, the exact amounts owed not having been determined. But in any event, at that point the government decided that it had enough and did not seek further review. After that, the amount of the COLAs was agreed to by the parties in the Court of Federal Claims, and the judges received their back pay. Since then, the judges have continued to receive their COLAs. The compensation for members of Congress had always been the same as that of federal judges. As a result of *Beer*, our pay has changed but congressional pay has not. Congress is not happy. The judges are happy. They thanked members of our court. I say: don't thank me. I dissented.

Two First Amendment cases in our court were also significant. Both concerned trademark registration. In the *Tam* case, our court held (and the Supreme Court agreed) that a prohibition on registration of marks that "disparage" persons or groups was unconstitutional (*In re Tam*, 808 F.3d 1321 (Fed. Cir. 2015) (en banc), *affirmed, Matal v. Tam*, 582 U.S. ——, 137 S. Ct. 1744 (2017)). The case arose in the context of the mark "Slants" to ironically self-describe an Asian American band. In this context, I agreed that the mark was protected free speech, because it was conveying a message in an important issue. But I dissented as far as the decision applied to purely commercial speech such as the mark "Redskins" (*In re Tam*, 808 F.3d at 1363 (Dyk, J., dissenting)). The other case involved the ban on "immoral" or "scandalous" marks. Our court again invalidated the ban, and the Supreme Court agreed (*In re Brunetti*, 877 F.3d 1330 (Fed. Cir. 2017), *affirmed, Iancu v. Brunetti*, 588 U.S.——, 139 S. Ct. 2294, 2302 (2019)). I would have construed the statute as limited to obscenity, thereby saving it for limited use (*In re Brunetti*, 877 F.3d at 1358 (Dyk, J., concurring)). In both cases, our now chief judge Kimberly Moore wrote our court's majority opinion.

Another case that went to the Supreme Court from our court was *Oil States Services LLC v. Greene's Energy Group, LLC*, 639 F. Appx 639 (2016), *affirmed*, 584 U.S.——, 138 S. Ct. 1365 (2018), involving the constitutionality of the Patent and Trademark Office post-grant review process for patents, created by a Congressional statute to eliminate bad patents that had been initially granted. The statute was the brainchild of Senator Hatch, among others. At the Federal Circuit Judicial Conference on March 16, 2018, Chief Justice Roberts (who was then hearing the case) and Hatch (then fondly remembering his legislative accomplishment) both spoke. Roberts spoke first but waited to hear Hatch, who launched into a broadside warning Roberts not to invalidate his statute. Pure ex parte and inappropriate. Roberts sat stone-faced. The rest of us slid under the tables. The Court agreed with Hatch, but Roberts dissented.

There have been numerous other important patent cases during my time on the court, many of which have gone to the Supreme Court. These include cases concerning the patenting of generic material (*Association for Molecular Pathology v. Myriad Genetics, Inc.*, 569 U.S. 576 (2013)); cases setting the standards for determining patent eligible subject matter as to laws of nature (*Mayo v. Prometheus Laboratories, Inc.*, 566 U.S. 66 (2012)) and abstract ideas (*Alice Corp. v. CLS Bank International*, 573 U.S. 208 (2014)); cases setting the standard for patent obviousness (*KSR International Co. v. Teleflex Inc.*, 550 U.S. 398 (2007)); and many others too numerous to describe here.

In the veterans area, we dealt with the use of evidence in rape cases where the victim is seeking VA benefits. I wrote an opinion holding that the victim's failure to report the assault and the absence of service records documenting the assault could not be used as evidence that the assault did not occur, given the reluctance of rape victims to come forward (*AZ, AY v. Shjinseki*, 731 F.3d 1303 (Fed. Cir. 2013)). In another case, we established that lawyers behave unethically when they transmit to clients and prospective clients compliments from judges suggesting that the counsel has a special relationship with the court (*In re Reines*, 771 F.3d 1326 (Fed. Cir. 2014)).

Finally, in one case my decision as a district judge was reviewed by the Federal Circuit, and I was affirmed. In another, I was reversed by the circuit. I tell my colleagues on the district court that I am now one of you.

## COVID-19

The process I have described is pre-COVID. I first began to be aware that COVID would affect our lives when in early March of 2020, I traveled to Puerto Rico to sit with the First Circuit. On the flight south a few passengers were already wearing masks. I was then more worried about coming down with the flu rather than COVID. My wife had just been admitted to Georgetown Hospital with the H1N1 flu. I left for Puerto Rico after being assured by her doctors that she was in no danger. I did not get the flu or COVID while away but returned to a lockdown that lasted for over a year. In the beginning,

I worked from home, but in June 2020, I returned to work in my chambers with two out of four clerks at a time. The clerks felt comfortable coming in, as did my judicial assistant. Oral arguments continued, but by telephone. Quite unsatisfactory, but not as bad as everyone thought. There are disadvantages. Most of us think that counsel are often less well prepared, less candid and less accurate in telephone arguments. Most judges on our court and elsewhere continued to work from home, and all of us missed meeting in person. To our great relief we resumed in-person arguments last September, though a few counsel elected to appear remotely, only to pause again in January. No one knows for sure when things will return to normal nor whether there will be a new normal. One suspects that there will be some difficulty getting the lawyers back to Paree after they have been down on the farm—that is, getting them back to big city offices, when they have worked remotely at their vacation homes..

## The Ten Most Difficult Things about Being an Appellate Judge

Reflecting on my experience on the court over the past 20 years, I end with what I think are the 10 most difficult things about being an appellate judge, not necessarily in order of their importance.

1. The first is that you leave very little in the way of personal legacy. You may think that you are going to play a distinctive, memorable role in shaping the law for generations to come after the nomination and confirmation process. But in fact, that is a delusion, as you quickly learn. Most circuit opinions are read only by the winning lawyer, the losing lawyer and the winning lawyer's mother. This is something that very much concerned Holmes when he was a judge on the Massachusetts Supreme Judicial Court. As one commentator has noted, "Holmes saw the role of a state appellate judge as that of a contributor to a collection, a collective enterprise, destined soon to be forgotten in name, and having any useful effect only in the incremental improvement of judicial reasoning that he would add to what judges had done before."[21] The same thing can be said of federal court of appeals judges. The shelf life of a court of appeals opinion is short. Very few of them are relevant even after a few years' time. The shelf life of the public's memory of the judges is short too; occasionally when I am reading an old case, I check the front of the volume that lists the names of the judges active at the time. After 20 years most names are forgotten. So, any court of appeals judge has to think of his or her contribution to the law modestly, without any expectation that you are going to leave a significant personal legacy. This is unlike the experience of a Supreme Court justice, almost all

of whom leave a legacy of opinions that are cited year after year and have a very long shelf life. For me, the satisfaction of being a court of appeals judge lies in contributing to the collective enterprise of the judiciary generally and of our court in particular, and the legacy that that represents.

2. The second difficult aspect of being a court of appeals judge concerns the relationship with your colleagues. When I first took the bench, I was not fully cognizant of the importance of relationships. Since we typically decide cases in panels of three, unlike trial judges, you can only act by getting at least one of your colleagues to agree with you. Most judges find that dealing with colleagues who have an equal say in resolving the matter to be a new experience. Even in a law firm, partnership equality is only equality in theory. On a court of appeals, it is equality in fact. The process of reaching agreement can be difficult and frustrating at times. It is important to remember that the colleague who declined to join you in an opinion last month may be a vote that you want on another opinion the following month. It is even more important to remember that collegiality and respect is the glue that binds the institution together and makes happy coexistence possible. The process requires attention and considerable effort. The fact that our chambers are in a single courthouse in Washington, DC, helps foster collegiality.

Courts of appeals have not always been successful in maintaining a collegial atmosphere. The D.C. Circuit years ago and the Fifth and Sixth Circuits today are examples of courts where internal collegiality became seriously frayed. One example of how angry confrontations can fracture a court concerns Judges Mikva and Silberman on the D.C. Circuit. After word of this confrontation leaked in the press, Judge Silberman recounted that in response to certain remarks that Judge Mikva made to him, he said, "If you were ten years younger, I would be tempted to punch you in the nose." But he also pointed out, "Judge Mikva did not become 10 years younger, our tempers receded, and we continued our discussion of the case."[22] Whatever else, this is an example of the passions that can exist in deciding cases. There are also numerous instances in the history of the Supreme Court where that was the case. The tensions between Chief Justice Warren and Justice Frankfurter gave me firsthand experience of this.

The primary source of discord lies in differences as to judicial philosophy, and deeply held views as to how the cases should be decided. There are other manifold potential sources of friction. Lobbying by colleagues for votes can be a major irritant. Tensions often arise because judges take too long in producing opinions, particularly dissents, or take too long in voting on other judges' opinions or insist on non-substantive changes to another judge's opinion. Another source of potential friction (not evident on our court) is when a judge cannot reach a decision or changes positions during the course of a case.

Another opportunity for discord lies in the succession of chief judges. The rule is automatic—the most senior judge under the age of 65 becomes the new chief judge (unless he or she declines). But there is an opportunity for the retiring chief judge to affect who will be his or her successor by leaving the position early. Bad feeling has resulted from such manipulation. Another source of conflict involves chief judges who depart from the random assignment of cases and panels. Chief Judge Markey did that on our court (unbeknownst to the other judges at the time). Scholarly and anecdotal sources point to the Ninth Circuit's also having an issue with the use of random assignments.[23]

The chief judge typically sets the tone, and if the chief judge sets a poor tone, this will contribute to friction. If the chief judge sets a good tone, the court will more likely be a happy court. To name only those still on the bench, our last chief judge Sharon Prost did an outstanding job, as did our former chief, Bob Mayer. We have recently transitioned to a new chief judge, now chief judge Moore, with hope and expectation that she will also contribute to a good tone and a happy court. She is off to a good start.

Fostering collegiality requires a willingness to discuss cases, listen to and learn from colleagues and, sometimes, to suppress one's own views in the interest of unanimity. Developing relationships with your fellow judges outside of court can be an important promoter of a collegial relationship. There is not always an easy path to that goal. As an example, we have weekly lunches to which all judges are invited. Only a half dozen regularly attend. There is an understanding that cases will not be discussed. The lunches are awkward at times. I was struck by Brandeis's description of a Supreme Court justices lunch: "The main discussion at luncheon was of shirts—where, when and how satisfactory ones may be secured."[24] To me, individual socializing is more rewarding. For years I played tennis with Judge Rader; I continue my efforts to get Judge Chen to play competitively. Sally and I often have a casual dinner with one or more of the other judges. My former colleague Art Gajarsa used to organize art trips.

When you join the bench, you are told that it takes five years to learn to become a judge, a theory that I think is quite accurate. To learn to be a good judge, you need to learn from your colleagues. In my early years on the court, Ray Clevenger was most helpful in showing me the ropes. Sharon Prost, though junior to me in seniority, helped me to learn to navigate an institution like the Senate from which she came, where the members are both equal and prickly. Polly Newman and Dan Friedman occupied different ends of the spectrum in taking fairness into account in judging cases, and their examples led me to a middle path. I also learned from many others too numerous to name here. Among the things I learned was not to be too hard on counsel and to reduce the number of rhetorical questions ("Is it the case that?" instead of "Isn't it the case that?"). In numerous individual cases, colleagues have caused me to reexamine my premises and sometimes to change my initial approach.

3. Another difficult thing about being an appellate judge is dealing with cases in which friends, former colleagues, or former law clerks are arguing. The challenge there is to not allow those relationships, good or bad, to influence the outcome of the case. I strive very hard to neither favor friends, colleagues and former law clerks, nor to bend over backwards to avoid favoring them. The outcome should not depend on the identity of the counsel. It is a difficult process and the difficult challenge is not always met.

4. A significant challenge is how to write opinions, a subject that I have already discussed. My first rule is to write simply and clearly, and to avoid trying to be cute or funny. I cringe every time I read Justice Blackmun's opinion in *Flood v. Kuhn*, 407 U.S. 258 (1972), where he attempts humor by calling up the names of baseball greats. Avoiding cuteness is only one aspect of good opinion writing; clarity, pragmatism, respect for precedent and the parties and their counsel are even more important.

We have many very able lawyers appearing before us producing briefs that help greatly in the writing of opinions, but many other cases are often not that well briefed and argued. With patent lawyers, there is sometimes myopia, unfortunately—that is, a lack of interest or knowledge of other areas of the law that turn out to be highly relevant. Some briefs therefore leave more work for the court to do than others.

It is fairly easy to winnow out the bad arguments that are made and set them aside. The more difficult problem arises when counsel fail to include good arguments in their briefs and oral arguments. It is startling how frequently this happens. That presents a challenge to courts of appeals. In the district court, there is more of a sense of being a referee in the case, but in the court of appeals, there is a feeling of greater responsibility for the development of the law. We are not just deciding the individual case: we are also articulating precedent that is going to govern future cases. Because you are creating precedent, it becomes important to get the law right. Most judges do not want to make bad law just because counsel may have argued the case badly. When I was in private practice, having poor counsel on the other side caused anxiety; to what extent would the judges after argument do the job that counsel should have done without giving me a chance to respond?

There is not much that a court of appeals can or will in most cases do if the lawyer in the case simply does not raise the issue at all, which happens with some frequency. So, we make a distinction between issues that are not raised, which are waived or forfeited (and where the opinion will not create precedent on the issue), and arguments that are not made concerning issues that were properly preserved (where the opinion will create precedent). Drawing the line between those two can be difficult and is one of the challenges for any appellate judge. There is the related challenge of whether to write narrowly or broadly and the extent to which the fairness of the outcome should play a role in the process. The risk is that in hard cases, we sometimes make bad law. The risk also is that in hard cases (or cases where the judges cannot reconcile their positions), we end up making sausage. This does not happen frequently, but we are embarrassed when it does.

5. Another difficult issue is when to dissent. I think in my own case, and perhaps this is true of most court of appeals judges, you tend to dissent more when you are new to the court. After a period of years, I think you learn that dissents do not always serve a useful purpose, and that it is better to grit your teeth and join the majority opinion, perhaps asking for changes in that opinion so that it is less sweeping or problematic. The maturing process is something that happens not only with individual judges, but with the court as a whole. I think our court has matured, so that there are fewer dissents than there used to be. When I dissent, I try to keep it short. A related issue is dealing with losses and the ability to realize that you cannot be on the winning side of every issue in every case. You have to deal appropriately with the fact that you are not going to prevail sometimes when you think the law is on your side, and not let yourself become too discouraged when it happens.

6. Despite the fact that there are many fine advocates in this country and many of the best argue in our court, another difficulty is dealing with counsel who are poor advocates, acting inappropriately at oral argument—that is, interrupting, not listening, not responding, misrepresenting facts of law—or not being prepared. That happens fairly frequently. Sometimes it seems as though the lawyers arguing the case looked at the brief for the first time on the plane ride to Washington and did not completely familiarize themselves with the authorities they rely on. Also, lawyers have come to oral argument unfamiliar with the record. Sometimes the lawyers forget even to bring the appendix (which contains excerpts from the record with them). Many have difficulty answering our questions as to where the record supports their arguments. Some lawyers, with a wave of their hand, assert "it's in there some-where," when, in fact, it is not.

There is a common saying in Washington that when you go to court, it is the only place that you have to actually answer the question that is asked of you. Despite the lawyers' best efforts to avoid some of the questions, our judges are insistent on having their questions answered. And those answers often have a significant effect on the outcome of the case. Lawyers are legitim-ately concerned that they could lose their cases by an admission that they make in oral argument. But the fact is that your case can be even more adversely affected by the lawyer's failure to answer the questions or to address the issues the court cares about. Bad lawyering tests the patience of the judges, but it is important to avoid abusing counsel for their failures. My own experience as an advocate has had a significant effect on my work as a judge. I try to recall how I did not like being abused. At the same time, in private practice, as a partner or associate, I was always deeply involved in the drafting of the briefs. I was intimately familiar with their content and theory. At oral argument, I always viewed the questions as a gift and welcomed the opportunity to engage with the judges. I expect the same approach from lawyers who appear before us.

Sometimes counsel engage in pandering to the court. My favorite example is in the Supreme Court in the *Quill* oral argument, concerning whether states could require out-of-state retailers to collect sales or use taxes, where Nicholas Spaeth, then attorney general of North Dakota, was arguing on behalf of North Dakota. He began the argument by noting that he was wearing a Colorado Buffaloes tie that Justice White would appreciate, being a Colorado native and graduate of the University of Colorado, home of the Buffaloes. Spaeth said he had worn the tie because he hoped that that would "sway" Justice White's vote in the case. This was viewed by most as rather inappropriate, and Justice Kennedy's response was to ask, "Do you have any better reasons?"[25]

With all this said, one of the great pleasures of being a judge is reading good briefs and hearing good oral argument, which are frequent. We are most grateful.

7. Another difficulty is the lack of feedback about the impact of the decision that you are rendering. Unless the case comes back for a second time after a remand, court of appeals judges often do not know the consequences of their decision for the individual litigants. That is very much unlike the experience in private practice where you are acutely conscious of the impact of the work that you do in the real world of clients and opponents. The same lack of feedback is often true about the impact of court of appeals decisions on future cases decided by other courts. In 20-plus years, I have had perhaps two or three calls from judges on other circuits commenting on my decisions. Mostly, we float our opinions on the waters, not knowing where they will go and what consequences they will have outside our own court. You do get feedback from follow-on cases in your own court and from the academy, and sometimes from blogs, and sometimes from bar conferences. You are pilloried by the bar if what you do is unpopular. You hear back from the Supreme Court if it grants cert in one of your cases. Compliments are nice, criticisms not so much. With those exceptions, the amount of feedback is limited.

The news media pay a great deal less attention to what the courts of appeals do than what district courts do (our decisions are only rarely discussed in the mainstream media). When I was in private practice, as I have described earlier,

I worked on a number of high-profile cases, which resulted in a significant amount of newspaper, television and radio coverage. Since I have been on the Federal Circuit, I have not had a single request for a media interview about my work on the court, and I probably would not accede to such a request. I have been on television once, in a C-SPAN program about the Supreme Court's decision in *Gideon*.[26] Relative obscurity comes with the privilege of judging. As discussed earlier, we have declined to allow our proceedings to be televised, while the Second, Third, and Ninth Circuits regularly allow television coverage. I do not see in the near future either a great demand for television coverage of our court, or if there were such a demand, that we would allow it. We do make audio recordings of the oral arguments available on the court's website soon after the argument, and during COVID we have livestreamed the audio. Partly as a result of the limited coverage, the general public lacks information on what we do. Our docket and our work are not a topic for cocktail party conversation.

Unlike district judges, our contact with lawyers in case adjudication is limited. As noted earlier, we typically hear oral argument in a maximum of four cases a day for four days out of the month. And in each of those cases, we will have an argument that lasts somewhere between half an hour and an hour per side, but it is a very different experience from being a district judge, where you are constantly in court and seeing lawyers, witnesses and jurors. There are various organizations, such as the Federal Circuit Bar Association, which convene conferences and invite us to attend. So, we do see quite a bit of the bar outside of court, especially the patent bar. But it is a very specialized audience, and that contact does not help us feel significantly less isolated. While I have friendships with other courts of appeals judges, district judges and Supreme Court justices, those friendships do not involve any real communication about our work. Because of the specialized nature of our docket, the problems that we are facing are very different from the problems that are faced by other courts of appeals. We live in an ivory tower even more than other court of appeals judges. I do not participate in social media.

The good side of this isolation is that there are many friendships and social relationships among the judges on the court, as I mentioned earlier, and with current and former clerks. We often joke that the only people that we can discuss politics with are other judges on the court.

8. Another challenge to courts generally and our court in particular is the complexity of technology. The patent cases deal with innovative technology, and to understand the case, you have to understand the technology. If you pick up one of our patent opinions, sometimes—perhaps most of the time—it can be difficult to understand the opinion because it is difficult to understand the technology. None of us on the court is an expert in all of the areas

of mechanical, electrical, pharmaceutical or computer technology that come before us. Understanding the technology well enough to decide the case is one of the great challenges on our court, and to courts generally, as Judge Posner has noted at some length.[27] Patent law, always arcane, has become even more complicated. These problems exist in other areas of the law or in other circuits, but to a lesser extent.

9. One significant decision that any justice or judge must make is how to use law clerks. I describe in detail above my own practice. The use of law clerks has been controversial almost from the time that justices and judges started using clerks. Generally speaking, the use of clerks varies depending on the level in the judiciary. In the district courts, the clerks typically play a central role in chambers administration—dealing with counsel, keeping track of deadlines, and coordinating with the clerk's office and courtroom personnel. Because of the load, judges delegate to clerks the preparation of orders and opinions subject to the judge's review. At the courts of appeals, there is less delegation because judges (unlike district judges) do not have to preside over extensive, pretrial, trial and posttrial proceedings, including civil discovery and criminal sentencing, and have more time for individual opinions. In the Supreme Court the workload is even less than on courts of appeal. Most clerks spend a significant amount of time on what is known as the cert pool (preparing memoranda for the justices on applications for certiorari) and doing in-depth research for the justices' opinions. You can see issues of delegation if you read the tell-all books of former Supreme Court law clerks. The difficult task of each judge is to find a happy medium between excessive delegation and the failure to use clerks to the judge's best advantage.

10. The most consequential decision for any Article III judge is whether and when to retire. Under the statute, a retiring judge has a choice between outright retirement and taking what is known as senior status—that is, remaining a judge with a reduced workload. As a result of statutory changes made in 1937 and earlier to encourage judicial retirements, justices and judges can now retire with full salary if they meet the rule of 80, whether they take senior status or leave the bench entirely.[28] The rule of 80 requires 10 years of active service, attaining the age of 65, and a combined total of years of service and age that adds up to 80. The result of full salary on retirement has been that the decision to stay or go is only occasionally influenced by financial considerations. I cannot recall a Supreme Court justice in recent years whose retirement was influenced by monetary considerations (the opportunity to return to private practice or to advocate or be an arbitrator or mediator) though this happens occasionally in the district courts and courts of appeals. Sometimes young judges leave and are spectacularly successful in practice. This was true of Thurman Arnold (one of the founders of Arnold & Porter), Simon Rifkind

(one of the founders of Paul Weiss) and, recently, John Gleeson who left the district court in New York to join Debevoise & Plimpton.

Although not leaving to make more money, justices leave voluntarily for a wide variety of reasons, including ill health (e.g., Reed), the ill health of a spouse (O'Connor), the desire to enable a particular president to choose a replacement (Warren, Kennedy), perceived impropriety (Fortas) or because they are simply tired of the job or the court (Souter, Stevens). There are sometimes unusual reasons for leaving—the decision to run for president (Hughes), the desire to serve in the executive branch (Byrnes) or as an ambassador (Goldberg). Others in the modern Court choose to die with their boots on, as with Scalia or Ginsburg. I recall that when Chief Justice Rehnquist was very ill, he spent time with our mutual barber (Diego D'Ambrosio), with whom he had developed a friendship. Diego later told me that shortly before he died, the chief justice began to cough up blood and implored Diego not to tell anyone so his ability to continue judging would not be questioned. He died a few days later. It used to be that Supreme Court justices would rarely retire early unless there were serious health problems. Now you have Justices O'Connor, Souter, Stevens and Kennedy all deciding to retire early while they were still able to do the work. In addition to the considerations mentioned above, maybe there is another: that the job of being a Supreme Court justice is not as much fun as it used to be.

In the courts of appeals, judges have ceased judging for other reasons: impeachment or criminal conviction (Manton), scandal (Kosinski), health issues (Posner) and even, unfortunately, suicide (Friendly). Given that the differences between being a senior court of appeals judge and an active judge is not as great as between a retired justice and an active justice, retirement of a circuit judge is not as big a deal as a justice's retirement. Circuit judges are largely immune from public pressure to retire (as unhappily occurred with Justice Ginsburg and now with Justice Breyer), though I have heard that the Trump administration urged circuit judges to take senior status (to create a vacancy) and Senator Arlen Spector used to call judges from Pennsylvania that he helped get appointed to demand that they take senior status as soon as they were eligible, so that he could influence a new appointment for one of his protégés. Judge O'Malley of our court has (unfortunately) decided to resign later this year, and (fortunately) Judge Leonard Stark of the District of Delaware has been nominated to take her place.

The most difficult situations involve judges who are unable to do the job and must be asked to leave. This was true of the judge for whom my wife Sally clerked (J. Skelly Wright) who had Alzheimer's, Justice Douglas (dementia) and Lincoln-appointee, Justice Stephen Field. When the first Justice Harlan approached Justice Field to remind Field that he had served on a committee recommending the retirement of Justice Robert Grier, who had suffered three strokes while on the Court, Field responded, "Yes, and a dirtier day's work I never did in my life." Field refused to submit his resignation and stayed on another year.[29] Even Justice Holmes had to be asked to resign, as he was showing increasing signs that he was incapable of dealing with the Court's workload. The task of convincing Holmes to retire fell to Chief Justice Charles Evans Hughes, who visited Holmes on a Sunday morning at home. The chief justice left in tears after completing this "highly disagreeable duty."[30] Some judges ask a family member or former clerk to tell them when it is time to leave. The decision about leaving is generally very closely held. I recall that the weekend before Justice O'Connor retired, we played tennis with her and her husband; no hint of what was to come the following Friday.

But at least with life tenure, the choice is yours to make, unlike those who serve in the executive branch. Walter Lippman wrote of the latter: "One day you are at the pinnacle. The next day you are back in Lincoln, Nebraska, with nothing to do. One day your every word counts. The next day you are considering how to make a living at the bar. [...] [S]o, men think twice, and then think again, and find reasons of the highest public order for not passing from greatness into obscurity."[31] Similar concerns have had more relevance to retiring justices and judges than you might think.

With all that, I think life tenure is essential to judicial independence. With term limits, the judge would inevitably be looking over the shoulder to see the next post-judging job, and that could affect decision-making. The judge risks asking: how will this decision affect my future prospects? That only happens now with district judges aspiring to be circuit judges and circuit judges aspiring to the Supreme Court, and that is not a happy circumstance.

## Notes

1 Frank M. Coffin, *The Ways of a Judge: Views from the Federal Appellate Bench* (New York: Houghton Mifflin, 1980), 7.

2 Interestingly very few appellate judges failed to comply with these obligations. There is no suggestion that those district judges who sat on cases where they should have recused were in any way motivated by a desire to financially benefit themselves. James V. Grimaldi, Coulter Jones and Joe Palazzolo, "131 Federal Judges Broke the Law by Hearing Cases Where They Had a Financial Interest," *The Wall Street Journal*, September 28, 2021, https://www.wsj.com/articles/131-federal-judges-broke-the-law-by-hearing-cases-where-they-had-a-financial-interest-11632834421

3 *Confirmation Hearing on the Nomination of John G. Roberts, Jr. to be Chief Justice of the United States before the Senate Committee on the Judiciary*, 109th Cong. 55–56 (2005) (statement of John Roberts), https://www.govinfo.gov/content/pkg/GPO-CHRG-ROBERTS/pdf/GPO-CHRG-ROBERTS.pdf.

4 Frank M. Coffin, *The Ways of a Judge: Views from the Federal Appellate Bench* (New York: Houghton Mifflin, 1980), 12.

5    Coffin, *The Ways of a Judge*; and Frank M. Coffin, *On Appeal: Courts, Lawyering and Judging* (New York: W.W. Norton, 1994).

6    "Court Jurisdiction," United States Court of Appeals for the Federal Circuit, last accessed June 5, 2021, http://www.cafc.uscourts.gov/the-court/court-jurisdiction.

7    Robert J. Dole, Federal Courts Improvement Act of 1981, S. Rep. No. 97–275, at 6 (1981), reprinted in 1983 U.S.C.C.A.N. 11, 16 (explaining that the court of appeals for the Federal Circuit would have jurisdiction over a wide range of subject matter).

8    See, for instance, Timothy B. Dyk, "Federal Circuit Jurisdiction: Looking Back and Thinking Forward," *American University Law Review* 67, no. 4 (2018): 973.

9    John R. Thomas, "The Leahy-Smith America Invents Act: Innovation Issues," *Congressional Research Service* (2014), https://fas.org/sgp/crs/misc/R42014.pdf.

10   See, for instance, Dyk, "Federal Circuit Jurisdiction: Looking Back and Thinking Forward," 983; Dyk, "Thoughts on the Relationship Between the Supreme Court and the Federal Circuit," *Chicago-Kent Journal of Intellectual Property* 16, no. 1 (2016): 78.

11   Paul R. Gugliuzza, The Federal Circuit as a Federal Court, 54 Wm. & Mary L. Rev. 1791 (2013), 1857.

12   Jennifer Senior, "In Conversation: Antonin Scalia," *New York Magazine*, October 4, 2013, https://nymag.com/news/features/antonin-scalia-2013-10/index6.html.

13   Richard A. Posner, *Reflections on Judging* (Cambridge, MA: Harvard University Press, 2013), 240–43.

14   Dean Acheson, *Morning and Noon: A Memoir* (Boston, MA: Houghton Mifflin, 1965), 80.

15   Address of Paul Freund, Proceedings in Memory of Mr. Justice Louis Memorial, 317 U.S. xx.

16   Leon Heppel, the owner of the clutter, found two letters side by side, saw through the chaos and started a future exchange of letters between David Lipkin and Earl Sutherland, who were independently studying the same molecule and had both written to Heppel at the same time. Heppel's endeavor eventually resulted in Sutherland's earning the prize in 1971. See Maxine Singer, *Leon Alma Heppel 1912–2010. A Biographical Memoir* (Washington, DC: National Academy of Sciences, 2011), 13–14.

17   General statistics about the court's activity can be found on the court's website at "Statistics," United States Court of Appeals for the Federal Circuit, last updated May 31, 2021 http://www.cafc.uscourts.gov/the-court/statistics.

18   A recent study of en banc decisions, expected to be published in the *NYU Law Review* this year, found an increase in disagreement. Neal Devins and Allison O. Larsen, "Weaponizing En Banc," SSRN (2021), https://papers.ssrn.com/sol3/papers.cfm?abstract_id=3782576.

19   A summary of the visit is available on the court's website: "A Historic U.S.A-China IP Event," United States Court of Appeals for the Federal Circuit, last accessed June 5, 2021, http://www.cafc.uscourts.gov/announcements/historic-usa-china-ip-event-0.

20   *Beer v. United States*, 696 F.3d 1174, 1187 (Fed. Cir. 2012) (Dyk, J., dissenting).

21   David J. Seipp, "Oliver Wendell Holmes, Jr.: The Judge as Celebrity," *Supreme Court Historical Society Quarterly* 27, no. 1 (2006): 3–4.

22   James Rowley, "Mikva's Political Skills to Be Tested as Clinton's New Counsel," *Associated Press*, August 12, 1994.

23   Marin K. Levy and Adam S. Chilton, "Challenging the Randomness of Panel Assignment in the Federal Courts of Appeals," *Cornell Law Review* 101, no. 1 (2015): 38–40, http://scholarship.law.cornell.edu/clr/vol101/iss1/1; also, Ronald D. Rotunda, "The Mystery of Case Assignment in the Ninth Circuit," *Verdict: Legal Analysis and*

*Commentary from Justia*, December 1, 2014, https://verdict.justia.com/2014/12/01/mystery-case-assignment-ninth-circuit.

24   Alpheus Thomas Mason, *Brandeis: A Free Man's Life* (New York: Viking Press, 1946), 533.

25   Recording and transcript available at "*Quill Corporation v. North Dakota*," Oyez, last accessed June 6, 2021, https://www.oyez.org/cases/1991/91-194.

26   Available at "*Gideon v. Wainwright* and the Right to Counsel," *C-SPAN*, 10 May 2017, https://www.c-span.org/video/?428269-1/gideon-v-wainwright-counsel&playEvent.

27   Richard A. Posner, *Reflections on Judging* (Cambridge, MA: Harvard University Press, 2013), 54–55, 75–77.

28   On the retirement issue, see Judge Glock, "Unpacking the Supreme Court: Judicial Retirement, Judicial Independence, and the Road to the 1937 Court Battle," *Journal of American History* 106, no. 1 (2019): 47–71.

29   Donald R. McClarey, "'Yes! And a Dirtier Day's Work I Never Did in My Life!,'" *The American Catholic*, 17 January 2019, https://www.the-american-catholic.com/2019/01/17/yes-and-a-dirtier-days-work-i-never-did-in-my-life/.

30   David J. Garrow, "Mental Decrepitude on the U.S. Supreme Court: The Historical Case for a 28th Amendment," *University of Chicago Law Review* 67, no. 4 (2000): 1018.

31   Ronald Steel, *Walter Lippmann and the American Century* (London: Routledge Taylor & Francis Group, 1999), 574.

# Chapter 12

# EPILOGUE

On the eve of a class reunion, Judge Silberman, one of my classmates at Harvard Law School, had his clerks research the various Harvard classes and discovered that our class of 1961 had the largest number of federal appellate judges of any class that had graduated from the Harvard Law School. With Justice Kennedy's retirement from the Supreme Court in 2018, all five of my classmates who became appellate judges have taken senior status or have died (Williams in 2020). Almost all my classmates who joined private firms have also retired, though some have found meaningful work to do after retiring from their firms.

In all courts of appeals, at some point in the judge's tenure on the court there is a portrait painted of the judge which is presented to the court for hanging in one of its courtrooms. Unlike the D.C. Circuit, for example, in our court, the portrait presentation ceremony occurs before the judge leaves the court or takes senior status. In my case, that portrait presentation took place in October 2015 and resulted in a ceremony at which some of my former law clerks spoke. The transcript of the ceremony appears in 878 F.3d. The artist was British, named Brendan Kelly. He has painted portraits of members of the British government and has done the official portrait for Justice Breyer. His portrait of me appears on the cover of this book.

There was an amusing episode about my portrait. My wife and I went to London. Brendan had just finished the portrait. We went to his studio in London to look at it. Brendan had said that if there was something about the portrait that I wanted to have changed, he would address it. When we arrived, Brendan said that he wanted to give us the opportunity to look at the portrait in private, so he would walk around the block and come back. Before leaving, he unveiled the portrait. Both my wife and I were delighted with it—a uniform reaction by those who saw it later. As we talked about it, my wife noticed that one of my hands seemed to be lighter than the rest of the portrait. And so, when Brendan came back, she suggested that he could darken that part of the hand. They got into a disagreement about whether that was desirable or not, and it became clear to me that this was not my portrait, but was Brendan's portrait which, of course, is always the mark of a great artist. The hand stayed as it was. I see the portrait whenever I sit in Courtroom 402.

Having your portrait painted and presented brings to focus whether you would like to continue and that raises once again the question why I wanted to be a judge in the first place. The answer is the same. The federal judiciary is one of the gems of our democratic government. Helping to make it work is a privilege.

Having now authored over four hundred precedential opinions and having heard over three thousand cases, I choose to labor on. My education continues.

# Appendix

# TIMOTHY DYK'S CLERKS BY YEAR, LAW SCHOOL AND CURRENT POSITION

2000–2001    **John Cuddihy**, GWU 1999, SVP & Deputy General Counsel, Scientific Games Corporation.

         **Troy Grabow**, GWU 2000, Associate General Counsel, IP & Product, Pax Labs, Inc.

         **Nathan Judish**, Harvard 1996, Senior Counsel, Computer Crime and Intellectual Property, U.S. Department of Justice.

2001–2    **Mark Bellermann**, Columbia 2000, Principal, Brake Hughes Bellerman.

         **Tiffany P. Cunningham**, Harvard 2001, Judge, Court of Appeals for the Federal Circuit.

         **Laura (Huntington) Donoghue**, U. of Chicago 2000, wife and mother.

2002–3    **Michael B. Eisenberg**, GWU 2001, Partner, Steptoe & Johnson.

         **Samuel F. Ernst**, Georgetown 2002, Professor of Law, Golden Gate University School of Law

         **Nicholas F. Joseph**, U. of Michigan 2002, Partner, Kauff Laton Miller.

2003–4    **Stephanie Ives**, Boston U. 2003.

         **Michael A. Valek**, U. of Texas 2003, Administrative Patent Judge, Patent Trial and Appeal Board, USPTO.

         **Scott Weidenfeller**, Georgetown 2003, Partner, Covington & Burling.

2004–5    **Corey B. Blake**, U. of Texas 2004, Director and Assistant General Counsel, Bank of America Merrill Lynch.

         **T. J. Chiang**, U. of Chicago 2004, Professor of Law, George Mason University Scalia Law School.

         **Ruthanne Deutsch**, Georgetown 2004, Partner, Deutsch Hunt PLLC.

2005–6      **Jonathan Wells Andron**, Georgetown 2005, Senior IP Counsel, Signify (formerly Philips Lighting).

            **Varu Chilakamarri**, Georgetown 2004, Deputy Assistant Attorney General, Civil Division, US Department of Justice.

            **Garrick B. Pursley**, U. of Texas 2004.

2006–7      **Jessica R. Hauser**, Georgetown 2004, Senior Tax Counsel, US and Global Controversy General Electric Co.

            **Greg Reilly**, Harvard 2006, Associate Professor of Law, Illinois Tech-Chicago-Kent College of Law.

            **Gabriel Taran**, U. of Chicago 2006, Deputy Chief Counsel for Cybersecurity, Cybersecurity and Infrastructure Security Agency.

2007–8      **Dennis J. Abdelnour**, Northwestern 2007, Partner, Honigman, LLP.

            **Melanie Bostwick**, Harvard 2007, Partner, Supreme Court & Appellate, Orrick, Herrington & Sutcliffe.

            **Nathan C. Brunette**, Georgetown 2006, Partner, Stoel Rives, LLP.

2008–9      **Joel Dillard**, Georgetown 2008, Dillard & Associates.

            **Jennifer Librach Nall**, U. of Texas 2008, Partner, DLA Piper.

            **Ajeet Pai**, UVA 2007, Senior Corporate Counsel, Amazon.com Inc.

            **Heather D. Schafroth**, Harvard 2008, Associate, Caplin & Drysdale.

2009–10     **Jeffrey T. Han**, Northwestern 2009, Counsel, Vinson & Elkins.

            **Elizabeth A. Laughton**, Duke 2009, Counsel, Smith, Baluch.

            **Una Lee**, Georgetown 2009, Chief Counsel, Health Subcommittee, Democratic Staff of the Committee on Energy and Commerce.

            **Sarah Tran**, Georgetown 2009, Formerly Professor, Southern Methodist U. Dedman School of Law; died February 28, 2014.

2010–11     **Christopher Abernethy**, Stanford 2010, Partner, Irell & Manella.

            **Stephanie DeBrow**, U. of Texas 2010, Partner, Norton Rose Fulbright.

            **Patrick Hughes**, Georgetown 2010, Chief Counsel for Opinions & Advice, Office of the Maryland Attorney General.

            **Janice Ta**, Yale 2010, Partner, Perkins Coie.

2011–12     **Brittany Blueitt Amadi**, Harvard 2010, Partner, WilmerHale.

            **Nathan R. Curtis**, Brigham Young 2011, Associate, Gibson, Dunn & Crutcher.

            **Lisa Larrimore Ouellette**, Yale 2011, Professor of Law, Stanford Law School.

**Brett J. Thompsen**, U. of Texas 2010, Partner, Baker Botts.

2012–13    **Christopher Dryer**, Georgetown 2011, Principal, Fish & Richardson.

**Haninah Levine**, Yale 2012, Attorney-Advisor, US Department of the Interior.

**Jessica Palmer Ryen**, Harvard 2012, Associate, Williams & Connolly.

**Christopher Suarez**, Yale 2011, Associate, Steptoe & Johnson.

2013–14    **Hannah Brennan**, Yale 2013, Associate, Hagens Berman Sobel Shapiro.

**Sharonmoyee Goswami**, NYU 2012, Partner, Cravath, Swaine & Moore.

**Sanjiv Laud**, U. of Minnesota, Partner, Jones Day.

**Alexandra H. Moss**, Stanford 2013, Executive Director, Public Interest Patent Law Institute.

2014–15    **David J. Bender**, GWU 2013, Associate, Covington & Burling.

**Stanley H. Chen**, Harvard 2014, Senior Counsel, Shef.

**Elissa Knoff**, Northwestern 2014, Attorney, Bookoff McAndrews

**Andrew Robb**, U. of Chicago 2013, Associate, Gibson, Dunn & Crutcher.

2015–16    **Aaron Frumkin**, Harvard 2015, AUSA, National Security Division, Central District of California.

**Christopher J. Morten**, NYU 2015, Associate Clinical Professor of Law, Columbia Law School.

**Oliver James Richards**, NYU 2015, Associate, Fish & Richardson.

**David Yin**, NYU 2014, Counsel, WilmerHale.

2016–17    **Giovanni S. Saarman González**, UCLA 2016, Associate, Munger Tolles & Olson.

**Anthony Sheh**, Georgetown 2015, Associate, Williams & Connolly.

**Alexander Trzeciak**, Duke 2014, Associate, Covington & Burling.

**Jimmy Zhuang**, Yale 2016, Senior Corporate Counsel, Ginkgo Bioworks, Inc.

2017–18    **Abigail L. Colella**, Harvard 2016, Managing Associate, Orrick, Herrington & Sutcliffe.

**Laura Dolbow**, Vanderbilt 2017, Associate, Covington & Burling.

**James A. Flynn**, Yale 2015, Managing Associate, Orrick, Herrington & Sutcliffe.

> **Zachary E. Shapiro**, Harvard 2016, Assistant Professor of Medical Ethics Research in Medicine, Weill Cornell Medical College, Co-Chair of the Ethics Committee at The Rockefeller University Hospital, Senior Research Fellow and Senior Advisor at Yale Law School.

2018–19  **Marta M. Chlistunoff**, U. of Texas 2016, Senior Associate, WilmerHale.

> **Christopher Marth**, U. of Chicago 2018.

> **Matthaeus Martino-Weinhardt**, Stanford 2016, Associate, Durie Tangri.

> **Katherine E. Rhoades**, Northwestern 2016, Associate, Bartlit Beck, LLP.

2019–20  **David Cho**, U. of Michigan 2017, Associate, Covington and Burling.

> **Lidiya Mishchenko**, GWU 2016, Visiting Assistant Professor of Law, Duke University School of Law.

> **Adam Pan**, Yale 2019, Associate, Williams & Connolly.

> **Parth Sagdeo**, Harvard 2018, Associate, Orrick, Herrington & Sutcliffe.

2020–21  **John R. Boulé III**, American 2018, Associate (Issues & Appeals), Jones Day.

> **Kim Do**, NYU 2018, Associate, Gibson, Dunn & Crutcher.

> **Edward Nugent**, Stanford 2019, Deputy Attorney General, California Department of Justice.

> **Lauren Matlock-Colangelo**, Columbia 2019, Associate, WilmerHale.

2021–22  **Nathanael Andrews**, Northwestern 2019, Current law clerk.

> **Rocky Li**, Harvard 2020, Current law clerk.

> **Haley Tuchman**, USC 2020, Current law clerk.

> **Crystal Weeks**, Georgetown 2018, Current law clerk.

# INDEX

CPSIA information can be obtained
at www.ICGtesting.com
Printed in the USA
LVHW102028150622
721333LV00003B/6